Y0-BYL-776

MAKERS

OF

MODERN MEDICINE

PASTEUR

MAKERS

OF

MODERN MEDICINE

BY

JAMES JOSEPH WALSH, M.D., Ph.D., LL.D.

Essay Index Reprint Series

BOOKS FOR LIBRARIES PRESS
FREEPORT, NEW YORK

First Published 1907
Reprinted 1970

STANDARD BOOK NUMBER:
8369-1538-0

LIBRARY OF CONGRESS CATALOG CARD NUMBER:
70-107741

PRINTED IN THE UNITED STATES OF AMERICA

TO

DR. WILLIAM OSLER

WHO EXEMPLIFIES FOR THIS GENERATION THE FINEST QUALITIES OF
THESE MAKERS OF OUR MODERN MEDICINE, THIS VOLUME IS
WITH HIS KIND PERMISSION DEDICATED AS A
SLIGHT TOKEN OF THE ADMIRATION
OF A DISTANT DISCIPLE.

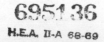

"If in some things I dissent from others, whose wit, industry, diligence and judgment I look up at and admire, let me not therefore hear presently of ingratitude and rashness. For I thank those that have taught me, and will ever; but yet dare not think the scope of their labor and inquiry was to envy their posterity what they also could add and find out. If I err, pardon me. I do not desire to be equal with those that went before; but to have my reasons examined with theirs, and so much faith to be given them, or me, as those shall evict. I am neither author or fautor of any sect. I will have no man addict himself to me; but if I have anything right, defend it as Truth's, not mine, save as it conduceth to a common good. It profits not me to have any man fence or fight for me, to follow or take my part. Stand for truth, and 'tis enough."

PREFACE.

THE present volume is published at the solicitation of
many friends who have read the articles contained in it as
they appeared at various times in magazines and who
deemed that they were worth preservation in a more permanent form. The only possible claim for its filling a want
lies in the fact that it presents these workers in medicine
not only as scientists but also and especially as men, in
relation to their environment, social, religious and educational.
I have to thank the editors of the *Messenger*, *Donahoe's
Magazine*, *The Catholic World* and the *Records of the
American Catholic Historical Society*, for permission to
reprint the articles which appeared in their periodicals.

The opening chapter, The Making of Medicine, is an
abstract from the introductory lecture of the course in the
history of medicine at the Fordham University Medical School,
New York. Much of the material for the article on the Irish
School of Medicine was gathered for a lecture before the
Historical Club of Johns Hopkins University and the District
Medical Society of the District of Columbia. The sketch of
the life of Dr. Jenner has not hitherto been published. All
of the other articles have been considerably lengthened and
revised.

There are other makers of modern medicine who deserve
a place beside those mentioned here, but as the material had
reached the amount that would make a good-sized volume it

was thought better to proceed with the publication of the first series of sketches, which will be followed by others if conditions conspire to encourage any further additions to our not very copious English medical biography. A subsequent volume will contain sketches of the lives of old-time makers of medicine in the fifteenth, sixteenth and seventeenth centuries, the men who laid the firm foundations of our medical science of the present day.

I have to thank my friend of many years and brother alumnus of Fordham University, Dr. Austin O'Malley, of Philadelphia, for reading the proofs and for suggestions while the book was going through the press.

CONTENTS.

THE MAKING OF MEDICINE

Without History a man's soul is purblind, seeing only the things which almost touch his eyes.—FULLER, *Holy and Profane State*, 1641.

THE MAKING OF MEDICINE.

Our generation, in this no more self-concentrated than many another, has prided itself so much on the progress it has achieved in science that it has in its interest in the insistent present rather neglected the claims of the history of science. There has been the feeling that our contemporaries and immediate predecessors have accomplished so much as to put us far beyond the past and its workers, so that it would seem almost a waste of time to rehearse the crude notions with which they occupied themselves. In no one of the sciences is this truer than in medicine. Yet it seems likely that no more chastening influence on the zeal for the novel in science, which so often has led this generation astray, could possibly be exerted than that which will surely follow from adequate knowledge of scientific history. In medicine there is no doubt at all that an intimate acquaintance with the work of the great medical men of the past would save many a useless investigation into problems that have already been thoroughly investigated, or at least would help modern workers to begin at a place much farther on in their researches than is often the custom.

There are other reasons why the knowledge of the history of medicine cannot but prove of great service to the present generation. We are entering upon a time when original research as the main business of selected lives, in contradistinction to the few hours a day or even a week that the medical practitioners of a few generations ago could steal from their busy lives, is becoming more and more the rule. A consideration then of the methods by which advances in

medicine were made in the past, of the character of the men
to whom we owe the ground-breaking discoveries, of the way
in which such discoveries were accepted or rather rejected
by contemporaries, for rejection was almost the rule, will
serve as a mirror for reflections that will surely be helpful
in this day of great institutions of research. It must not be
forgotten, however, that only too often in the past it is in the
large institutions that routine work has been done, while the
occasional genius has sprung up in circumstances that seemed
quite unlikely to be the fostering mother of originality,
and there has taken for the world the precious step into the
unknown which represents a new departure in medical
science.

Prof. Osler's declaration that the world's best work was
mainly done by young men was not well received, but
no one knew better than he that this is the most salient
fact in the history of medical progress. There is practically not a single great discovery in medicine that was
not made by a young man under thirty-five. As a rule,
indeed, the new departures in medicine came from men
who were well under thirty, some of them in fact only at
the beginning of their third decade of life. Morgagni's
great germinal idea, which made him the father of modern
pathology, came to him when he was a student scarcely more
than twenty. He then began to take notes on all the morbid
appearances that he found in bodies, recognizing very clearly
that he must trace out not only the main cause of the disease, but also the subsidiary pathological factors that were
at work in the production of the various symptoms of the
special case as he had studied it clinically. This idea is so
obvious now as to seem impossible to be missed; yet scarcely
a century ago it constituted the foundation-stone of modern
pathology.

Auenbrugger, who laid the foundation of modern physical diagnosis by his observations upon percussion, began the work when he was under twenty-five, at the Spanish Hospital in Vienna, and carried it out to a completely successful issue absolutely without any encouragement from the great masters of the Vienna school. As a matter of fact, they rather pooh-poohed the idea that this foolish drumming, as one of them is said to have termed it, could ever amount to anything in enabling physicians to recognize pathological conditions within the chest. For twenty-five years after the publication of his little book, Auenbrugger's discovery attracted no attention. Laennec, who followed Auenbrugger in the development of physical diagnosis, set himself the much harder problem of constructing a system of auscultation when he was in his early twenties, studied the subject for twelve years and then published the book on it when he was as yet scarcely thirty-five. He accomplished the revolution in medicine that is due to him, though he was never strong and died at the early age of forty-six.

These are only striking examples which show what the young man has accomplished. The same thing was true in other countries. Corrigan wrote his famous essay on the "Permanent Patency of the Aortic Valve" when he was only twenty-nine years of age, and the work for it had been done during the preceding three years, at a hospital in which there were beds for only six medical patients. Trousseau declared this the greatest medical work, from a clinical standpoint, that had ever been accomplished, and hailed young Corrigan as one of the masters of clinical medicine. He maintained that disease of the aortic valve should receive the name Corrigan's disease. Stokes, Corrigan's contemporary and friend in Dublin, wrote his little book on the stethoscope when he was not yet twenty-one, and at a time when the distinguished clinicians of the day were all asking if these young men expected the old physicians to carry this toy about with them and use it for any serious purpose. Graves, also of the Irish school of medicine, made some of the clinical observations on which his reputation is founded, including a short description of characteristic cases of the affection that still bears his name, when he was well under thirty-five.

Further examples might well be cited, but they will be met with in the course of this book. The history of most of the sciences is like medicine in this respect, and it is to young men that the great ground-breaking ideas come. How true this is in biology can be noted even from the lives of the physician-biologists that are included in this volume. Theodore Schwann, the father of the cell doctrine, did all the work for which he deserves the name of founder of modern biology when he was scarcely more than thirty. Part of the best of it was accomplished before he was twenty-five. Claude Bernard had shown the precious metal of his originality before he was far on in his twenties. Pasteur, the most original genius of them all, began his work when he was scarcely more than a boy, and though every five years of a long life was filled with original observations of the most precious kind, his genius had received the bent which it was to follow from the successful accomplishment of observations during his third and fourth decades.

In these modern days, when the education of the young man for medicine is not supposed to be finished until he is nearly thirty, it is easy to understand that perhaps the precious years in which originality might manifest itself are already past before he gets out of the swaddling clothes of enforced instruction from others. As has been very well said, it is possible to smother whatever of the investigating spirit and original initiative there may be in a young man by attempting to teach him too much of what the present generation knows. Unfortunately, it happens only too often even in this wise generation of ours that it is not so much the ignorance of mankind that makes them ridiculous as the knowing so many things that are not so. The number of things that the young man has to learn and that are taught him, often with the assurance that they are almost gospel truth in medicine, and yet that he finds before he has been long out of school or indeed sometimes before he leaves school, to be at best opinions, is entirely too great. The saving grace for the correction of this constantly recurring fault in education is undoubtedly a knowledge of the development of medicine in the past and a recognition of the fact that the accepted truth of any one generation proves after all often enough to be only apparent.

After the false impression that it is to older men we owe progress in medicine, perhaps the most universally accepted apparent truth is that the investigating spirit is communicable, and that the pupils of a great master may be expected to carry on his work and add almost as much as he has done to the great body of medical knowledge during the generation immediately following his work. It would naturally be expected, for instance, that Morgagni having laid the foundations of modern pathology and connected pathological observation with clinical observation the great development in modern diagnosis would have come down in Italy. This was not true, however. The next great step connecting bedside observations with postmortem appearances was made by Auenbrugger in Vienna in distant Austria. Auenbrugger's work having been successfully accomplished it might reasonably be supposed that he himself or some of those who had seen his successful diagnosis of thoracic con-

2

ditions by percussion would take the next step and discover auscultation. This, however, did not happen in Germany, but in France. It is true that Laennec's work was done under the influence of Corvisart, who revived Auenbrugger's work and gave it to the world once more, and that in a way, therefore, Laennec may be considered an indirect pupil of Auenbrugger; but the fact stands that the two discoveries of percussion and auscultation were made at an interval of nearly fifty years and at a distance of more than a thousand miles from each other.

On the other hand, Laennec having solved the wonderful mystery of the significance of the sounds within the chest as far as they concern pulmonary diseases might have been expected to do as much also for heart disease. Even genius, however, is able it seems to take only one step into the unknown. Auenbrugger did not discover auscultation, though it apparently lay so near at hand. Laennec did not solve the riddle of heart murmurs, though for most of us they do not present any more difficulty than the wonderfully successful recognition of the significance of *râles* of various kinds in which Laennec never failed. The problem of heart diagnosis was to be solved by Corrigan and the Irish school of medicine hundreds of miles away, though they were doing their work about the same time that Laennec was making his observations in Paris. Curiously enough just during the same decade Richard Bright, in England, was studying out the problem of kidney disease, and, as a young man, teaching the world nearly as much about it as it has ever learned, though, in the seventy-five years that have passed since, so much of investigation has been devoted to the subject.

No one nation can claim the palm of superiority in the matter of original investigation. The spirit of genius breathes where it will, and unfortunately it is incommunicable. Students may think they absorb all that the master has to give them, and that they are ready to go on with his work where he left it. They do actually seem to their own generation to make distinct progress in medicine. When the situation is analyzed fifty or a hundred years afterward, however, it is found that only the master's work counts, and that much of what seems to be advance was only a skirmishing here and there along the lines laid down by him, but without any material progress for true science.

This same peculiarity is manifest, also, not only in the history of sciences allied to medicine, but in that of all the physical sciences. A very striking example is to be found in the story of the rise of electrical science, which took place almost at the same period as that which saw the rise of clinical medicine. Origins in electricity date from Franklin's work here in America and Galvani and Volta's observations in Italy. It might quite naturally have been expected that the further progress of electrical science would come in either of these countries. The next great discoveries, however, were separated by long distances and a considerable interval of time. After Volta came the demonstration by Oersted, in Denmark, of the identity of magnetism with electricity. It was not in Denmark, however, that the problems connected with this principle were worked out, but by Ampère in France. In the mean time, Cavendish and Faraday, working quite independently of their Continental colleagues, were making significant strides in electricity in England.

When the problem of the resistance to the passage of electricity in a conductor was to be studied, another nation supplied the man for the opportunity. Ohm had never been in contact with any of these great contemporaries and did his work entirely by himself. It is a curious confirmation of what we have stated with regard to the young man in medicine and the making of great discoveries that practically all these founders in electricity were under thirty-five when their best original work was accomplished.

From a series of biographies of great medical discoverers, certain salient traits stand out so as to attract attention even from the cursory reader. The essence of significant work in medicine consists of observation, not theory. It has always been the custom to theorize much and unfortunately to observe but little. Long ago John Ruskin said that the hardest thing in the world for a man to do is to see something and to tell it simply as he saw it. Certainly this has been true in medicine. The men who have had eyes, and have used them, have impressed their names upon the history of progressive scientific advance. The theorists have never contributed anything worth while to the body of medical truth.

While this is readily acknowledged by every generation, with regard to the past, it is curious to note how different is the appreciation of each generation for the theorist as opposed to the observer. Medical theorists have always been honored by their contemporaries unless their theories were utterly outlandish, and even then they have had many disciples, and have seldom been without honor and never, with sorrow for the foolishness of men be it said, without emolument. The observer, however, has but rarely been in favor with his contemporaries. Not infrequently the observation that he made appeared to be so obvious that his fellows could not think that it represented a great truth. As a consequence they have usually derided him for attempting to make them see a significance in his observation that they could not think was there. Huxley once stated the phases through which a new scientific truth ordinarily passes. At first it is said to be trivial and insignificant, then as it attracts more attention it is declared to be in contradiction with hitherto known truth. Finally it is declared to be after all only in other terms what the world has always believed in the matter. Certainly through these stages all the great discoveries in medicine have gone. So true is this, that if what seems to be a new truth in medicine is accepted at once, and willingly, there is more than a suspicion that it is not really a new discovery but only a modification of something hitherto well known.

All the great discoverers in medicine have practically without exception met, if not with opposition, surely with neglect of their work. We smile complacently now at the generation that considered the stethoscope a toy, and asked derisively if they should be expected to carry it about with them. The next generation, however, having grown accustomed to the stethoscope, refused quite as inconsequentially to have anything to do with the thermometer. They refused to carry these glass things around with them in order to test the fever that patients might have, since they claimed they were able to accomplish this purpose quite as well by means of their educated touch. The generation of medical men is not yet passed who refused to credit the thought that the diagnosis of diphtheria would ever be made only by the microscope and culture methods, and who considered that they could tell very well what was diphtheria, and what not, from the appearance of the throat.

Of course similar opposition was the fate meted out to every distinguished scientific discoverer, and so I suppose medical men cannot complain. His contemporaries said of Galvani that he had made of himself a dancing master for frogs, because he continued his observations on the legs of these animals in order to solve the problems of animal elec-

tricity. Pasteur's demonstration that there was no such
thing as spontaneous generation, served at first only to bring
down on his devoted head the aspersions of most of the
distinguished scientific men in Europe. When that genius,
the physician Robert Mayer, discovered the conservation of
energy as the result of his acute observation, that blood drawn
by venesection in the tropics was redder than that drawn in
colder climates, he found that scientific circles were not only
not ready to accept his demonstration, but that he was
looked upon as a visionary, somewhat as one who thought
that he had solved the problem of squaring the circle or
the endless puzzle of perpetual motion.

Fortunately these men have as a rule had a physical
and mental force that enabled them to go on in spite
of the opposition or derision of their contemporaries. It
is rather a curious fact that most of the great medical
discoverers were born in the country and were as a rule the
sons of rather poor parents. Many of them were so situated
that they had to begin to make their own livelihood to some
extent at least at the beginning of their third decade of life.
Far from proving a hindrance to their original work, this
necessity seems rather to have been one of the sources of
inspiration that spurred them on to successful efforts in
their investigations.

Most of them were what would be called handy men, in the
sense that they could use their hands to work out their ideas
mechanically. This was typically true of Galvani, who had to
construct his own first electrical instruments, and of Laennec,
who took pride in making his own stethoscopes. So many
of them made by his own hands are still extant, that a number
of museums have the opportunity to hold specimens of his
handiwork. Auenbrugger and Johann Müller and Pasteur
are further examples of this same handiness. Claude Ber-

nard exhibited this quality very early in life and continued to exercise it all during his career.

Nor was their ingenuity limited to material things. Many of them were interested in literary and artistic work of various kinds. Morgagni was considered a literary light in his generation. Auenbrugger composed a musical comedy which had a distinct success, even in music loving Vienna. The Empress Maria Theresa said that she supposed he would now continue to write musical comedies; but Auenbrugger replied, with more candor than gallantry, that he had something better to do. Claude Bernard composed a play that shows distinct evidence of literary talent. It seems fortunate indeed that he was diverted from his original intention of following literature as a career, and took up medicine. Many of the others, as, for instance, Graves and Stokes, were excellent judges of art, critics of real knowledge and genuine appreciation; and indeed it may be said that none of them was ever so absorbed in his vocation of medicine as not to have much more than a passing interest in some of the great phases of intellectual activity quite apart from his professional work, or from scientific knowledge: an avocation to which he turned for the only true recreation of mind there is—a change of work.

This seems all the more worth while calling attention to in our strenuous age, because it is sometimes considered a mistake for a physician to show that he is interested in intellectual pursuits of any kind apart from his professional work. It is supposed that no one is capable of dividing his attention in this way and yet do justice to his profession and his patients. As a matter of fact it has well been said that no really great physician has ever been a narrow specialist in the sense that he knew only medicine well; there was always at least one other department of intellectual attainment with which he had made himself so familiar as to be an authority in it. It is not the lopsided who make great athletes, and it is not the one-sided man who succeeds in doing really great work. Practically all the great physicians have had favorite hobbies to which they have turned for relaxation, for surely no one understands better than physicians that recreation consists not in that impossibility, the doing of nothing, but in resting the mind by doing something quite different from what it has been engaged at before.

There is another phase of the lives of these great men of medicine that is so different from what is ordinarily thought to be the rule with physicians, that it seems worth while emphasizing at the end of this introduction. All these great discoverers have been men of constructive imagination, men who might have been distinguished litterateurs very probably, had they applied themselves in that field. All of them have had too much imagination to be materialists, that is, to consider that they could know nothing except what they learned from the matter with which their studies were taken up. All these great discoverers in medicine have been simple, sincere, faithful believers, ready to express their trust in an overruling Providence, and in a hereafter that they knew only by faith, it is true, but which was for that reason none the less distinctly recognized. While it is usually considered that medicine leads men's minds away from orthodox thinking in the great matter of the relationship of the creature to the Creator, all these men have been not only ready to acknowledge their personal obligations to Him, but have furnished exemplary models of what the recognition of such obligations can make of human lives.

There is an old proverb that runs *Ubi tres medici ibi duo athei,*—where there are three physicians there are at least two atheists. This has made many a heartache for fond mothers when they found their sons had determined on becoming physicians. If the present series of sketches is to be taken as any argument, however, it is only the small minds among physicians who become atheists. They are not able to see their way clearly from the material they work in to the higher things that prove a source of strength and con- solation to the great minds while they are busy making medicine for their own and subsequent generations. Certainly no more thoroughly representative group of the makers of nineteenth century clinical medicine could have been selected than those whose sketches are here given. They are from all the nations who have contributed materially to modern medical advance, yet all of them were deeply religious men.

There is another and equally important point with regard to them. It is their relations to their fellows. Without exception they were men beloved by those around them for their unselfish devotion not only to science, but also to their brother men. In the midst of their occupations the thought that has been the profoundest consolation for all of them without exception has been that they were accomplishing something by which their fellow-men would be saved suffering and by which human life would be made more happy. A study of their careers cannot fail to show the young physician the ideals he must cherish if he would have real and not apparent success and happiness in life.

MORGAGNI, THE FATHER OF PATHOLOGY

Let us then blush, in this so ample and so wonderful field of nature (where performance still exceeds what is promised), to credit other men's traditions only, and thence come uncertain problems to spin out thorny and captious questions. Nature herselfe must be our adviser; the path she chalks must be our walk; for so while we confer with our own eies, and take our rise from meaner things to higher, we shall at length be received into her closet-secrets.—Preface to *Anatomical Exercitations concerning the Generation of Living Creatures*, 1653. WILLIAM HARVEY.

MORGAGNI, THE FATHER OF PATHOLOGY.

"VIR INGENII, MEMORIAE, STUDII, INCOMPARABILIS."—
HALLER.

IN 1894, when the International Medical Congress met at Rome, Prof. Virchow of Berlin, the greatest living pathologist at the time, was asked to deliver the principal address. He chose as his subject John Baptist Morgagni, the distinguished Italian physician and original investigator of the eighteenth century, whom he hailed as the Father of Pathology. No medical scientist of the nineteenth century was in a better position than Virchow to judge who had been the founder of the science for which he himself did so much. Virchow besides, through long and faithful study of the history of medicine, knew well whereof he spoke. In pathology especially modern medicine has made its sure advances, so that Morgagni's ground-breaking work may well be considered the beginning of the most recent epoch in medical science. As a matter of fact, medicine lost much of its obscurity by losing all its vagueness when Morgagni's methods came into general use.

As a medical student scarcely twenty years of age, he revolutionized medical observation by studying his fatal cases with a comparative investigation of their clinical symptoms and the postmortem findings. This had been done before, but mainly with the idea of finding out the cause of death and the principal reasons for the illness which

(29)

preceded. Morgagni's investigations in pathology consisted
in tracing side by side all the clinical symptoms to their
causes as far as that might be possible. This looks so
simple now as to be quite obvious, as all great discoveries
are both simple and obvious once they have been made; but
it takes a genius to make them, since their very nearness causes
them to be overlooked by the ordinary observer so prone
to seek something strange and different from the common.

How much Morgagni's studies from this new viewpoint
of the investigation of all the symptoms of disease has meant
for modern medicine, may be best appreciated by a quotation
from an address delivered before the Glasgow Pathological
and Clinical Society in 1864, by Professor Gairdner, who
thus tersely describes the character of the distinguished
Italian pathologist's work:

"In investigating the seats of disease, Morgagni is not
content to record the coincidence of a lesion in an organ with
the symptoms apparently due to disordered function in that
organ.

"For the first time almost in medical inquiry, he insists
on examining every organ, as well as the one suspected to be
chiefly implicated; not only so, he marshals with the utmost
care, from his own experience and that of his predecessors,
all the instances in which the symptoms have existed apart
from the lesion, or the lesion apart from the symptoms. He
discusses each of these incidents with severe exactness in the
interest of truth, and only after an exhaustive investigation
will he allow the inference either that the organ referred to
is or is not the seat of the disease.

"And in like manner in dealing with causes: a group of
symptoms may be caused by certain organic changes—it
may be even probable that it is so—but, according to Morgagni's method, we must first inquire into all the lesions of

organs which occur in connection with such symptoms; in the second place, we must know if such lesions ever occur without the symptoms; and again if such symptoms can be attributed in any cases to other causes in the absence of such lesions."

During over sixty years of a long life Morgagni continued to follow out the idea that he had developed as a boy, and his works contain the first definite account of pathological lesions and clinical manifestations that attracted attention.

As a proof of the striking difference between the value of observation and theory in medicine, it may be said that many hundreds of volumes containing the most elaborate medical theories were published during the eighteenth century, and that practically none of these is ever read now, except for curiosity's sake by some seeker after the quaint and distant in medicine, while Morgagni's books still contain a precious fund of information, to which pathologists at least, and not a few clinicians, turn often with interest and come away always with profit. They are not infrequently quoted from, and, as we shall see, have been highly appreciated by some of the best medical authorities of the present and the immediately preceding generations.

To the modern thinker, accustomed to look rather to the northern nations or to France for great advances in science, it may prove somewhat of a surprise to have an Italian thus put forward as the founder of modern medicine, and especially of the most scientific department of it. Those who are familiar with the history of medicine since the revival of civilization after the Dark Ages will realize what a prominent place Italy has always held in the development of medical science. The first great Christian medical school was founded at Salerno, not far from Naples, in the tenth century. The first regular practical teaching of anatomy by means of dissections of human bodies and demonstrations on the cadaver was done at Bologna by Mondino at the beginning of the fourteenth century. The great Father of Modern Anatomy, Vesalius, was a Belgian, but he did all the work for his epoch-making book, the *De Fabrica Humani Corporis*, at the Universities of North Italy, especially at Padua, Bologna and Pisa, during the first half of the sixteenth century. Every student of medicine in those times who was desirous to secure wider opportunities for medical education went down into Italy, and on the rosters of the Italian medical schools of the sixteenth century are to be found the names of most of the men who in all the countries of Europe became famous for their medical attainments.

Morgagni only forms a final link in the chain of great Italian medical scientists, connecting medieval with modern medicine. From the time of Vesalius to that of Morgagni there was never a period when Italy did not possess the leading medical investigator of Europe. We need only mention such names as those of Fallopius, who added so much to our knowledge of abdominal anatomy; Eustachius, to whom we owe many important details of the anatomy of the head; Spigelius, whose name is forever associated with the liver, and Malpighi, to whom the whole round of the biological sciences allied most closely to medicine owes more than perhaps to any other single investigator, to show the complete justification for this claim. As a matter of fact, every encouragement to the progress of medicine was extended both by the secular and the ecclesiastical authorities in Italy during these centuries, and the Italian peninsula was from the beginning of the sixteenth to the end of the eighteenth centuries the mecca for ardent medical students desirous of exhausting the medical knowledge of their time, quite as Germany has been in our day.

John Baptist Morgagni was born on February 25, 1682. His birthplace was Forli in Romagna. It was the capital of a little papal state, lying at the foot of the Apennines to the southeast of Bologna. The modern American traveler is likely to know something about it, because it is one of the principal stopping places on the road from Bologna to Rimini, for at least the feminine portion of any travelling party will want to make a pilgrimage to the home of Dante's poor Francesca and to the scene of the heroic exploits of Catarina Sforza, the great woman of the Renaissance, to whom in all honor, and without any tinge of the discredit it has since come to convey, was given the proud title of the Virago of Forli. The little town is noted for the beauty of its situation, and well deserves a visit for itself, for it contains a famous palace built after designs made by Michael Angelo. The town had decreased in importance and population at the end of the seventeenth century, when Morgagni was born there, but it was favorably known for the high standard of cultivation among its inhabitants, possessed a good library, a number of schools and a well-known college.

Like many another great man, Morgagni seems to have been especially fortunate in his mother. He was left an orphan at a very early age. His mother, however, whose maiden name was Maria Tornieli, not only bore her loss bravely, but devoted her life and talents to the education of her gifted son. She seems to have been a woman of uncommon good sense and remarkable understanding. Morgagni often spoke of her during the course of his life, and attributed much of his success to the training he had received from her. It is the custom sometimes to think that women have come to exert great cultural influence only in these latter days. Nothing could be more untrue. All through history are abundant traces of women exerting the high-

3

est intellectual influences in their own sphere, and the
North Italians in their era of highest cultural development
seem to have been happier in nothing more than their recognition of the possibilities that lay in providing educational
facilities for women.

These times and this part of Italy are famous in history
for some of the opportunities afforded women in the matter
of higher education. It has been suggested that it is perhaps
to the liberal culture of the mothers we owe the fact that this
part of Italy furnished for one hundred and fifty years about
this time the greatest men in science of the time. It is well
known that women occasionally held professorships at the
University of Bologna, not far from Morgagni's birthplace.
The general culture of the women of this section was very
high. Modern masculine historians have even been un-
generous enough to point out that Bologna was famous for
two things—the opportunities provided for the higher education of women and the extensive manufacture of various
forms of prepared food, the best known of which, the classical
Bologna sausage, has come down as a precious heritage to
hurried housekeepers in our own time.

After an excellent preliminary education at Forli, always
under the careful supervision and enlightened encouragement
of his mother, Morgagni, as might have been expected from
the place of his birth, went to the neighboring university town
of Bologna for his higher studies. Bologna was at this time
at the very acme of its reputation as the greatest of existent
medical schools. The science of anatomy had been especially
developed here as the result of important investigations and
discoveries made by some of the greatest men in the history
of medical science. Mondino had, very early in the fourteenth century, recreated the modern science of anatomy as
we know it. He was the first to realize the importance

and urge the necessity for the dissection of human bodies, if any real lasting progress in human anatomy was to be made. Medical teaching before this time had been largely by lectures and disputations upon the work of Aristotle, Hippocrates and Galen, but actual observation on human tissues and organs now replaced the older method. Bologna became a papal city in 1512, and it is especially after this date that, under the fostering care of the Popes, the University of Bologna became the centre of medical teaching for the whole world for several centuries.

As the result of actual observation and patient study instead of idle theorizing there came a large number of great discoveries in anatomy. From Mondino to Morgagni there is a continuous series of great men in connection with the University of Bologna such as no other institution can show. About midway between the first and last came the great Vesalius, who taught at Bologna as well as at Padua and Pisa, and whose work on anatomy was to be a treasure for anatomists of all countries for many generations. It was while teaching at Bologna that Vesalius made the famous series of dissections which formed the subjects of the illustrations for his great work on anatomy. Titian, the celebrated Venetian artist, who had come down from Venice in order to study anatomy for artistic purposes at the famous school of anatomy and under the supervision of its great teachers, is said to have executed the plates for the book. The work remains a worthy monument of the two great masters in their respective professions whose collaboration created it.

During the century before Morgagni's entrance into the University of Bologna, the distinguished English physician Harvey, who was to lay the foundation of modern physiology by the discovery of the circulation of the blood, was attracted to Bologna because of the opportunities it presented for

advanced work in the studies in which he was so much
interested. While repeating some of the dissecting work
that Vesalius had done Harvey was led to suspect the
existence of the circulation and had his thoughts directed
in the channel which finally led to his masterly exposition
of the subject. In a word, here at Bologna the study of
the physical side of life, so important a characteristic of
latter-day science, became a distinct and recognized branch
of science. As Professor Benjamin Ward Richardson said,
in his sketch of the life of Morgagni, "Since that time there
has been no decline in interest in these studies and medicine
has been developed in a manner as daring in project as it
has been useful in application."

Bologna was, at the time, certainly an excellent place for
Morgagni. He went there as an inquiring youth of fifteen
and began his medical studies at once. He became a student
of two of the most celebrated professors of the time—Albertini,
a leader in his day, though since more or less forgotten, and
Valsalva, whose investigations into the anatomy of the ear
assure him a permanent place in the science of anatomy for
all time. When Morgagni went to the university, Valsalva
was at the zenith of his brilliant career as an anatomist.
He was in the midst of his great work on the organ of hearing.
This extremely intricate piece of human mechanism had
never been understood before his time, and the working out
of its details proved a time-taking but intensely interesting
investigation.

It was not long before the genial insight of Valsalva picked
out Morgagni as a person excellently fitted to assist him in
his dissecting work. Morgagni had not only an enthusiasm
for the work, but had, what is much more precious under the
circumstances, untiring patience and industry and unswerving
perseverance. These were the qualities that were after-

ward to prove the foundation of his reputation. His genius consisted certainly in the faculty for hard work, and his special talent was an infinite capacity for taking pains. Nearly all of the dissections which Valsalva required for his demonstrations during lecture hours, or for the illustrations of his books, are said to have been made by Morgagni under the master's personal supervision.

After four years of this precious training and study at the university, Morgagni took his degree as Doctor of Medicine and of Philosophy. The late Benjamin Ward Richardson, one of the great English medical men of the end of the nineteenth century, says that this is a happy combination of qualifications which might, with great advantage, be required of the graduate in the present day, when so much of medicine and so little of philosophy is demanded of the student, to the manifest detriment of both departments of knowledge.

Some idea of the estimation in which Morgagni was held at this time may be gathered from the fact that, though scarcely more than twenty-one years of age, he was sometimes allowed to assume Valsalva's lecture obligations during the master's absence. After graduation he spent some time at the university doing special work in connection with the science of anatomy, in which he was so much interested, and as an assistant professor and tutor. Bologna at this time enjoyed as wide a European reputation as at any period of its history. Students from all countries in Europe flocked here, especially to make their legal and medical studies. Among the medical students Morgagni was always a moving spirit, a leader in the phases of thought in many lines that were occupying students' minds at the time.

He was the founder and director of a society of young professors and maturer students, whose object was the discussion of scientific subjects of many kinds. The standard of the new society was personal investigation and observation as a means of arriving at scientific truth. The principal maxim that guided their discussions seems to have been that nothing was to be accepted on authority, merely because it was authority. In the physical sciences thought had been frequently cramped to fit the old theories inherited from Galen and Pliny and Aristotle and Hippocrates. A quotation from one of these classic authors on a point at issue was supposed to throw light on any difficulty that might be the subject of discussion.

Morgagni's society was called the Academia Inquietorum— "The Academy of the Restless"—the idea of the curious name being that the members were not satisfied to rest peacefully in the knowledge to be gleaned from the older authors, but preferred to get at science for themselves by direct observation and planned experiment. Morgagni's idea in founding the society seems to have been premature. The fate of the Academy of the Restless is involved in some obscurity, but biographers seem to hint that it failed of its purpose. Neither the university nor the times were yet ready for such freedom of thought as this. Even in our own day such a scheme would be considered radical and chimerical. The discouragement met with finally led to the abandonment of the meetings, and Morgagni gave up his attempt to inspire others with his own industry and enthusiasm for original investigation in the physical sciences.

For some years after this he seems to have been absent from Bologna. His time was spent especially at the medical schools of the great universities of Pisa and of Padua. Students who wished to make some special branch of medicine such as physiology, or anatomy, or the, then as yet scarcely known, science of pathology, their prime object in life, had to visit various universities in order to find opportunity and

suggestion for study. Morgagni devoted himself so faithfully to his work that his eyesight failed him for a time and
very probably his general health also. For some years he
returned to his native town to recuperate. Here he took
up the active practice of medicine. As so often happens,
this period of rest after years of study proved especially
broadening in its influence upon Morgagni. After his rest
his contemporaries begin to realize his great possibilities as
a scientist.

His first publication was a series of notes on anatomy.
These were published in the form of collected essays, with
the title *Adversaria Anatomica.* The title has a pugnacious
sound, but Morgagni did not indulge in controversy and
adversaria is only the Latin name for note-books. The
first articles thus collected were really communications
made by Morgagni to the "Academy of the Restless" during
his presidency of that body. This opened his career as a
writer, and it is interesting to note that his last book was to
be published some sixty-three years later—a period of fecund
authorship almost unprecedented.

As the result of the reputation gained by this work he was
offered a teaching position at the University of Padua and
later was transferred to the chair of the second professorship
of anatomy. After a few years he succeeded to the first
professorship of anatomy at the university, at that time the
most important post in the medical school. This gave him,
at the age of about thirty-five, one of the greatest university
professorships in the world. Opportunities for research
were now amply provided. He was in a position where his
communications would be received with due attention and
his reputation was secure.

A university professorship in those days was a position of
more importance than even in our own, and Morgagni was

especially favored in the fact that it had come early
in life, so as to enable him to round out his career. His work
was eminently congenial to him, and the labor it involved
was that which constituted for Morgagni the highest form
of recreation. He made many friends among professors
and students. The lectures which Morgagni delivered to
the university became so popular that his lecture-room was
overcrowded and new quarters had to be provided. Many
foreign students were attracted to the university by his widespread reputation as a great and suggestive teacher. These
students came in great numbers especially from the northern
countries of Europe. At one time there were over a thousand
German students at the University of Padua, and when they
organized into a guild for mutual help and social purposes,
Morgagni was chosen by them to act as their patron.

Here at the University of Padua Morgagni was to
found the new science of pathological anotomy. Normal
anatomy had received its development at the hands of the
other great masters in the schools of North Italy. To
Morgagni was to be given to describe the changes which
take place in organs as the result of disease. Needless to say,
this is the most important practical branch of modern medical
science. The symptoms of disease mean very little unless
we know just what organs are affected and what changes
have taken place. Morgagni's work on *The Seats and Causes
of Disease* contains the foundation of modern pathology.
Modern advances might seem to put it out of date, but
the acuity of its author's observations and the truth of his
investigations make it an enduring classic.

Of this work of Morgagni's, Professor Benjamin
Ward Richardson, said: "To this day no medical scholar
can help being delighted and instructed by the study of this
wonderful book. To move into it from the midst of a body

of current medical literature, is like passing from the peri-
odical flux of current general literature to the perusal of a
Shakespearean drama, the *Pilgrim's Progress,* or *Paradise
Lost.* It is a transition from the mediocrity of incessant
repetition of well-known truths told in long and hackneyed
terms, back to descriptions derived direct from nature and
fresh from her treasury. It matters not where the book is
opened, it is always good and instructive reading, full of
suggestion and rich in original narrative."

Some of Morgagni's work in clinical medicine and in
pathology, as detailed in these volumes, remains of perennial
interest and is often referred to. Many an after-time discovery, proclaimed loudly by its author, will be found, at
times only in embryo but often enough in entirety, in its
pages. There are frequent surprises to the reader in the
anticipation of what are supposedly much later thoughts in
medicine. Some of these passages of more general interest
I venture to present here.

It was Morgagni who first realized that minute connections
between parts of the nervous system might very easily provide
the basis for symptoms quite distant from the site of actual
disease. He gives, for instance, a detailed account of a
curiously interesting case in which the patient, a man somewhat beyond middle life, was annoyed on a number of
occasions by violent sneezing. These attacks of sneezing
became more and more frequent and finally were accompanied by difficulty of breathing and a sense of pressure over
the chest. These symptoms became more and more marked,
until finally, during an especially violent attack of sneezing,
the man suddenly died.

Up to this time anatomists generally had declared that
there was no direct nervous connection between the mucous
membrane of the nose and the diaphragm. Sneezing is

due to a violent contraction of the diaphragm and is almost
invariably caused by the presence of an irritant in the nose.
This is, in fact, nature's method of getting rid of irritant
material on the sensitive nasal mucous membranes by
an explosive expulsion of air through the nose. This expulsion of air is brought about by a convulsive contraction
of the diaphragm. It had always been supposed that the
sneezing was due to irritation transmitted through the brain
to the diaphragm.

Morgagni, in discussing the reason why the diaphragm
should be excited into sympathetic reaction by the presence
of an irritant in the nose, pointed out a fact that had been
forgotten or the significance of which had not been appreciated. The membrane of the nose concerned in smell is
supplied by the first pair of cranial nerves, the so-called
olfactory nerves. Between this olfactory nerve and the nerve
which supplies the diaphragm, the phrenic nerve, which is
a cervical and not a cranial nerve, that is to say, comes from
the central nervous system through the spinal cord in the
neck and not directly from the brain, the older anatomists
declared there was no connection. Morgagni pointed out
that the mucous membrane of the nose is partly supplied
also from the fifth pair of cranial nerves. From the fifth
nerve, small branches of connection with the cervical nerves,
as low even as the intercostal nerves, had been traced by
Meckel. This shows the possibility of a nervous reflex;
that is, of a communication of nerve impulses without the
necessity for the intervention of the central nervous system.

This was the first direct tracing of distant reflex nervous
action in human physiology. The problem of nervous reflexes was to remain obscure for more than a century later,
until light was thrown upon it by the investigation of the
French physiologist, Claude Bernard. Here, however, was

the pregnant suggestion of the explanation of the seeming mystery. In subsequent cases Morgagni looked for the confirmation of his theory in this matter and found it. He pointed out that there was a relationship between the abdominal viscera and the olfactory mucous membrane of the nose. In one of his cases an epileptic siezure was always accompanied by a sense of discomfort in the upper abdominal region and a fetid odor. This odor was entirely subjective; that is, though extremely annoying to the patient it could not be noticed by any one else, even though the patient was close at hand and exhaled his breath at the moment of the observation.

This would seem to point to the fact that Morgagni suspected there were other connections between the special senses and important organs besides those which had been discovered by anatomists up to that time. As a matter of fact the so-called sympathetic nervous system does place all the organs of special sense in direct connection with the other important organs of the body. Morgagni's suspicions were to be confirmed by the discoveries made in this sympathetic system during the succeeding century.

Morgagni first of all seems to have realized what was the mechanism by which alcohol injures the human system. He pointed out that the excitation of the heart due to the action of alcohol was reflected in an overdistention of the arteries. This overdistention gradually led to degenerations in the arterial walls. The loss of elasticity thus induced brought on a disturbance of the circulation in the important organs of the body, and so gave rise to symptoms of widespread interference with organic functions.

Morgagni's studies in aneurism, that is, in the dilatation of bloodvessels, show how thoroughly he understood the mechanism of the formation of this serious pathological condition. He pointed out that the first noticeable disease change that occurs is a degeneration of the inner coat of the artery. This leads to the formation of furrows on the inner wall of the vessels and finally brings on weakness of the middle coat of the artery. He realized that the progress of these arterial changes is due to a large extent to blood pressure within the arteries. He felt, too, that blood pressure could be kept from being dangerously high by strict attention to diet limitation. If aneurisms are discovered in early stages the patient's life may well be prolonged by these simple measures. This idea contains the germ of the Tufnell treatment, which has been the most successful therapeutic measure for the treatment of aneurism in the nineteenth century.

The Italian anatomist's acumen led him to appreciate better than ever before in medical history the influence of the mind on the circulation. He pointed out that emotions have a powerful influence on the circulatory system in all its parts. How much the peripheral bloodvessels are affected can be seen in the tendency to blushing during certain forms of excitement, involving shame or embarrassment; on the contrary, pallor in anger, or indignation, or fright. He pointed out, too, that the heart is affected by such emotions and is sometimes strenuously excited and sometimes very much retarded. Morgagni understood that the influence of such emotions in especially excitable individuals leads to wear and tear on the bloodvessels and so to a shortening of lives. He thought of some aneurisms, even those affecting the large bloodvessels, might be caused by sudden intense emotions, and especially by violent efforts to suppress or conceal emotions. We know now, however, that these pathological conditions are due to human passions, but quite other than those which Morgagni had in mind.

It is interesting to note that comparative pathology—

that is, the study of the diseases of animals as illustrating corresponding conditions in human beings—had already attracted the attention of the Bolognese school of medicine. Albertini, who had been a professor of Morgagni's, pointed out that aneurisms are rarely found in animals, because brutes were not subject to emotions as are human beings. Morgagni made still further observations in this line to confirm his own conclusions in the matter. For a time in his earlier life he devoted himself to the study of fishes, because they seemed to promise to throw light on certain problems in human anatomy and pathology.

How closely he studied pathological changes in tissues can be gathered from the fact that his observations led him to point out that aneurism of the aorta occurs most frequently at that part of the curvature of the aorta against which blood is constantly projected by the heart. The realization of the importance of this mechanical factor in the production of aneurism is one of the first successful results of carefully applied observation and knowledge of physical laws in the causation of changes in the tissues as opposed to elaborate theories with very little foundation in fact.

Variations in the pulse attracted his attention, and he was among the first to point out that the occurrence of flatulency is liable to cause disturbance of the heart's action and to bring on noticeable cardiac palpitation in the absence of any organic affection of the heart itself. Morgagni also pointed out that intermittence of the pulse may be due to nervous conditions. He showed that severe mental shock or trying emotions may cause irregularity of the heart's action and pulse intermittency. Some of his observations in this matter show an intuition with regard to the nerve supply of the heart that is quite beyond the anatomy of his time, and seems to indicate that he suspected the existence and function of the sympathetic system and also the existence of a special nerve supply to the small arteries.

Perhaps Morgagni's most penetrating evidence of insight in pathology and its relations to clinical medicine is with regard to tuberculosis. Over a century and a half ago he insisted on its contagiousness. He refused to make autopsies on patients who had died of tuberculosis, and his position in the matter was undoubtedly of the greatest service in directing the attention of his contemporaries, and especially those closely in contact with him, to the important question of intimate association with tuberculous patients as a potent factor in the acquirement of the disease, more potent even than heredity which then occupied all men's minds on this subject.

It might be deemed that this advanced position of Morgagni was due rather to intuitive abhorrence of the disease than to the conviction of actual observation, and that his conclusions were the result more of prejudice than of real knowledge. Any such opinion, however, is absolutely contradicted by the fact that he knew and understood better than any one of his generation the pathology of consumption. He pointed out at a time when any chronic affection of the lungs was liable to be considered consumption that there are a number of forms of chronic bronchitis that are not due to pthisis pulmonalis, but to other slow-running conditions within the lungs.

He anticipated very completely the present position of surgery with regard to the treatment of cancer. He advised the operative removal of these malignant tumors whenever possible. As Benjamin Ward Richardson points out, this advice was given evidently not with the idea that the disease could be always thus completely cured, but because early operation gave speediest relief of annoying symptoms and assured the greatest prolongation of life. Many other methods of removal of cancerous growths were suggested in Morgagni's time, as in our own, and many false promises made and false hopes raised by their advocates. He pointed out that the quickest, the safest, the surest and in the end, for the patient, the easiest method of removal is by the knife in the hands of the bold and skilful surgeon. After a century and a half of vauntedly great advance, especially in surgery, we are practically in the same position as when Morgagni's advice was penned, and his opinion remains practically as valuable to-day as then.

In another important point of medicine Morgagni seems to have anticipated the opinion of our own time. It was the custom to practise venesection very freely. On one or two occasions in his own lifetime Morgagni fell ill and venesection was recommended. His biographer says that he constantly refused this method of treatment, adding very naïvely, "and he who had often cured others by venesection would never allow this remedy to be used upon himself because, as I believe, he had a natural abhorrence to it."

It was an index of thoroughgoing independence of thought in those days to stand out, even for personal reasons, against the overwhelming tradition in favor of blood-letting. But Morgagni had well-grounded doubts as to the remedial efficacy of abstraction of blood, and at least avoided it in his own case.

Besides his skill in practical and theoretic medicine, Morgagni was a man of cultivated taste in art, and he was conversant not only with the literature of his own language, but also of French, Latin and Greek. He was always welcomed in the literary circles of the cities of Northern Italy, and counted among his friends many of the great writers of the time. His success in winning the friendship of rulers was especially noteworthy, and had not a little influence for the advantage of education and science. The patricians of Venice were proud to consider him as a personal friend, and to the Venetian Senate he owed his professorship at Padua. The King of Sardinia, Emanuel III, looked upon him as an intimate acquaintance. All the Popes, five in number, of the second half of his life were on terms of personal intimacy with him, and his advice was asked on many important questions with regard to educational matters in his own day.

Some of these Popes are among the most influential pontiffs that ever occupied the Roman See. The great Benedict XIV, himself a native of Bologna and an intimate friend of the scientist, in his classic work "De Beatificatione Servorum Dei" mentions Morgagni in terms of special commendation. His scarcely less famous successor, Clement XIII, had often consulted Morgagni professionally at Padua before his elevation to the See of Rome. After his election as Pope he assures Morgagni of his continued esteem and friendship, and asks him to consider the Vatican always open to him on his visits to Rome. In an extant letter Clement praises his wisdom, his culture, his courtesy, his charity to God and men, and holds him up as an example to others, since with all his good qualities he had not aroused the enmity or envy of those around him.

Morgagni's life must have been in many ways ideally happy. Rewards for his scientific success began early in life, even before his professorship, and continued all during his long career. The Royal Society of England elected him a fellow in 1724; the Academy of Sciences of Paris made him a member in 1731. In 1735 the Imperial Academy of St. Petersburg conferred a like honor upon him. In 1754 the Academy of Berlin elected him to honorary membership.

His English biographer, Dr. William Cook, says quaintly

that all the learned and great who came into his neighborhood did not depart without a visit to Morgagni. He was in
correspondence with most of the great men of his time, and
the terms of intimate relationship that this correspondence
reveals are the best evidence of the estimation in which
Morgagni was held, especially by the prominent scientists of
his time. Among them were such men as Ruysch, Boerhaave, Sir Richard Mead, Haller and Meckel. This wide
acquaintanceship of itself was a great distinction at a time
when the means of communication were so much more
limited than at present.

It is gratifying to think that Morgagni must have been
enviably content in his private life, though, as usually happens
when this is the case, very little is said explicitly on this subject.
His untiring labor deserved the compensation of a loving
domestic circle. During his retirement at Forli, after his
graduation from the university and when, from overwork, his
health failed him for a time, he married the descendant
of a noble family of the town, Paola Vergieri by name, a
companion for him who, biographers declare, could not have
been surpassed in judgment or in affection. They had a
family of fifteen children, eight of whom survived their father
though he lived to the ripe age of eighty-seven years. There
were three sons, one of whom died in childhood; another
became a Jesuit and taught in the famous Jesuit school at
Bologna whose magnificent building has now become the
municipal museum, the Accademia delle Belle Arte. The
third followed his father's profession, married and settled
in Bologna, but died before his father, who assumed the care
of his grandchildren. All Morgagni's daughters who grew
up to womanhood, eight in number, became nuns in various
religious orders.

The spirit of science had not disturbed the development

4

of a homely simple faith in the family. The great Father of
Pathology, far from being disturbed by the unselfish self-
sacrifice of so many of his children, bore it not only with
equanimity but even rejoiced at it. His relations to his
children were ever most tender. After the suppression of the
Jesuits, his son, who had been a member of the order, worked
at science with his father at the University of Bologna and not
without distinction.

The estimation in which Morgagni was held by his contemporaries can be judged from the fact that twice when invading
armies had entered the Emilia and laid siege to Bologna, their
commanders, as in old Greek history did the Grecian gen-
erals with regard to Pindar and Archimedes, gave strict orders
that special care was to be taken that no harm come to Morgagni, and that his work was not to be hampered. Having
lived his long life amidst the reverent respect of all who knew
him, he died full of day and honors.

Succeeding generations have not been backward in acknowledging Morgagni's merits. I have already spoken of
Virchow's tribute to his greatness. The Italians have long
considered him as one of their most brilliant names in medicine. One of the best known of the representative Italian
medical journals is *Il Morgagni*, published at Milan. To
its pages the foreigner seeking to know the progress of Italian
medicine turns almost as the first resort. *Il Morgagni* was
founded some fifty years ago, and continues to uphold its
reputation as one of the world-known medical periodicals.

The great medical scientist whose work was to prove the
foundation of modern pathology, and thus be the source of
more blessings to mankind than ever even he dreamed of,
remained in the midst of the reverence and gratitude of his
generation, one of those beautifully simple characters whom
all the world delights to honor. As a teacher he was the

idol of his students. No great scientist who came to Italy felt that his journey had been quite complete unless he had had the privilege of an interview with Morgagni. This friend of Popes and of many of the European rulers was the happy father of a houseful of members of religious orders, and considered himself blest that so many of them had chosen the better part. He was himself all during his long life the ardent seeker after truth, who did well the work that came to his hand and followed his conscience in sincere simplicity of heart and reaped his personal reward in the peace that is beyond understanding to those who have not the gift of faith to appreciate the things that are beyond the domain of sense.

AUENBRUGGER, THE INVENTOR OF PHYSICAL DIAGNOSIS

While medicine is your vocation, or calling, see to it that you have also an avocation—some intellectual pastime which may serve to keep you in touch with the world of art, of science, or of letters. Begin at once the cultivation of some interest other than the purely professional. The difficulty is in a selection and the choice will be different according to your tastes and training.—OSLER, *Aequanimitas and other Addresses.*

AUENBRUGGER,

THE INVENTOR OF PHYSICAL DIAGNOSIS.

AT the present time the most interesting development in medicine is the gradual reduction of the death rate from tuberculosis. This is entirely due to the fact that the disease can now be recognized very early in its course, and that, as a consequence, the treatment may be begun before serious damage has been inflicted on the lungs. Under the circumstances, the disease formerly supposed incurable has become according to all the best modern authorities one of the most tractable of infectious diseases. In their recent lectures in Philadelphia, before the Phipps Institute for the Prevention and Cure of Consumption, such distinguished medical authorities as Dr. Trudeau, of Saranac; Professor Osler, of Johns Hopkins, and Professor G. Simms Woodhead, of Cambridge, England, insist on the absolute curability of tuberculosis when it is taken in time. Professor Woodhead particularly asserts that there has been entirely too much pessimism in this matter, even among physicians.

This present confidence with regard to the successful treatment of pulmonary consumption is due to the fact that the diagnosis can be made early. The glory of this early recognition depends entirely on two men—Auenbrugger, of Vienna, and Laennec, of Paris. To Auenbrugger, whose work was done nearly half a century before that of Laennec, must be given the credit of having first approached the problem of differentiating diseases of the lungs from one

(55)

another by methods which were so objectively practical that every practitioner of medicine could, after having become expert in their employment, use them with absolute confidence in his diagnosis.

Modern medical science and practice acknowledges very gratefully its deep obligations to what is known as the Vienna school of medicine. It is not a little surprising to find that it was the practical side of medicine particularly which was developed at Vienna, since the inhabitants of the Austrian capital, while supposed to have artistic tastes far above the average, are usually considered to be among the most impractical people in Europe. For over one hundred and fifty years, however, the medical department of the University of Vienna has always ranked among the first in the world. Many of the Viennese professors of medicine have been acknowledged as the greatest teachers of their time. Beginning with Van Swieten and De Haen during the second half of the eighteenth century, the medical department of the University of Vienna has scarcely ever been without at least one of the leading lights of medicine in Europe. Wunderlich, Rokitansky and Skoda were, in the middle of the nineteenth century, the greatest medical men of their time. Hebra, Billroth and Nothnagel worthily continued the tradition of medical greatness in the Austrian capital. Even at the present time, notwithstanding the great advance in medicine and medical teaching that has come over all Europe, it is generally conceded that the best place in the world to study clinical medicine—that is, to study illness at the bedside of the patient—is the famous Allgemeines Krankenhaus, the General Hospital of Vienna.

The clinical teaching of medicine developed much later in the history of medical education than might naturally have been expected. There is a tradition of bedside instruction

in medicine in old Grecian times at the various shrines of
Æsculapius, but this is not well authenticated. Early in the
sixteenth century came the modern birth of clinical medical
instruction at St. Francis's Hospital, in Padua, in connection
with the University there, which in every line did so much
for modern medicine. The first clinic that attracted widespread attention, however, did not come until Boerhaave's
time, at the end of the seventeenth and the beginning of the
eighteenth century. The bedside instruction in medicine
by this distinguished master drew hosts of students to the
hitherto comparatively unimportant University of Leyden,
in Holland. Two rulers—just the two who, to modern
minds, would perhaps appear least likely to do so—at once
recognized the immense practical value of this innovation
in medical teaching and immediately set about securing its
benefits for their people. Pope Benedict XIII and the
Empress of Austria put themselves in communication with
Boerhaave, and the Pope was the first to avail himself of the
advice in the matter which the great Dutch master gave.
The Roman clinic became, in the first half of the eighteenth
century, under the direction of the distinguished Lancisi,
one of the best known in Europe.

The Austrian Empress, Maria Theresa, interested in everything that could prove to be for the benefit of her people,
invited the distinguished pupil of Boerhaave, Van Swieten,
to become her family physician, and encouraged him in the
foundation of a clinical medical school at Vienna. Van
Swieten soon came to occupy a very prominent place at
Court. When he was invited from Holland, on the recom-
mendation of the sister of the Empress, there was no heir to
the Austrian crown, though one had been anxiously looked
for for several years. Heirs to the number of sixteen in all
blessed the imperial family in the next twenty-five years,

and Van Swieten became the confidential adviser of the
reigning monarchs in polity as well as in medicine. Accordingly, when he suggested the invitation of De Haen, who
had also been a pupil of Boerhaave, the suggestion was
promptly accepted, and the Leyden colleagues became the
founders of the Old Vienna School of Medicine, as it is called.
They established the tradition of bedside teaching, of actual
practical experience in the treatment of patients, and of the
collection of detailed information of every feature of cases
that could possibly be helpful for diagnosis. They also
established the custom of demonstrations on pathological
material with confrontation of the diagnostic conclusions
during life and the findings of the postmortem examination
in fatal cases, which, down to our own day, makes Vienna
an ideal place for serious post-graduate work in clinical
medicine.

It was not long after the establishment of the clinic on
these broad lines at Vienna before the first important fruit
of the new teaching method was to be gathered. Curiously
enough, however, this initial advance in practical medicine
did not come from one of the distinguished heads of the clinic,
but from a comparatively young man of no previous reputation. The greatest discovery ever made at Vienna is due
to Auenbrugger, an unassuming practitioner of medicine,
who came from the Austrian province of Styria, or, as it
is called in German, the Steiermark, about the middle of the
eighteenth century. He was the son of a small hotel keeper
of Gratz, and, after making his medical studies in Vienna,
he remained at the capital for some years, doing hospital
work.

While thus engaged, the young Styrian, who attracted very
little attention except for his affability, and who made no
pretension to special knowledge or genius in observation,

laid the first stone in the structure of modern exact diagnosis of pulmonary disease, and cleared up many of the obscurities in which all affections of the chest had been shrouded before his time. Having accomplished this noteworthy achievement before he was forty years of age, Auenbrugger then quietly settled down to be an ordinary medical practitioner in the Austrian capital, with a special reputation for his knowledge of chest diseases, and for kindly ways that gave him as much interest in his poor patients as in those that could afford to pay handsomely for his services.

Leopold Auenbrugger, afterward Edler von Auenbrug—a term about equivalent to the English "Knight of Auenbrug" —who thus stands at the head of modern medical diagnosis, was born on the 19th of November, 1722, at Gratz, in Lower Austria. His early education was received at Gratz, and it seems to have been of rather a comprehensive character, for Auenbrugger, later in life, was a member of the elegant literary circles in Vienna and a welcome friend at the tables of cultured and distinguished fellow-townsmen. It will be recalled, by those who remember German literature, that at this time Vienna was the centre of culture in Germany, attracting many literary men—as, for instance, the two Schlegels—from other parts of Germany.

Auenbrugger's father was of the lower middle class, the proprietor of the Gasthaus Zum Schwarzen Mohren, in one of the suburbs of the city of Gratz, but also the owner of another hotel in the city itself, so that he was able, by making some sacrifices, to afford his son a university and medical education in Vienna. The family were not in very affluent circumstances, however, and in this Auenbrugger was in the same condition as many other of the distinguished medical men who have made important original discoveries. Volta, Laennec, Johann Mueller, Helmholtz, Pasteur and

Virchow were all the sons of comparatively poor parents, and had to eke out their university education by doing teaching work as soon as they were considered capable.

Auenbrugger's studies in medicine were pursued under the well-known Baron Van Swieten. Van Swieten was, as has been said, one of the most distinguished of Boerhaave's pupils, and devoted most of his life to writing a set of commentaries on Boerhaave's aphorisms and editing his master's work. Van Swieten's greatest ambition was to make the Austrian capital the home of the great clinical school of medicine and a pilgrimage at least as attractive for physicians seeking to study practical medicine at the bedside as had been his own alma mater at Leyden. He was of so great administrative ability that Maria Theresa made him one of her state counsellors.

With all the influence of the government behind him, then, it is not surprising that Van Swieten succeeded in his very laudable project of establishing a great medical school at Vienna.

It was fortunate that Auenbrugger made his medical studies under such good auspices. We have no details of his student life nor of his success in his examinations. Even as a student his engagement of marriage to Marianna von Priesterberg was announced. The formal marriage ceremony took place in 1754, when Auenbrugger was about thirty-two years of age. His wife seems to have had a dowry, and this enabled Auenbrugger to begin his medical career in Vienna. Some years before this, as a young graduate physician, he had accepted the position of resident medical attendant at the Spanish military hospital of the Holy Trinity in Vienna. This hospital was large and important and provided manifold opportunities for clinical study. Its wards were frequently drawn on by the clinical department of the University of Vienna for cases to be demonstrated before the students.

This fact was sufficient to make Auenbrugger's position of great educative value for him. Mistakes in diagnosis would be apt to be discovered, since the interesting cases were reviewed by some of the best physicians of the time in Europe. His position carried with it no salary beyond his maintenance, but proved well worth the time he gave it, since it developed in him habits of careful investigation. Just ten years after he began his work at this hospital he published the little book called "Inventum Novum," or new discovery, on which his reputation depends. It was written in Latin, and its full title ran: "A New Discovery that Enables the Physician, from the Percussion of the Human Thorax, to Detect the Diseases Hidden within the Chest."

Altogether his little manual probably does not contain much more than ten thousand words. It is perhaps two or three times as long as thousands of medical articles published every year in our modern medical journals. It contains, however, one of the most important discoveries in the whole history of medicine. One of the best diagnosticians of the nineteenth century, Skoda, the distinguished head of the Vienna school of sixty years ago, calls the discovery that Auenbrugger outlined so unpretentiously "the beginning of modern diagnosis," and hailed Auenbrugger himself as the founder of the new science of diagnosis that was to prove so fruitful of good in the prevention of human suffering.

It is interesting to compare Auenbrugger's little book with Van Swieten's commentaries on Boerhaave's works, which were published in some eight huge volumes. Van Swieten's successor, De Haen, an equally illustrious contemporary of Auenbrugger, published about the same time some eighteen volumes on the science of medicine. Neither of these works is ever consulted now, except by some enthusiastic student of the history of medicine, who wishes to clear up a point in medical historical development; but Auenbrugger's unpretending monograph is, and will ever remain, a classic. Practically nothing has been needed to complete the clinical usefulness of his discovery. Like Laennec, whose work was done just half a century later, he had the genius to realize what the possibilities and the limitations of his discovery are, and he completed it in all its details before giving it to the public.

Auenbrugger's discovery consisted in recognizing that diseases of the chest can be distinguished from one another and their varying character differentiated by the sounds elicited when the chest is tapped with the finger. To this tapping he gave the technical name, since become classic in medicine, of percussion. Wherever there is air in the chest, that is all over the healthy lungs, the sound elicited by percussion resembles that given out by a drum over which a thick woolen cloth has been placed. Over the heart, where there is no air, the sound given out, when the chest is percussed, corresponds very nearly to the sound produced when the thigh is tapped. The sound elicited by percussion of the thigh Auenbrugger took as the standard of dulness and applied to it the term Schenkel-ton, or thigh sound.

When the lungs become consolidated because of an inflammatory process such as pneumonia or tuberculosis, then the percussion note over the consolidated area resembles the sound over the leg or that found over the heart. As a rule the heart is somewhat covered by the lungs, and the sound produced by percussion over it is not quite as dull as that over the solid muscular structures of the legs. Whenever fluid finds its way into the thorax, as in pleurisy, then the sound produced on percussion is very dull.

Auenbrugger further showed that by means of the sound thus obtained he could demonstrate the size of the heart under varying conditions, and so determine whether it is larger than normal or not. This gave the first inkling as to the discernment of hypertrophy and dilatation of the heart, and was the first step in the modern differential diagnosis of heart diseases. He showed, moreover, that he could, by percussion, outline very exactly the extent to which a consolidation of the lung has taken place, or the height to which an effusion into the pleural cavity reaches. These conclusions and demonstrations require not only the greatest care but the most deliberate confirmation of every detail by comparison of the diagnosis during life with the condition found after death in fatal cases.

Auenbrugger seems to have spared neither time nor labor in this work of confirmation. He made a number of experiments upon dead bodies, injecting fluid into the pleural cavity and then demonstrating by percussion the line of demarcation that indicated the level of the fluid within the chest, as well as the pulmonary conditions that developed because of its presence. In the study of pneumonia and tuberculosis particularly, Auenbrugger spent many hours of patient investigation during his ten years of hospital service. He succeeded not only in demonstrating the presence of consolidation, but also the existence of cavities in the lungs and their size and general character.

Vienna was an ideal place for the development of Auenbrugger's ideas of confirmation. At this time, it must have been one of the most unhealthy places in Europe as regards pulmonary diseases. The city was surrounded by walls that occupied the ground now taken up by the magnificent Ring Strasse and the inhabitants were packed into extremely narrow quarters. The modern municipal sanitary conscience is lax enough in our own day, but at that time it had not been awakened to the slightest sense of duty toward the citizens. Narrow, wandering streets lined by high buildings that made an attaché of the British Legation of Vienna speak of the houses of the city, scarcely more than fifty years ago, as "well-like," were the universal rule.

It must be remembered that the present magnificent Austrian capital, containing, perhaps, the handsomest single street and some of the finest buildings in the world, is entirely a creation of the last half-century. The old city had every cause to be unsanitary. Situated in the valley of the Danube, liable in the spring-time to serious floodings from the capricious, mighty river, which has been brought under control only in recent years at great expense; in an exposed situation, which makes it a veritable temple of the winds during the autumn and winter; it is not surprising that tuberculosis should have been very frequent. Even with all its improvements in recent years, sanitary, hygienic, municipal and domiciliary, Vienna has at the present time one of the highest death rates from tuberculosis in Europe. In Auenbrugger's time there must have been practically unlimited opportunity for the study of pulmonary diseases of all kinds.

How well the brilliant young medical observer took advantage of the opportunities thus afforded him can be judged very well from the passages of his book that refer to chronic pulmonary diseases. He divides the chronic diseases of the thorax in which abnormal percussion sounds are heard into two classes. In the first place, he places those in which the thoracic organs are rendered less capable of resisting disease and become actually affected, because of insidious influences, such as hereditary conditions, depressing circumstances, poverty and poor nutrition. Without really calling it tuberculosis, it is evident that in this group pulmonary con-

sumption is included. The second class consists of affections
in which the thoracic organs become diseased from definite,
easily recognizable causes. Such are disturbances of the
general health in pulmonary affections that follow thoracic
disease not completely recovered from. By these diseases
Auenbrugger evidently intends cases of pneumonia or other
affections of the lungs, or trauma and the like, which are
followed by tuberculous processes.

With regard to cavities in the lungs, Auenbrugger was
able not only to demonstrate their presence and to show by
autopsy records that his localization and determination of
their approximate form and size were correct, but he also
understood the method of their formation and explains the
reasons for certain varieties of cavities that occur. He
speaks of two classes of cavity formations. From one kind
there is an ichorous discharge; from the other variety the
evacuations are purulent. Cavities with non-purulent secretions are situated only in the lung. Abscesses of various
kinds—that is, cavities with purulent secretions—may occur
in any part, or in any of the organs of the thorax. The lung
cavities are usually due to the breaking down of what he calls
crude tubercles. Both kinds of cavities may either be closed
or have an opening into the bronchi.

Auenbrugger showed very well how to distinguish, by
percussion, cavities of various kinds, and set it down as a
principle, that before the evacuation of the contents of the
cavity percussion over it gave a distinctly dull note, resembling that obtained when the thigh is percussed, while after
evacuation, as by copious expectoration, a distinctly resonant
note occurred. It is clear from his discussion of the symptoms noted in cavities (at least in the opinion of Dr. Merbach,
who wrote a sketch of Auenbrugger's life for the Jahres-
bericht der Gesellschaft für Natur und Heilkunde in Dresden,

5

in 1861), that Auenbrugger was very near the discovery of auscultation in his study of pulmonary cavities. Auenbrugger says that when a cavity has been located by means of percussion, if the hand be laid over the place beneath which it lies and the patient is asked to cough, the fremitus produced by the pus in the cavity can be felt as it moves under the coughing impulse. This is what we now know as palpation. If instead of using his hand Auenbrugger had applied his ear to the chest, auscultation would have been discovered nearly half a century before Laennec began his work upon the subject. Perhaps Merbach, who was himself a native of Styria and a professor at the University of Gratz, was for patriotic motives more ready than others might be to give Auenbrugger credit for practically discovering auscultation.

Auenbrugger's and Laennec's observations were made on exactly the same sort of clinical material. They were both studying advanced cases of tuberculosis in the hospitals of a great city. Laennec's work was actually not anticipated in the slightest degree however. How Auenbrugger could have made the careful examinations of the chest that he did in thoracic diseases without acquiring some knowledge of the value of the further application of the sense of hearing, which Laënnec was to employ so fruitfully in the diagnosis of affections of the lungs and heart, seems to us almost impossible to understand. Discoveries once made, however, always seem so obvious that the wonder is they were not made long before. It takes genius to cross the line into the realm of the hitherto unknown, and the contemporary generation usually occupies itself mainly with making little of the new discovery. Even genius very rarely makes more than one original observation in a lifetime, and it would be too much to expect more from Auenbrugger.

The preface to Auenbrugger's little book is a model of concise directness typical of the man and his ways. 'As the modest introduction to a work that will ever be a classic in medicine it seems to deserve a place here:

"I present to you, kind reader, a new sign for the detection of diseases of the chest, which I have discovered. It consists in the percussion of the human thorax and the determination of the internal condition of this cavity by the varying resonance of the sounds thus produced. My discoveries in this subject are not committed to paper because of an itch for writing, nor an inordinate desire for theorizing. Seven years of observation have put the subject in order and have clarified it for myself and now I feel that it should be published.

"I foresee very well that I shall encounter no little opposition to my views and I put my invention before the public with that anticipation. I realize, however, that envy and blame and even hatred and calumny have never failed to come to men who have illuminated art or science by discoveries or have added to their perfection. I expect to have to submit to this danger myself, but I think that no one will be able to call any of my observations to account. I have written only what I have myself learned by personal observation over and over again, and what my senses have taught me during long hours of toil. I have never permitted myself to add or subtract anything from my observations because of the seductions of preconceived theory.

"I would not wish, however, that any one should think that this method of diagnosis, which I suggest, has been developed to its utmost perfection. I confess with all candor that there are defects in the system which conscientious observation will, I hope, amend with time. It is possible that there are even other important truths for the recognition

of disease still hidden from this method of diagnosis.   Some
of these may prove of great usefulness for the differentia-
tion, prognosis and cure of diseases of the chest.

"This was the reason why in my personal experience,
after I had succeeded in finding the signs in the chest and
proceeded further to the investigation of their causes so
far as my own observation could help me, I have always
afterward had recourse to the commentaries of the illustrious
Baron Van Swieten, since I have considered that whatever
can be desired by an observant man is sure to be found in
his work. I have thus been able to spare you a long
disquisition. I have found in his work a sure basis of
knowledge on which my slight superstructure may be raised
up to view.

"I do not doubt, however, that I have accomplished a
work which will earn the gratitude of all true devotees of
the art of medicine, since I have succeeded in making clear
certain things which shed not a little light on our knowledge
of the obscure diseases of the chest, a subject hitherto very
imperfectly understood.

"I have omitted many things that seem doubtful because
they are as yet not sufficiently elaborated.   I shall endeavor,
however, faithfully to devote myself to [literally to sweat
over] the further development of these points.   Finally, it
has not been my effort to write in any elegant diction.   I
have chosen a style in which I may be thoroughly understood.
Vale;
    "December 31, 1760."

Auenbrugger's own realization of the importance of his
work and of its significant value for medicine kept him faithfully investigating his chosen subject, though he seems to
have met with very little encouragement from members of

the medical profession near him. It is extremely difficult to understand how his practical observations and thoroughly conservative claim failed to attract more attention than they did from really great physicians who were deeply interested in the progress of medicine. At least two distinguished writers on medicine, Van Swieten and De Haen, compiled treatises on medical subjects that included the consideration of diseases of the chest within a few years after Auenbrugger's *Inventum Novum* appeared, and yet neither of them devotes any space to the question of percussion nor hints at its possible value.

Van Swieten's work consisted of commentaries upon the aphorisms of Boerhaave. The Vienna professor did not, however, limit himself to the consideration of the aphorisms alone, but made his work also a compendium of his own clinical experiences with acute and chronic diseases. As a matter of fact his commentaries on the aphorisms are each a monograph on some special disease. The two last volumes of this commentary appear after the publication of Auenbrugger's book on percussion, one volume being published in 1772, the other in 1774.

The first of these articles contains a long article on pulmonary consumption, and the other an almost equally long chapter on pleurisy with effusion. In neither of the volumes, however, is there any mention of percussion, or of Auenbrugger's work, though if Van Swieten had given any serious attention to the subject, he must have become convinced how valuable Auenbrugger's invention was in the diagnosis of these conditions.

This omission is all the more surprising as Auenbrugger was a pupil of Van Swieten's and practically dedicated his *Inventum Novum* to his master. He mentions Van Swieten's work several times in his little book. Auenbrugger's investigations were not unknown to Van Swieten then, and the only conclusion to be drawn from his neglect to mention Auenbrugger's methods is that he deliberately omitted reference to them because of his failure to recognize the value of the discovery. This constitutes one of the most serious blots on Van Swieten's medical career. He was succeeded as the head of the clinic in Vienna by De Haen, who also came from Leyden and brought with him the methods of Boerhaave's clinical school. As the time during which Auenbrugger was making his valuable observations at the Spanish military hospital coincides with the years when De Haen was professor of clinical medicine, and when he was frequently indebted to his colleague of the Spanish hospital for his cases for demonstration, it is impossible to conceive that Auenbrugger or his work should have remained unknown to the distinguished head of the clinic.

There is not a single mention, however, to be found anywhere in De Haen's voluminous writings of Auenbrugger or his work. De Haen's principal work is his *Ratio Medendi (System of Medicine)*, published at Vienna during the years from 1757 to 1779. It consists of eighteen volumes, in which all the important forms of disease as well as the rarer types of affections that came to the clinic are thoroughly discussed. De Haen treated of pneumonia, of consumption, of pleurisy with effusion, which he calls dropsy of the chest, but never suggests the use of percussion. On the contrary, he complains in a number of places how very obscure and difficult of diagnosis are thoracic diseases and especially dropsy of the chest, pleuritic and pericardial exudates, and insists on the ease with which errors of diagnosis may be made in these subjects. He failed completely to recognize how much light had just been thrown on this subject by Auenbrugger's work, and how much easier the differential diagnoses of these conditions were to be as the result of systematic percussion.

Some of the commentaries on Auenbrugger's work are not entirely depreciative, however. In Ludwig's *Commentaria de Rebus in Scientia Naturali et Medicina Gestis* for the year 1762, published at Leipzig, there is an excellent notice of Auenbrugger's work within a year after its appearance. It is not known who the reviewer was, but he calls Auenbrugger's discovery "a torch that was designed to illumine the darkness in which diseases of the thorax had up to this time lain concealed." A brilliant future was prophesied for the new method of examination. It is evident that the writer not only thoroughly comprehended Auenbrugger's work, but had himself applied the percussion method for purposes of diagnosis.

This is almost the only favorable and reasonably intelligent review of Auenbrugger's work to be found in the medical journals of the time. In the new Medical Library, issued by Rudolph Vogel, Professor of Medicine in Göttingen, published in six volumes in 1766, there is a short mention of Auenbrugger's book and his new discovery. This reference is, however, an extremely curious affair. The good professor completely failed to understand in what the new discovery really consists. It is clear that he had never read Auenbrugger's book. He seems to have heard of the subject from some medical friend, and to have obtained an entirely wrong notion. He talks of Auenbrugger's new diagnostic method as if it were an imitation of Hippocrates's succussion method of recognizing the presence of fluid in the chest by shaking the patient till the liquid gave the characteristic splash.

Other medical writers of the time perhaps, as the result of reading Professor Vogel's book, made the same mistake in their appreciation of Auenbrugger's work. Vogel himself insisted that Auenbrugger did wrong to claim any originality for his invention, since it had been used so long before by Hippocrates. He adds that what is original with Auenbrugger is of very little value, the older ideas being the only ones worth while considering with regard to the application of this so-called new method of diagnosis. Vogel was an authority in medicine at the time and other commentators took the key note from him in this matter, and in many parts of Germany it was generally accepted that Auenbrugger's method of percussion was only an elaborated method of the so-called succussion of Hippocrates.

Under these circumstances it is perhaps not surprising that Auenbrugger's work attracted very little attention in the German-speaking countries. In Vienna itself, as we have already said, Van Swieten and De Haen failed utterly to recognize its value. Outside of Vienna their example was naturally followed, for the Vienna school was considered authoritative, and surely, if any one, the professors of the University of Vienna might be expected to know whether Auenbrugger's new discovery was really of any value or not.

It is interesting to compare Auenbrugger's state of mind, with regard to the neglect of his discovery, with Laennec's remark in the preface of his book. Laennec said: "For our generation is not inquisitive as to what is being accomplished by its own sons. Claims of new discoveries made by contemporaries are apt for the most part to be met by smiles and mocking remarks. It is always easier to condemn than to test by actual experience." Auenbrugger seems to have suffered from more than the neglect of which Laennec complains. When he speaks of envy and calumny in no uncertain terms, the only conclusion possible is that his representations as to his discoveries must have been set down as pretensions that his contemporaries considered unjustified by what they knew of his work.

It is interesting also to note that both men found their prospects of reward, not in the good will of their contemporaries, nor even the prospect of fame, but in the hope that their work would be useful in lessening the sum of human suffering. Laennec said: "It suffices for me if I can only feel sure that this method will commend itself to a few worthy and learned men who will make it of use to many patients. I shall consider it ample, yea more than sufficient reward for my labor, if it should prove the means by which a single human being is snatched from untimely death."

Laennec's words are almost an echo fifty years afterward of Auenbrugger's expressions, just quoted: "I console myself," he said, "with the thought that I have accomplished a work which will earn the gratitude of all true devotees of the art of medicine, since I have succeeded in making clear many things which shed not a little light on the chapter of the obscure diseases of the chest, in which our knowledge has hitherto been so very incomplete."

As a rule it may be said that medical observers whose genius leads them to step across the narrow line that separates the known from the unknown are likely to lack the appreciation of their own generation. Long before Auenbrugger or Laennec, Harvey, the discoverer of the circulation of the blood, said to friends that he did not expect any one of his generation to accept the new doctrine, and it is well known that the great medical men of the time did not accept it. Harvey is not an isolated example, and even in our own time real medical progress sometimes waits for years for recognition, while well-advertised pretended advances are occupying the centre of the stage. Auenbrugger's discovery made its impress, however, and was never entirely lost to sight. Even before his death there was the consoling prospect of its meeting with adequate attention.

De Haen's successor in Vienna, Maximilian Stoll, treated Auenbrugger's work very differently from his predecessors, and was the first to introduce it practically into clinical medical training. Stoll did not hesitate in his clinic, on the strength of what was discovered by means of percussion, to attempt the evacuation of fluid from the pleural cavity on a number of occasions. It can be easily understood that with their lack of knowledge of the necessity for thorough cleanliness in the surgical sense, such an operation might readily be followed by discouragingly fatal results. This actually happened in Stoll's own experience. He does not, however, seem to have abandoned his practice of tapping the chest because of this. He insisted to his students that Auenbrugger more than anyone else had experience in removing fluid, and especially purulent collections, from the chest, and he recommended the practice to them. He added that medicine owed as much to Auenbrugger for his rational method of treating effusions into the pleural cavity, whether of pus or serum, as for his diagnostic sign by which the presence of the fluid could surely be recognized.

Some of Stoll's pupils took up the work of commending Auenbrugger's method, and a little book written by one of them, Eyerel, came into the hands of the distinguished French physician, Corvisart. Eyerel did not hesitate to say, in his treatise on empyema, that the practice of percussion of the thorax, a diagnostic method introduced by the very distinguished Vienna physician, Auenbrugger, had been of great help to them in the study of this disease.

Once the great French professor of medicine, Corvisart, took it up, the new method of diagnosis was destined to have an immediate and world-wide vogue. Corvisart was not only a power in medicine because of his faculty of observation and his thorough appreciation of the work of others, but he was the court physician of the first Napoleon, and this gave any ideas that he favored many adventitious chances for publicity. Napoleon's well-known faculty for selecting men for special positions whose genius was calculated to be of service to him was never less at fault than when he violated most of the court medical traditions in Paris and chose Corvisart for the imperial physician. Corvisart's selection was the result of Napoleon's appreciation of his new method of diagnosis, namely, that of percussion, in chest diseases.

The Emperor himself was suffering from a persistent cold and was told that Corvisart, instead of following the traditional method of feeling the pulse, looking very wisely at the tongue and then gazing learnedly into space, conducted an actual examination of the chest and sounded it carefully all over, in order to determine where abnormal conditions might exist. This struck Napoleon as a very practical and possibly valuable feature of diagnosis. Accordingly Corvisart was summoned to give his professional opinion. After the consultation he was made the Emperor's private physician.

When Corvisart took up the subject of percussion of the chest, it was practically unknown in Europe outside of Vienna. Even in the city of its origin, as we have seen, it was not well appreciated. Auenbrugger's little book had fallen into oblivion. Corvisart obtained his hint as to the possible value of percussion from Stoll's and Eyerel's appreciative remarks with regard to it. The Frenchman used the method to some extent and, realizing its value, resolved to call the attention of his countrymen and the medical world to this very helpful aid in diagnosis. It was at this time that he came upon Auenbrugger's original monograph. Instead then of writing himself on the subject, he translated

Auenbrugger's little book into French and made a commentary on it.

Corvisart was Laennec's patron in medicine, his favorite teacher, and the man to whom the great French physician owed much of his early inspiration   It is no little merit in Corvisart's career thus to have been the connecting link between the men who did most for the practical science of medicine, and especially for the important but obscure chapter of diseases of the chest.   He did not attempt at all to claim for himself any of the merit that he felt should rightfully go to Auenbrugger, and while his own observations and writings established percussion upon a firm basis and extended its knowledge, he shares the immortality of his discoverer, and comes down to us in medical history as an example of the reward of having rendered faithfully what was due, where it was due.   It has been the custom to praise Corvisart for his justice toward Auenbrugger.   Mere justice seems scarcely a worthy reason for praise of a great man, yet the history of medicine is so full of failures on the part of subsequent observers to acknowledge priority of discovery, that perhaps the praise does not seem quite as futile as it otherwise would.

It is not surprising then that Corvisart's pupil Laennec should have appreciated very thoroughly the value of Auenbrugger's discovery.   In the preface of his book on Mediate Auscultation, Laennec bewails the fact that men are generally neglectful of discoveries made in their own time, and fail to give them the attention they deserve.   He attributes this neglect rather to the well-known carelessness of men than to any deliberate failure to recognize the merit of contemporary work.   He says:

"Lack of attention is an extremely common failing of all men.   What it takes years and hard labor to acquire, is not infrequently passed over without notice. Auenbrugger's method, published some fifty years ago, though capable of being learned in a few days, and without difficulty, and of being put into practice without the use of any instruments, although snatched from oblivion by my illustrious preceptor, Professor Corvisart, and made clearer than it had been left even by the author himself, is not as yet in ordinary use among physicians. Even the wonderful invention of the illustrious Jenner, though received with so much praise, and with regard to whose efficaciousness numberless confirmatory observations have been made, is already somewhat less prominent in the minds of men than it should be, or at least it would be, only for the fact that the governments of many countries, provinces and cities, the foresight of the clergy, of the authorities of all kinds, and the advice of the best physicians have exerted all their influence to keep it at public expense constantly in practice."

After about ten years of service at the Spanish military hospital, Auenbrugger resigned his position there and took up private practice. In this he was eminently successful, being, as might be expected, especially in demand for cases involving affections of the thorax. His practice appears to have been to a great extent among the better class of people, but he seems never to have neglected the poorer patients whom he had come to know during his hospital experience. There are traditions in Vienna of his unfailing willingness to assist the poor and even to put himself to considerable inconvenience in order to be of service to them.

Tradition tells that he was very conscientious in the pursuit of his vocation as a physician, and among the family relics there is preserved a small lantern which he kept always by his bedside, to light him on his visits to the sick when called out at night. It must not be forgotten that city streets were not regularly lighted at the end of the eighteenth century, and night calls even in city work must have been a source of great annoyance and discomfort. There is a family tradition, too, that the night bell at his house was connected directly with Auenbrugger's room, so that the others of the household might not be disturbed when night callers came for him. Every tradition points to him as a man among men in his unselfish readiness to save others trouble, and do all the good in his power.

Auenbrugger was, according to well-grounded traditions, especially admirable in his relations toward other members of the medical profession. This may not seem a very significant sign of amiability to those outside the profession, but it is well recognized that even great physicians have not always been known to get on well with brother practitioners. Auenbrugger has, besides, the pleasant reputation of having been of great material assistance to a number of needy medical students during the time of their university careers, and to have frequently lent a helping hand to young practitioners in the city, who probably found it quite as discouraging, beginning practice in those days, as any of their young confreres of this generation find it at the present time.

To physicians and medical students when ill, Auenbrugger was almost unceasing in attention. Two or three physicians of the generation immediately after his attributed to his unselfish care and devotion to them their recovery from what would otherwise have been mortal illnesses. In this way Auenbrugger seems to have been a man whom everyone who came to know him, even slightly, learned to love and respect. His relations to his family and relatives were always of the most happy, kind character, and family traditions show that his fatherly care was befittingly returned to him in his old age. The number of his friends was very great, and he counted among them some of the most distinguished inhabitants of the Austrian capital.

Notwithstanding his devotion to his practice, Auenbrugger did not cease to make observations that occasionally he considered worthy of being committed to paper. He was especially careful in the study of his cases, and left fully written records of over 400 important cases that he had studied very faithfully. His attention seems to have been attracted particularly to certain mental diseases. This work was done half a century before even the first beginnings of the modern classifications of mental diseases were attempted. He wrote a short article with regard to mania and its treatment, and a longer article on melancholia. How well he recognized the essential feature of this latter affection and the main symptom that must be guarded against, can be gathered very well from the title of his paper, which he called "The Still Madness, or the Impulse to Self-Murder."

It is about the time that he was engaged in the study of melancholia, perhaps as a contrast to sadder things, that he wrote a comic opera, of which we shall have more to say presently. His description of the conditions that he saw during an epidemic of dysentery that occurred in Vienna show how exact and careful a clinical observer he could be, and that the demands of his practice did not absorb all his attention to the detriment of his faculty for observation. He seems himself to have suffered from a severe attack of typhus fever which raged epidemically in Vienna in 1798.

Auenbrugger had a wide circle of interests beyond the subject of medicine. There is a family tradition that he had a magnificent library. He seems with true Viennese spirit to have been a great devotee of the opera, and to have had an especial liking for music. He wrote the text, score, and libretto of a comic opera with the title, "The Chimney Sweep." This operetta evidently enjoyed more than a *succes d'estime*, and further writing in this line was confidently expected from him by his friends. There is even a story to the effect that the Empress Maria Theresa, of whom he was an intimate friend, and who made use, it is said, of his counsel in political matters more than once, asked him why he did not follow up his first success in operatic writing. His blunt reply shows how intimate must have been his relations with the great empress. He said he had things much better with which to occupy himself than the writing of comic operas.

Seeing that he was so favored at court, it is not surprising to find the family tradition that Auenbrugger was associated with many of the most prominent persons in the Austrian capital during his lifetime. He was a special friend of and spent a great deal of time with the famous philosopher, Werner. As he grew older he delighted especially in music, and spent many hours at the house of Baron Zois, where many of the distinguished European musicians were to be found and where famous matinee concerts were given every Sunday from twelve to two. The day and the time may seem strange to foreigners, but Vienna still has concerts at this time on Sunday, and after the Viennese have gone to Mass in the morning they think that they could not occupy themselves better than with listening to good music in the middle of the day.

Toward the end of his life, Auenbrugger lived during the summer time in the suburb of Rossau and cultivated a little garden, taking the greatest pleasure in spending his time at this simple occupation. It is a source of satisfaction to find that though Auenbrugger's medical work failed during his life to attract the attention it deserved, he had his reward, for his patient investigations in earlier life, in a peaceful and contented ending to a career that had been so worthy of what was best in the man. He lived to celebrate his golden wedding in 1804 and was especially happy in the almost constant companionship of the good wife who had proved so faithful a helpmate during her long life. After her death, which took place the year following the celebration of their jubilee, his vitality and his contentment with life seemed to abandon him. He was a changed man and kept himself for the most part to his room. He went to bed very early and did not care to see anyone but his near relatives. His last illness was the result of a cold, and his advanced age, eighty-seven, left him little resistive vitality. He retained his consciousness until the very end, and said the day before his death that the next day would be his last.

Shortly before noon of the day of his death he looked at the clock in his room and said that when the hands would point to two o'clock he would be no more. His prophecy came true.

Vienna has never had the reputation of honoring its great geniuses during their lifetime, unless they happened to belong to the higher nobility. The exclusiveness of court society at the capital made itself felt in all circles, and the consequence was that genius sprung from the lower orders was almost sure not to receive its due share of attention. The comparative neglect of Auenbrugger does not seem so bad when we recall the case of Mozart. Music has always been one of the special fads of the Austrian and the Viennese pride themselves on their appreciation of it. Mozart, however, perhaps the greatest musical genius that ever lived, received some attention during his life, but passed away almost unnoticed at the early age of thirty-five, was buried in a common trench with the poor people of the city, and now Vienna cannot

6

find his resting place. There is a magnificent monument to him, but his bones lie with his own people forever.

Outside the circle of his personal friends Auenbrugger did not receive much attention, so that even the year of his death was until recently more or less uncertain and the resting place of his remains continues to be unknown. The present generation of medical men has done more to afford the due meed of praise to Auenbrugger than any preceding generation. The interest in tuberculosis particularly has led medical men to appreciate all the significance of Auenbrugger's work, and the practical importance of his discovery for the early recognition and consequently for the cure of the disease. The appreciation of Auenbrugger in our time has been so flattering as quite to make up for previous neglect. His name has been linked with that of Laennec as the great discoverers of physical diagnosis in chest diseases.

At the opening of his address as President of the American Climatological Association, some five years ago, Dr. Edward O. Otis, of Boston, said:

"It is quite improbable, I think, that we should be here to-day, or, indeed, have an existence as a society largely devoted to the consideration of diseases of the chest, were it not for the methods of thoracic examination which Auenbrugger and Laennec have given us in their discoveries of percussion and auscultation. Without these two precious methods of investigation we could scarcely have arrived at any degree of precision or certainty in thoracic pathology and might have been not unlike the old physicians and surgeons, 'who would swear,' as Morgagni says, 'that there was fluid in the chest when in reality there was not a single drachm, or perform paracentesis of the thorax upon a duke for an empyema which did not exist.' "

His tribute is only an echo of many others not less appreci-

ative of Auenbrugger's important original work than have
been expressed by modern medical men of all nations. The
simple old German practitioner, who had the annoyance of
seeing his discovery neglected by his contemporaries for so
many years, has at last come into his own. There is scarcely
an important medical meeting held anywhere in the world
in which diseases of the chest are discussed without a
mention of Auenbrugger's name. This is not surprising in
Germany, but is quite as true of France, and England, and
America. As Dr. Otis said, in closing the address from
which we have just quoted:

"Although we possess but meagre and fragmentary records
of Auenbrugger's life, there is yet enough to enable us to fill
in the lines and gain a distinct idea of his personality
and character. With some persons one does not need to be
acquainted with much of the detail of their lives in order to
know what manner of men they are; a few characteristic
illustrations here and there in their career redeem the spirit
and motives of their lives, and show the kind of men just as
they are, quite as well and clearly as an extended and continuous biographical narrative. Always enthusiastically devoted to the study of disease, Auenbrugger escaped the not
infrequent misfortune of the student, a loss of sympathy with
one's kind. His love for his fellow-men, for suffering humanity, for struggling students in his own profession, kept pace
with his love for medical study. He never sacrificed the man
for the scientist, nor did he lose his interest for other things
in life, as happens sometimes with men intensely devoted to
one pursuit. A man of original powers, as some one has truly
remarked, can never be confined within the limits of a single
field of activity.

"He was interested in music, philosophy and the drama,
and well illustrates what Dr. Da Costa has so happily styled

'the scholar in medicine.' With dignity, sympathy, enthusiasm in his profession, even to the last; ever seeking to improve and add to his art; modest, like most great men; never refusing to give what is best to suffering humanity, he richly lived out his long life. As we teach our students percussion, as a matter of just recognition and due honor let us tell them something of the life of the discoverer, and at least his name, which I fear but few, who avail themselves of the result of his long and arduous labors, know."

Auenbrugger's German biographer, Professor Clar, of Gratz, says of his early life that from his parents he received an excellent early training, especially edifying because of the exemplary Christian family life he saw about him, the piety of his father and mother, and of the other members of the family. The baptismal register of the parish church at Gratz is one of the important documents in his life history, for there is some dispute as to the exact date of his birth, as there is also with regard to his death. In 1798 he suffered from a severe attack of typhus fever, which at the time was epidemic in Vienna, and some of his biographers report his death in this year as a consequence of it. His descendants, however, have shown, by the burial register of the parish church in Vienna, that his death did not take place until May 17, 1807; from this church, of which he had been for half a century a faithful member, he was buried.

Few of the lives of the great discoverers in medicine have in them more of encouragement for the busy practitioner of medicine than that of Auenbrugger. He began his medical career by a series of practical observations that stamped him for all time as one of the great geniuses. When his discoveries failed to meet with the acceptance they deserved, he was not disturbed, and, above all, he did not insist on acrid controversy. He took up the practice of medicine and demonstrated how much his discovery could help in the diagnosis of the obscure chapter of the diseases of the chest. In the mean time he went on his way placidly doing the good that he found to do, taking care of his poor patients and faithfully tending brother-physicians who happened to be ill. He found an avocation to fill the moments spent apart from his vocation, and added to the pleasure of humanity by his work in music. All the time he remained a simple, faithful believer in the relation of Providence to man, and considered that somehow the inexplicable things of this life would find an explanation in the hereafter. He was probably the best-liked member of the profession in Vienna during his lifetime, and the profession of his native town are very proud to recall the example that he sets physicians generally in all the ethical qualities that make a physician's life not only successful in the material sense, but also in inspiration for those around him to do their duty rather than seek the fulfilment of merely selfish aims.

EDWARD JENNER, THE DISCOVERER
OF VACCINATION

"It helps a man immensely to be a bit of a hero worshipper, and the stories of the lives of the masters of medicine do much to stimulate our ambition and rouse our sympathies. If the life and work of such men as Bichat and Laennec will not stir the blood of a young man and make him feel proud of France and of Frenchmen, he must be a dull and muddy-mettled rascal. In reading the life of Hunter, of Jenner, who thinks of the nationality which is merged and lost in our interest in the man and in his work! In the halcyon days of the Renaissance there was no nationalism in medicine, but a fine catholic spirit made great leaders like Vesalius, Eustachius, Stenson and others at home in every country in Europe."—OSLER, *Aequanimitas and other Essays.*

EDWARD JENNER, THE DISCOVERER OF VACCINATION

A VERY striking life in its lessons for the serious student of medical problems is that of Edward Jenner, who first demonstrated to the world that a simple attack of mild, never fatal, cowpox, deliberately acquired, might serve as a protective agent against the deadly smallpox, which before that time raged so violently all over the civilized world. His successful solution of this problem has probably saved more lives and suffering than any other single accomplishment in the whole history of medicine. While this fact is apparently not generally appreciated, Jenner's discovery did not come by mere chance, but was the result of his genius for original investigation, which led him to make many other valuable observations covering nearly the whole range of medicine; nor indeed was his activity limited to medicine alone, but extended itself to many of the allied sciences, and even to scientific departments quite beyond the domain of medicine.

In medicine we owe to Jenner the first hint of the possible connection between rheumatism and heart disease. He pointed out, at a discussion in a little English medical society, how often affections of the heart occurred in those who had suffered from previous attacks of rheumatism. He was among the first, perhaps the very first, to hint at the pathological basis of angina pectoris. While Heberden's name is usually connected with this discovery, there seems good reason to think that already Jenner had independently noted and called attention to the frequency with which degenerative affections of the arteries within the heart muscle itself were to be found where during life heart-pang had been a prominent and annoying symptom.

Besides these important advances in medicine made by him, and his great discovery of the identity of cowpox and smallpox, Dr. Jenner was an interesting observer of phenomena in all the biological sciences, and in geology and palæontology. He was a great friend of Dr. John Hunter, who frequently suggested to him the making of such experiments and observations as were more likely to succeed in the country than in the city, and one cannot help but be struck with the determination evinced all his life to take nothing on authority, but to test everything by actual observation, and above all not to theorize where he did not have the actual data necessary for assured conclusions; and even where he thought he had them, his wonderful faculty for waiting until they had properly matured, and their true significance had become evident, stamped him for all time as a model for scientific investigators.

Undoubtedly Jenner's greatest work was that of determining the value of vaccination. His patient investigation of this subject, the thorough conservatism with which he guarded himself from publishing his conclusions until he had tested them in every way, the absence of that haste to rush into print so characteristic of most present-day medical investigators, and which is the cause of so much disappointment in modern medicine, all distinguished this country physician as one of the greatest investigating geniuses that medicine has produced. His life is a mirror for the medical student and the investigating practitioner of medicine. His discovery was so complete when he finally announced it that but very little has been added to it since. His invention came from his mind as Minerva from the brain of Jove fully armed for the conflict that was sure to come. In this Jenner resembled very much Laennec and the other investigating geniuses in medicine. As a matter of fact only one improvement has been made in the preparation of vaccine material since Jenner's time, and that is the incorporation of glycerin in very recent years, which gradually destroys any micro-organisms that may be present, leaving the vaccine virus itself unimpaired in its efficacy, though without the possibility of inflicting those secondary infections which for so long cast a shadow on vaccination.

Dr. Edward Jenner was the third son of an Anglican clergyman, his mother being the daughter of a clergyman who had been at one time prebend in the cathedral of Bristol. The family held considerable property in Gloucestershire. He received his early education at Wotton-under-Edge and later at Cirencester, the old Roman town in Gloucestershire. While he acquired a good working knowledge of the classics, from his earliest years he was interested in natural history. Before he was nine he made a collection of the nests of the dormouse. The hours that other boys spent at play he devoted to searching for fossils or other interesting natural curiosities.

After his preliminary education had been finished he was apprenticed to Mr. Ludlow, an eminent surgeon at Bristol, and after two years here he went to London, where he had the privilege of residing as a favorite pupil in the family of John Hunter for two years. At this time Jenner was in his twenty-first year, John Hunter in his forty-second. Hunter was not then a public lecturer, but he had been for two years surgeon to St. George's Hospital, and for nearly five years had been engaged in studying the habits and structure of animals in a menagerie and laboratory which he had established at Brompton. The inspiration of Hunter's original genius meant much for young Jenner. He learned not only to respect the teacher but to love the man. In Hunter's unquenchable desire for knowledge and love of truth there was something very congenial to the spirit of Jenner, who was himself, above all things, an inquirer.

After completing his two years of work with Hunter he still remained intimately associated with him by letter. Though later in life Jenner's correspondence became very voluminous, these letters from Hunter were always very carefully preserved in a special cover, and they serve to show how stimulating to the young man must have been Hunter's virile enthusiasm for truth as it could be deduced by observation and experiment.

It was to Hunter that Jenner once wrote that he had heard it said in Gloucestershire that the dairy workers who suffered from a certain disease caught from the udders of cows and called cowpox were protected thereafter from attacks of smallpox. He added that this tradition interested him very much and that he intended to think about it. "Don't think," wrote Hunter to him, in return; "make observations, investigate for yourself the truth of the tradition." Jenner did so, and the result is now known to all.

These letters from Hunter contained many other interesting suggestions. For instance, it was under Hunter's direction that Jenner succeeded in finding out that in hibernating animals the temperature is very much reduced and the respirations are very slow, while the rate and force of the pulse are often so much diminished as to be scarcely more than noticeable at the extremities. Between Hunter and Jenner it had already been discovered that the sap in trees will not freeze at temperatures much lower than that at which the same fluid freezes when withdrawn from the tree, and the same thing seemed to be true with regard to the blood of hibernating animals. He learned that notwithstanding the low temperature to which it is reduced the animals are not affected particularly by the cold, though their store of fat is consumed and they awake very hungry in the spring-time.

Besides hibernation Jenner also investigated the habits of the cuckoo, that crux of the biologist which insists on foisting its eggs upon other birds and allowing its orphan young to be brought up in alien nests, while the real young of the deceived foster-parents are often pushed out of their nests by this burly intruder which grows so fast and strong. It is needless to say, this subject interested John Hunter very much and there are a number of letters which passed between them on the subject.

It must not be supposed, however, that young Jenner was entirely occupied with his scientific work to the exclusion of social life and recreation. He was one of the best-known men of the county, and was looked upon as a genial companion from whom might be expected on almost any occasion pleasant jests and epigrams, not too biting, with regard to friends and acquaintances. Some of these have been preserved and we quote several of them as indicative of his special vein of humor.

ON THE DEATH OF A MISER.

"Tom at last has laid by his old niggardly forms,
And now gives good dinners; to whom pray?—the worms."

ON LORD BERKELEY'S HUNTSMAN, WHO DIED IN THE CHASE.

"Determined much higher to hoist up his name,
Than Nimrod the hunter, in annals of fame,
'Hark forward!' cried Charles, and gallantly whirled
His high-mettled steed o'er the gates of the world."

DEATH AND MR. PEACH.
A Short Dialogue.   N. B.—Mr. P. died in April.

"P.—Awhile forbear thy horrid gripe,
 Do pray, dread Sir! remember
Peaches are never fairly ripe
 'Till August or September."

"D.—To gratify my longing taste,
 And make thy flavour fine,
I had thee in a hot-house placed,
 And moistened well with wine."
"Mr. Peach had shortened his life by the too free use of the bottle."

We have said that Dr. Jenner's supreme accomplishment
in science was the working out of the vaccination problem
to a great humane conclusion.   His discovery was no mere
accident, nor chance confirmation of a medical tradition.
He devoted himself for many years to the study of cowpox,
as he had the opportunity to see it, and it is what we know
of this investigation, his patience and care in eliminating all
the factors of error, that stamped Jenner as a medical scientist worthy of honor.   When he began practice in Berkeley,
he made many inquiries among his professional brethren,
with regard to their opinion of the protecting power of cowpox, but most of them had either paid no attention to such
reports, or shook their heads at once, and said they were
at most popular traditions, due merely to coincidences and
unsupported by any credible evidence.   In the face of this,
Jenner began to follow John Hunter's advice to investigate.
The first careful investigation dates from about 1775, and
it took him more than five years to clear away the difficulties
surrounding the solution of the question, in which he was
interested.

As Pasteur found in the next century, when investigating
the silkworm disease, Jenner soon learned that there was

more than one disease called cowpox, and that the confusion consequent upon the existence of at least two specific diseases and a number of skin affections of the hands of various kinds, which existed among dairy workers, made the recognition of the protective power of true cowpox extremely difficult. After he had differentiated genuine cowpox, however, there was no difficulty in tracing its apparent protective power. He soon found, however, that the protection was not afforded unless the cowpox had been communicated at a particular stage of the disease. In other words, after the true vaccinia has run its course, secondary affections of the skin of the cows usually take place, and if dairy workers became infected from these lesions, then no protection against smallpox is afforded them. Another important observation that Jenner made at this time was that the disease known as grease in horses is the same affection as cowpox, and that both of these diseases are smallpox as modified by the organism in which they develop. It may be said at once that this opinion so difficult to arrive at, more than a century ago, when so little was known of comparative pathology, is held at the present day, and was confirmed by the last series of investigations made under the auspices of the Jenner Society, in England.

One difficulty that confronted Jenner in his researches was the fact that cowpox was scarce in his part of the country, and he had no opportunity of making inoculations with the disease in a proper stage, so as to put his suspicions to an absolute test. He collected much information, however, and stimulated others to the making of observations, so that when his discovery was announced the mind of the medical profession was more ready to receive it. In 1788 he carried a carefully made drawing of a case of cowpox as it occurred on the hands of a Gloucester milkmaid to London, and showed it to a number of medical men, whose opinions he wished to obtain. Among these was Sir Edward Holme, who agreed that there was a distinct similarity between it and certain stages of smallpox and considered that the question of a connection between the two diseases was an interesting and curious subject. He did not share any of Jenner's views, however, with regard to the practical importance of his discovery in this matter, and gave little encouragement to the idea that a possible prophylactic for smallpox might be discovered.

Something of Jenner's enthusiasm for experiment may be gathered from the fact that he did not hesitate even to inject various materials related to cowpox into the arm of his own children. We know Mrs. Jenner to have been a very wonderful woman, quite as deeply interested as the doctor himself in securing the great benefit to humanity that would result from the demonstration that cowpox protected against smallpox, but it is a little bit difficult for us in these days to understand how her mother-heart could have permitted some of the experiments which Dr. Jenner's biographer, Dr. Baron, describes.[1]

The subject is indeed so surprising that I prefer to quote the passage with regard to these experiments directly from Dr. Baron:

"In November, 1789, he inoculated his eldest son Edward, who was then about one year and a half old, with swine-pox matter. The progress of the disease seemed similar to that which arises from the insertion of true smallpox matter when

[1] The life of Edward Jenner, M.D., F.R.S., Physician Extraordinary to His Majesty Geo. IV, Foreign Associate of the National Institute of France, &c. &c. &c. With illustrations of his doctrines, and selections from his Correspondence by John Baron, M.D., F.R.S., Late Senior Physician to the General Infirmary, Consulting Physician to the Lunatic Asylum at Gloucester, and Fellow of the Royal Medical and Chirurgical Society of London. In two Volumes. London: Henry Colburn, 1838.

the disease is very slight. He sickened on the eighth day: a few pustules appeared; they were late and slow in their progress, and small. Variolous matter (this would mean material from a smallpox patient calculated to give that disease) was carefully inserted into his arms at five or six different periods, subsequently without the slightest inflammation being excited in the part.

"On Thursday, April 7th, 1791, variolous matter was again inserted by two small incisions through the cutis, [beneath the skin]. Then the following notes of observed conditions day after day are made: 9th, Evidently inflamed. 10th, An efflorescence of the size of a shilling spread round the inferior wound. 11th, The incision assumed a kind of erysipelatous elevation: the efflorescence much increased. 12th, These appearances much advanced. 13th, A vesicle, containing a brownish fluid, and transparent, about the size of a large split-pea on the superior incision, the inferior about twice as big; the surrounding parts affected with erysipelas. The erysipelas extended to the shoulder, and then pretty quickly went off. The child showed no signs of indisposition the whole time."

"March, 1792. E. Jenner was again inoculated: the matter was taken from a child that caught the disease in the natural way, and had it pretty full. It was inserted fresh from the pustule. The same evening an inflammation appeared round the incision, which, at the end of twenty hours, increased to the diameter of a sixpence, and some fluid had already been collected on the lips of the scratch, which the child had rubbed off."

It was not for five years after this time, however, that Jenner was able to make his crucial experiments in the matter. On the 14th of May, 1796 (the date is still recalled as Vaccination Day in Germany, especially in Berlin), vaccine

7

matter was taken from the hand of a dairy maid, Sarah
Nelmes, and inserted by two superficial incisions in the arms
of James Phipps, a healthy boy of about eight years of age.
The boy went through an attack of cowpox in a regularly
satisfactory manner. After this, however, it was necessary
to determine whether he was protected from smallpox.
After waiting two months Jenner inoculated him with variolous material. The result of this experiment can best be
learned from the following letter written to his friend
Gardner:

"DEAR GARDNER:

"As I promised to let you know how I proceeded in my
inquiry into the nature of that singular disease the Cow Pox,
and being fully satisified how much you feel interested in its
success, you will be gratified in hearing that I have at length
accomplished what I have been so long waiting for, the
passing of the Vaccine Virus from one human being to
another by the ordinary mode of inoculation.

"A boy of the name of Phipps was inoculated in the arm
from a pustule on the hand of a young woman who was
infected by her master's cows. Having never seen the disease
but in its casual way before; that is, when communicated
from the cow to the hand of the milker, I was astonished at
the close resemblance of the pustules, in some of their stages,
to the variolous pustules. But now listen to the most de-
lightful part of my story. The boy has since been inoculated for the smallpox which, as I ventured to predict, produced no effect. I shall now pursue my experiments with
redoubled ardour.

"Believe me yours, very sincerely,

"EDWARD JENNER.

"BERKELEY, JULY 19, 1796."

Notwithstanding the complete success of this experiment, Jenner did not rush into print with it. Two years later, at the end of June, 1798, his "Inquiry into the Causes and Effects of the Variolæ Vaccinæ" was published. In the mean time Jenner had succeeded in demonstrating the protective quality against smallpox of vaccination, contracted either casually or by direct inoculation, in some twenty-three cases. Sixteen of these had occurred accidentally in the course of occupations connected with cows and horses; the rest were done under Jenner's directions. Among the persons inoculated was Jenner's own little second son, Robert Fitts Harding Jenner, an infant eleven months old. Jenner demonstrated conclusively that the cowpox protects the human constitution from the infection of smallpox.

After Dr. Jenner had made his tests he prepared a pamphlet for publication. Before publishing, however, he thought it better to make a visit to London, so that he might have the opportunity to introduce the subject personally to friends, and demonstrate the truth of his assertion to them. He remained in London for nearly three months without being able to find any one who would submit to vaccination. The medical profession generally took very little interest in the subject and seemed to consider him sadly visionary. Under the circumstances it is not surprising that Jenner went back to Gloucestershire, and his country practice, rather disappointed. It happened, however, that soon after his return home, a distinguished London surgeon named Cline resolved to make a trial of the vaccine material which Jenner had left with his friends. The surgeon's purpose in using it, however, was not altogether to test its efficacy as a prophylactic against smallpox, but with the notion that the counterirritation thus obtained might be useful in a case which he had under treatment. Those

were the days when the seton and the issue were still in
common use, and counterirritation was considered one of
the most important remedial measures at the command of
the surgeon.

The patient was a child suffering from a form of chronic
hip-joint disease that at this distance of time, and with
rather incomplete descriptions, seems to have been the
ordinary tuberculosis of the hip. The vaccine material was
inoculated over the joint and, surprising though it may
appear now, the vaccine vesicle ran rather a normal course
and healed kindly. The little patient was afterward inoculated with smallpox and found to be incapable of
acquiring that disease. This case attracted considerable
attention. It is not, however, a matter for congratulation
as regards the openness of mind of the medical men of the
period to find that this was the only sort of a case that was
considered suitable for such an experiment. It is very
easy to understand that in a child in a run-down condition
the vaccine material might very well have provoked a rather
serious local reaction. In a way, the fate of vaccination
hung in the balance and good luck was in its favor. Mr.
Cline, however, after this, became a strong advocate of
vaccination, and brought it very decidedly before the London
physicians. There was still a feeling of opposition, as indeed
there always is against any novelty in medicine, but this
gradually disappeared, to give place to a suspenson of judgment, until more accurate and detailed information could
be obtained from further observations and tests.

It was not long before the opposition to the practice of
vaccination took definite form. One of the best-known
London physicians of the time, Dr. Ingenhouz, became the
leader of a strong faction of the medical profession of London,
who not only would have nothing to do with vaccination,

but proclaimed openly that it was a dangerous innovation, absolutely unjustifiable, and communicated a disease without protecting against any other. On the other hand, there were overzealous advocates of vaccination, who insisted on its value but did not know how to recognize the true cowpox from other lesions sometimes confounded with it, nor the exact stage of the disease in which the vaccine material obtained would prove effectively protective. A number of these used vaccine material so contaminated by secondary infections of one kind or another that no wonder serious sores were reported as a result.

Physicians who have for many years known how difficult it is to bring certain people to a recognition of the benefits that have been conferred on modern civilization by vaccination, will appreciate how many difficulties and prejudices and misunderstandings Jenner himself must have encountered during the original introduction of vaccination. Some of the supposed objections to vaccination wear a very modern air, and come from physicians whose only purpose apparently is to bring out the truth, and yet who are evidently led to the drawing of conclusions much wider than their premises by the fact that they know they will have an attentive audience among the anti-vaccinationists at least.

A fair example of one of these old-time objections against vaccination may be found in the following passage from a letter by Dr. Jenner written to Mr. Moore. Corresponding objections have been made in much more modern times, and the passage will arouse the sympathetic amusement of present-day physicians:

"You probably may not have seen a pamphlet lately published by Dr. Watt of Glasgow, as there is nothing in its title that develops its purport or evil tendency: 'An Inquiry into the Relative Mortality of the Principal Diseases of

Children,' &c. The measles, it seems, have been extremely fatal in the city of Glasgow for the last four or five years among children, and during this period vaccination was practised almost universally. Previously to this, the measles was considered as a mild disease. Hence Dr. Watt infers that the smallpox is a kind of preparative for the measles, rendering the disease more mild. In short, he says, or seems to say, that we have gained nothing by the introduction of the cow-pox; for that the measles and small-pox have now changed places with regard to their fatal tendency. Is not this very shocking? Here is a new and unexpected twig shot forth for the sinking anti-vaccinist to cling to. But mark me—should this absurdity of Mr. Watt take possession of the minds of the people, I am already prepared with the means of destroying its effects, having instituted an inquiry through this populous town and the circumjacent villages, where, on the smallest computation, 20,000 children must have been vaccinated in the course of the last twelve years by myself and others. Now it appears that, during this period, there has been no such occurrence as a fatal epidemic of measles. You would greatly oblige me in making this communication to the Board, with my respectful compliments."

Fortunately only a few colleagues were so illogical, and an excellent idea of how much Jenner's discovery was appreciated by his contemporaries may be obtained from the number of honors, diplomas, addresses and communications from public bodies and distinguished individuals which he received. A chronological list of these may be found at the end of Dr. Baron's Life of Jenner. Among them may be noted the diploma of LL.D. from the Senate of Harvard University, Cambridge, Mass., under the presidency of Dr. Willard; also the Diploma of Doctor in Medicine, honoris causa, which Jenner especially appreciated, as he says in one of his letters, because he understood that the University conferred this degree in this way only once or twice in a century. There is a diploma as Fellow of the American Society of Arts and Sciences in Massachusetts, as well as a Diploma as a member of the American Philosophical Society at Philadelphia. The diploma from Boston bears the signature of John Adams as president, that from Philadelphia the signature of Thomas Jefferson. Most of the prominent medical and scientific societies of Europe had elected him a member or had sent him some special token of recognition.

One of these documents, expressive of the gratitude of the senders for the great benefit his work had conferred upon the human race, which Jenner valued the highest, was an address from the Five Indian Nations which, with a Wampum Belt, was delivered to him on November 8, 1807. In reply to this Dr. Jenner wrote to the American agent through whom the insignia had been forwarded:

"SIR:
"Your kindness in delivering to the Five Nations of Indians my Treatise on vaccination, and in transmitting to me their reply, demands my warmest thanks.

"I beg you to make known to the Five Nations the sincere gratification which I feel at finding that the practice of vaccination has been so universally received among their tribes, and proved so beneficial to them; at the same time, be pleased to assure them of the great thankfulness with which I received the belt and string of Wampum, with which they condescended to honour me, and of the high estimation in which I shall for ever hold it. May the active benevolence which their chiefs have displayed in preserving the lives of their people be crowned with the success it deserves; and may that destructive pestilence, the small-pox, be no more known among them.

"You also, Sir, are entitled to the most grateful acknowledgments, not only from me, but from every friend of humanity, for the philanthropic manner in which you originally introduced the vaccine among these tribes of Indians.

"I have the honor to remain, &c.,

"E. JENNER."

The general trend of American appreciation for Dr. Jenner's work, at least among the intelligent classes, may be gathered from the following letter sent to Dr. Jenner by Thomas Jefferson while he was president, May 14, 1806:

"MONTICELLO, VIRGINIA, May 14, 1806.
"SIR:

"I have received the copy of the evidence at large respecting the discovery of the vaccine inoculation, which you have been pleased to send me, and for which I return you my thanks. Having been among the early converts in this part of the globe to its efficacy, I took an early part in recommending it to my countrymen. I avail myself of this occasion to render you my portion of the tribute of gratitude due to you from the whole human family. Medicine has never before produced any single improvement of such utility. Harvey's discovery of the circulation of the blood was a beautiful addition to our knowledge of the human economy; but on a review of the practice of medicine before and since that epoch, I do not see any great amelioration which has been derived from that discovery. You have erased from the calender of human afflictions one of its greatest. Yours is the comfortable reflection that mankind can never forget that you have lived; future nations will know by history only that the loathsome small-pox has existed, and by you has been extirpated. Accept the most fervent wishes for your health and happiness, and assurances of the greatest respect and consideration.

"Th. Jefferson."

Almost more interesting than the story of Jenner, the experimental scientist, the true harbinger of modern experimental medicine, the founder of experimental pathology, and the discoverer of the pregnant idea which was to mean so much for nineteenth century medicine in the hands of Pasteur and his successors, is the story of Jenner the man, the husband, the friend, and the physician of the poor. In spite of his intense preoccupation in his experimental work and the amount of time it must have required to make his observations, he found opportunities to care for the poor and to interest himself in all their concerns as well as their health. He made many firm friends among people of his own social status and generally was considered a most amiable, as well as a liberal, and humanitarian man. He was deeply religious, and, as we shall allow his earliest biographer Dr. Baron to tell, was not ashamed to exhibit his religious feelings by word and deed when the proper occasion presented itself. This part of his life deserves to be studied as carefully and remembered as faithfully as that in which he made his discoveries, since it is the complement that shows the character of the man in its entirety.

Jenner's personal character may be very well understood from a paragraph of his biographer, who had been his bosom friend for many years. He says:

"But Dr. Jenner was not only humble in all that concerned this, the greatest incident of his life (the successful discovery of vaccination); he continued so after success had crowned his labors, and after applause greater than most men can bear had been bestowed upon him. This most estimable quality was visible at all times; but it was particularly conspicuous when he was living in familar intercourse with the inhabitants of his native village. If the reader could in imagination accompany me with him to the dwellings of the poor, and see him kindly and heartily inquiring into their wants, and entering into all the little details of their domestic economy; or if he could have witnessed him listening with perfect patience and good humor to the history of their maladies, he would have seen an engaging instance of untiring benovolence. He never was unwilling to receive any one, however ·unseasonable the time may have been. Such were his habits, even to the latest period of his life. I scarcely know any part of his character that was more worthy of imitation and unqualified respect than that to which I have alluded. I have never seen any person in any station of life in whom it was equally manifest; and when it is remembered that he was well 'stricken in years;' that he had been a most indefatigable and successful laborer in the cause of humanity; and that he might have sought for a season of repose, and the uncontrolled disposal of his own time, the sacrifices which he made are the more to be valued. In the active and unostentatious exercise of kindness and charity he spent his days; and he seemed ever to feel that he was one of those 'qui se natos ad homines juvandos, tutandos, conservandos arbitrantur,' who consider themselves born to help, protect, and cherish their fellow men.

"His kindness and condescension to the poor was equalled by his most considerate respect and regard to the feelings and character of the humblest of his professional brethren. I have often been struck with the total absence of everything that could bear the semblance of loftiness of demeanor.

Few men were more entitled to deliver their sentiments in
a confident or authoritative tone; but his whole deportment
was opposed to everything of that description, and he did
not hesitate to seek knowledge from persons in all respects
his inferiors. All his younger brethren who have ever had
the happiness to meet him in practice, must have been deeply
impressed with this part of his character."

Many a member of the medical profession who is not a
genius will find an excuse for allowing disorder about his
rooms from the example which is said to have been set by
Jenner. He was interested in nearly every branch of science
and specimens from many departments were constantly
around him. He himself, it is said, had the key to the apparent confusion. Most of the others who allow themselves to
drift into careless habits in the same direction insist that
they too have the key. Some of their friends, however, are
inclined to doubt it. It is curiously interesting under these
circumstances to have Jenner's biographer tell of the confused state of affairs that existed in his room and yet his
defence of it. Perhaps in this matter it is well to remember
what Augustin Birrell says at the end of his essay on Car-
lisle: "Don't let us quarrel with genius; we have none of
it ourselves and the worst of it is we cannot get along without it."

"The objects of his studies generally lay scattered around
him; and, as he used often to say himself, seemingly in
chaotic confusion. Fossils, and other specimens of natural
history, anatomical preparations, books, papers, letters—
all presented themselves in strange disorder; but every
article bore the impress of the genius that presided there.
The fossils were marked by small pieces of paper pasted on
them, having their names and the places where they were
found inscribed in his own plain and distinct handwriting.

His materials for thought and conversation were thus constantly before him; and a visitor, on entering his apartment, would find in abundance traces of all his private occupations. He seemed to have no secrets of any kind; and, notwithstanding a long experience with the world, he acted to the last as if all mankind were as trustworthy and free from selfishness as himself. He had a working head, being never idle, and accumulated a great store of original observations. These treasures he imparted most generously and liberally. Indeed his chief pleasure seemed to be in pouring out the ample riches of his mind to everyone who enjoyed his acquaintance. He had often reason to lament this undoubted confidence; but such ungrateful returns neither chilled his ardor nor ruffled his temper."

It is interesting to note what was Jenner's opinion with regard to two subjects that are very much discussed at the present time. These are the questions of religious training in education, and the advisability of making nature study a part of the course for children. Jenner considered that no education could possibly be complete which did not include both of these subjects. Religious training he deemed absolutely indispensable. Nature study he advised for somewhat different reasons from those for which it is now urged. He thought there was a depth of interest in the study of the objects of nature that could scarcely fail to lessen the burden of education for the child, but the main reason for its study to his mind was that children intent on the wonders of nature could scarcely help but realize the power of the Creator and, learning to admire Him more and more, be thus drawn to respect His laws, to acknowledge His supremacy and to devote themselves to bringing about the fulfilment of His will in this world to the fullest extent in their power.

Jenner's religious opinions and beliefs must be left to the expression of the biographer already mentioned, who gives them very fully. He says:

"One of the most remarkable features in Jenner's character, when treating of questions of a moral or scientific nature, was a devout expression of his consciousness of the omnipresence of the Deity. He believed that this great truth was too much overlooked in our systems of education; that it ought to be constantly impressed upon the youthful heart, and that the obligations which it implied, as well as the inward truth and purity which it required, should be rendered more familiar to all. Mrs. Jenner was constantly occupied in teaching these lessons to the poor around her, in schools which she established for the purpose of affording a scriptural education. He, building upon this foundation, wished to add instruction of a more practical description, deduced from their daily experience, and illustrated by a reference to those works of wisdom and beauty which the universe supplies. He always contended that some aid of of this kind was necessary to impress completely upon the character of the lower ranks those maxims which they derived from their teachers. He had other views, too, in recommending such a plan; he thought that the lot of the poor might be ameliorated, and many sources of amusement and information laid open to them which they are at present deprived of; that the flowers of the field and the wonders of the animal creation might supply them with subjects of useful knowledge and pious meditation."

His wife, as is often, though unfortunately not always, the case, seems to have had that precious uplifting influence over him which served continually as an incentive to higher things and kept him from the sterile materialism which an exclusive absorption in scientific studies, with lack of the exercise of faith and of association with human suffering, seems to bring to many men. Dr. Baron says on this point:

"I remember, when discussing with him certain questions touching the conditions of man in this life, and dwelling upon his hopes, his fears, his pains, and his joys, and coming to the conclusions which merely human reason discloses to us; and when dwelling on the deformity of the heart, our blindness, our ignorance, the evils connected with our physical structures, our crimes, our calamities, and our unfathomable capacity both for suffering and for enjoyment; he observed, Mrs. Jenner can explain all these things: they cause no difficulties to her."

Toward the end of his life Jenner's feelings with regard to the importance of a confident other worldliness as the only fitting explanation for the mysteries of this, became emphasized. To quote his biographer once more:

"As he approached nearer to his own end, his conversations with myself were generally more or less tinged with such views as occur to the serious mind when contemplating the handiwork of the Creator. In all the confusion and disorder which appears in the physical world, and in all the anomalies and errors which deface the moral, he saw convincing demonstration that He who formed all things out of nothing still wields and guides the machinery of his mighty creation."

Jenner's feelings with regard to the relative importance of medical and religious ministrations may be very well appreciated from an expression of his on the occasion when he was being presented to a distinguished nobleman by the famous missionary, Roland Hill. The Reverend Mr. Hill said: "Allow me to present your Lordship my friend, Dr. Jenner, who has been the means of saving more lives than any other man." "Ah," responded Jenner, "were I like you I could save souls." In his sketch of Jenner's life in "The Disciples of Æsculapius," Sir Benjamin Ward Richardson considers that this incident shows a lack of appreciation of the dignity of the medical profession and a humility rather difficult to understand. Anyone who will place himself in Jenner's position of fervent belief that the one thing necessary is the salvation of souls will not fail to recognize, however, his sincerity or fail to appreciate its true significance.

After all, Jenner was so deeply impressed with the importance of other worldly things and the comparative insignificance of this that he found it even a little difficult to understand why men should not see the direct action of the Creator and all His providence in even some of the minutest details of life. Once he said, "I do not marvel that men are grateful to me, but I am surprised that they do not feel grateful to God for making me a medium of good."

Few men who have accomplished so much have felt so little vainglory over it as Jenner. There was not a jot or tittle of what is so rightly called conceit in him. He well deserves a place beside such beautiful characters as Morgagni, Auenbrugger, Laennec and Pasteur, whose work was done for others, not for themselves, and after all the most striking definition of a saint is one who thinks first of others and only second of himself.

GALVANI, FOUNDER OF ANIMAL ELECTRICITY

The world that I regard is myself; it is the Microcosm of my own frame that I cast mine eye on; for the other, I use it but like my Globe, and turn it round sometimes for my recreation. Men that look upon my outside, perusing only my condition and Fortunes, do err in my Altitude; for I am above Atlas his shoulders. The earth is a point not only in respect of the Heaven above us, but of that heavenly and celestial part within us; that mass of Flesh that circumscribes me, limits not my mind; that surface that tells the Heavens it hath an end, cannot persuade me I have any: I take my circle to be above three hundred and sixty; though the number of the Arc do measure my body, it comprehendeth not my mind; whilst I study to find how I am a Microcosm, or little World, I find myself something more than the great one. There is surely a piece of Divinity in us, something that was before the Elements, and owes no homage unto the Sun.—SIR THOS. BROWNE, M.D.

GALVANI, FOUNDER OF ANIMAL ELECTRICITY.

It is often thought and only too often stated that the impetus to the rise of our modern science which came during the last half of the eighteenth century was due to the spirit of the French Revolution, making itself felt long before the actual declaration of the rights of man, by the French Encyclopedists. It is the custom to conclude that the spirit of liberty which was abroad infected the minds of the rising generation to such an extent that they cast off the fetters of old traditional modes of thinking, refused to accept supposed truths on the strength of tradition or on authority as before, tested knowledge for themselves, and as a consequence made true progress in the sciences. Something doubtless there is in this, and yet a careful investigation of the lives of the men to whom especially the beginnings of the biological sciences are due, will show that not only were they men with the deepest respect for authority, the greatest reverence for old modes of thinking, but also they were typical representatives of the developing influence of methods of education which are sometimes unfortunately deemed to be narrowing in the extreme.

We have already studied the life of Morgagni, the great Father of Modern Pathology, to find that he least of all, in his generation, was affected by any of the liberalizing tendencies that are supposed to have led up to the freedom of the human mind and the consequent successful broadening of human science. We shall see that there were many others who did their work at the end of the eighteenth century of whom this same thing can be said, and no more

striking examples of this can be found than the lives of
two great Italians, Volta and Galvani, to whom the modern
world has paid the tribute of acknowledging them as founders
in electricity by taking their names to express important
basic distinctions in the science.

It was not in Italy alone, however, that this adhesion of
great scientific minds to the old orthodox teachings of Christianity constituted a notable characteristic of the history of
eighteenth century science. Everywhere the same thing was
true. Cavendish, Sir Humphrey Davy and Faraday, the
great English scientists, to whom so much of progress in
electricity and in physics is due, were very similar in this
respect to their Italian colleagues. Oersted the Dane be-
longs in the same category. In France such distinguished
names as Lamarck, the great founder of modern biology
and the first to broach the theory of evolution; Haüy, the
father of crystallography; Laplace, and many others might
be mentioned. The lives of the men who were contemporary workers in medicine as sketched in the present volume
will show this same thing to be true also in their cases.

A glance at the life of Aloysius Galvani will illustrate
how little the spirit of the revolution had to do with the
rise of electricity and the first discussions of its relations to
life. He was born at Bologna, September 9, 1737. A
number of his immediate relatives had been distinguished
as clergymen. The early years of Galvani's life were spent
in association with religious, and as a youth he wished to
become a member of a religious order whose special function
it was to assist the dying at their last hour. His father,
however, was opposed to his entrance into religion, and so
Galvani devoted himself to medicine at the University of
Bologna, and at length became a professor of anatomy in
his Alma Mater. Professor Galeazzi, who was at the time

one of the most distinguished professors in anatomy in Italy, was very much attracted to young Galvani and became his friend and patron in his student days. Galvani became a member of Galeazzi's household, and finally having fallen in love with one of his daughters, won her father's consent to their early marriage. The happiness in life that he thus prepared for himself became one of the often quoted exemplars of domestic felicity in Bologna, where Galvani's life was passed.

Medici, in his panegyric of Galvani, which we shall have occasion to quote from more than once, gives a very pretty story of the doctor's wooing and marriage with Lucia Galeazzi, which we prefer to repeat in the naïve simplicity with which it is related by the Italian panegyrist.

Galvani had been seriously thinking of matrimony for some time and had, it seems (strange as that might be considered in a rising young scientist in our day), even prayed for counsel in the matter. One of his favorite saints was St. Francis of Sales, the Archbishop of Geneva, the gentleman saint as he has been called, for whose charming personal character Galvani had a very devout admiration. One day while praying in one of the churches of Bologna before a statue of St. Francis of Sales he looked up after some moments of abstraction to find a young woman's face between him and the altar. The face proved to be that of Lucia. Galvani looked upon it as a sign from heaven of approval of some of his wishes, and applied for the hand of the fair Lucia. Anyone who has seen the offerings at the shrine of St. Anthony of Padua, not so far from Bologna, and has realized that the good patron of things lost seems also to be a special subject of recourse in cases of lost hearts among the northern Italians even at the present day, will realize that probably the story as told is the simple truth without any tincture of romance.

Galvani began original work of a high order very early in his medical career. His graduation thesis with regard to bones, treating specially their formation and development, attracted no little attention and is especially noteworthy because of the breadth of view in it, for it touches on the various questions relative to bones from the standpoint of physics and chemistry as well as medicine and surgery. It was sufficient to obtain for its author the place of lecturer in anatomy in the University of Bologna, besides the post of director of the teaching of anatomy in the Institute of Sciences, a subsidiary institution. From the very beginning his course was popular. Galvani was an easy, interesting talker, and he was one of the first who introduced experimental demonstrations into his lectures.

At this time the science of comparative anatomy was just beginning to attract widespread attention. John Hunter in London was doing a great work in this line which has placed him in the front rank of contributors to biology and collectors of important facts in all the sciences allied to anatomy and physiology. Galvani took up this work with enthusiasm and began the study particularly of birds. These animals, the farthest removed from man of the beings that have warm blood, present by that very fact many interesting contrasts and analogies, which furnish important suggestions for the explanation of difficult problems in human anatomy and physiology.

His experimental work in comparative anatomy, strange as it might appear and apparently not to be expected, led him into the domain of electricity through the observation of certain phenomena of animal electricity and the effect of electrical current on animals.

Like so many other great discoveries in science, his first and most important observations in electrical phenomena

were results of an accident. Of course, it is easy to talk of
accidents in these cases. The fall of the apple for Newton,
Laennec's observation of the little boys tapping on a log in
the courtyard of the Louvre, from which he got his idea for
the invention of the stethoscope, were apparently merest
accidents. Without the inventive scientific genius ready to
take advantage of them, however, these accidents would not
have been raised to the higher planes of important incidents
in history. They would have meant nothing. The phenomena had probably occurred under men's eyes hundreds of
times before, but there was no great mind ready to receive
the seeds of thought it suggested and go on to follow out the
conclusions so obviously indicated. Galvani's observation
of the twitching of the muscles of the frog under the influence of electricity may be called one of the happy accidents
of scientific development, but it was Galvani's own genius
that made the accident happy.

There are two stories told as to the method of the first
observation in this matter. Both of them make his wife an
important factor in the discovery. According to the more
popular form of the history, Galvani was engaged in preparing some frog's legs as a special dainty for his wife, who was
ill and who liked this delicacy very much. He thought so
much of her that he was doing this himself in the hope that
she would be thus more readily tempted to eat them. While so
engaged he exposed the large nerve of the animals' hind legs
and at the same time split the skin covering the muscles. In
doing this he touched the nerve-muscle preparation, as this
has come to be called, with the scalpel and little forceps simultaneously, with the result that twitchings occurred. While
seeking for the cause of these twitchings the idea of animal
electricity came to him.

The other form of the story of his original discovery is not less interesting and is perhaps a little more authentic. One evening he was engaged in his laboratory in making some experiments while some friends and his wife were present. By chance some frogs, the hind legs of which had been stripped of skin, were placed upon the table not far from an apparatus for the generation of frictional electricity. They were not in contact with this apparatus at any point, however, though they were not far distant from the conductor. While the apparatus was being used to produce a series of sparks, a laboratory assistant, without thinking of any possible results, touched with the point of a scalpel the sciatic nerves of one of the animals. Just as soon as he did this all the muscles of this limb went into convulsive movement. It was Galvani's wife who noticed what had happened and who had the assistant use the scalpel once more with the same result.

She was herself a woman of well-developed intellect, and her association with her father and husband made her well acquainted with the anatomy and physiology of the day. She realized that what had occurred was quite out of the ordinary. Accordingly, she called the attention of ner husband to the phenomena, and is even said to have suggested their possible connection with the presence and action of the electric apparatus. Husband and wife then together, by means of a series of observations, determined that whenever the apparatus was not in use the phenomenon of the conclusive movements of the frog's legs did not take place, notwithstanding irritation by the scalpel. Whenever the electric apparatus was working, however, then the phenomenon in question always took place. According to either form of the story it is clear that Madame Galvani had an important part in the discovery, and Galvani himself, far from making little of what she had accomplished, was always glad to attribute his discovery, or at least the suggestive hint that led up to it, to his wife.

After these first discoveries on the influence of artificial electricity, nothing seemed more interesting than to investigate whether ordinary atmospheric electricity as manifested in lightning would produce the same effects on muscular movements. In this matter Galvani showed much courage as an inventive genius. He dared to place an atmospheric conductor on the highest point of his house and to this conductor he attached a wire, which ran down to his laboratory. During a storm he suspended on this metallic circuit by means of their sciatic nerves frogs' legs and the legs of other animals prepared for the purpose. To the feet of the animals he attached another wire sufficiently long to reach down to the bottom of a well, thus completing a current to the ground.

All the phenomena took place exactly as if with artificial electricity. Whenever lightning flashed from the clouds the limbs of the animals experimented with underwent violent contractions, which were noticeable before the noise of the thunder, and were, so to say, the signal for it. These contractions took place, although there were no conductors from the muscles, and although the nerve conductors were not isolated. The muscular contractions were greater in proportion than the intensity of the lightning and the proximity of the storm. The phenomena were manifest whether the animal was in the open air or if, for greater convenience, it was enclosed in a room, or even in a vessel. The muscular contractions could even be noticed despite the fact that the nerves were separated somewhat from their conductor, especially whenever the lightning was violent. The sparks would leap over a small gap almost as in the case of artificial electricity, the muscular contraction of the animal being proportioned to the energy and the nearness of the sparks.

It is almost needless to say, these experiments upon the frog were not accomplished in a few days or a few weeks. Galvani had his duties as Professor of Anatomy to attend to, besides the obligations imposed upon him as a busy practitioner of medicine and surgery. At that time it was not nearly so much the custom as it is at present, to use frogs for experiments, with the idea that conclusions might be obtained of value for the biological sciences generally, and especially for medicine. There has always been an undercurrent of feeling that such experiments are more or less a beating of the air. Galvani found opposition not only to his views with regard to animal electricity as enunciated after experimental demonstration, but also met with no little ridicule because of the supposed waste of time at occupations that could not be expected to lead to any practical results. It was the custom among scientific men to laugh somewhat scornfully at his patient persistence in studying out every detail of electrical action on the frog, and one of the supposedly prominent scientists of the time even dubbed him the frog dancing master. This did not, however, deter Galvani from his work, though some of the bitter things must have proved cutting enough, and might have discouraged a smaller man, less confident of the scientific value of the work that he was doing.

There were even phases of physical science quite apart from physiology or animal electricity, which he was able to illustrate by his experiments. He called special attention, for instance, to the fact that the lightning does not excite a single contraction of the muscle as is the case with a spark of artificial electricity, but that there are a series of muscular contractions succeeding one another rapidly in diminishing energy and somewhat corresponding to the reiterated reports of thunder. This was Galvani's expression for the dying away of the electrical influence upon the muscle. He had thus evidently reached a hint of the pendulum-like swing with which electrical equilibrium is restored after its violent disturbance immediately following the lightning stroke. He noted, moreover, that for the production of muscular contractions the absolute appearance of lightning was not indispensable. Muscular twitchings were noted whenever the heavens were overclouded by a storm, or whenever clouds charged with electricity were passed above the conductor.

These experiments were made upon living frogs, as well as upon the separated legs, and in both cases the results obtained were very similar to those observed on the employment of some form of artificial electricity. In some of these observations, Galvani was anticipating ideas that became current truth in electrical science only many years after his time. In his observations upon the effects of lightning, he was forestalling Franklin's works to a certain extent. Both of these great scientists, however, had been anticipated by a clergyman in Austria; whose work attracted very little attention, however, because he was not in touch with the scientific bodies of the day. The demonstration of the identity of ordinary terrestrial artificial electricity and the lightning was in the air, as it were, and many workers, as is usually the case with any great discovery, came very close to it, and deserve at least a portion of the credit for it.

It is almost needless to say, many of these experiments with lightning thus conducted by Galvani were not without an element of serious personal danger. Not long after this time a Russian savant, Richman by name, while repeating Franklin's experiments with the kite, was struck dead by the charge received from his apparatus. Galvani, however, devoted himself only in passing to the physical problems involved, and kept always in view the physiological aspects of the problem of animal electricity; and, accordingly, made a series of most interesting observations on the ray fish or torpedo, as it is sometimes called, the fish which gives electrical shocks. His idea was to demonstrate that the shocks felt when this animal is touched are really due to sparks of electricity similar to those which can be obtained by artificial means. This had never been determined, and Galvani succeeded in showing the presence of sparks exactly as if the animal were one of the apparatuses by which the sparks of frictional electricity are developed. At this time this seemed surprising enough. Galvani also endeavored to demonstrate that the electricity in the electric torpedo differed only in degree, but not in quality, from certain electric manifestations that he had noted in the bodies of other animals, especially the frog. His idea always was to show the existence of a natural animal electricity, by means of which some of the complex mechanism of life was accomplished. He seems to have had some notion of the theory that has been suggested often enough since, and is not yet entirely disproved, that there is some very close relationship between nerve impulses and the electric current. In this, of course, he was far ahead of his time, and utterly unable to make absolute demonstration, because of the lack of proper apparatus.

The most interesting quality of Galvani's scientific career is the thoroughly experimental character of all his researches into natural phenomena. Few men have known so well how to vary their experiments so as to bring out new details of scientific knowledge. His experimental skill was of the highest order, and it is to this that we owe the development in his hands of the nascent science of electricity to a point where it became easy to continue its natural evolution. Galvani's work furnished the necessary stimulus to Volta, and then the real foundation of modern electricity was laid.

Almost more interesting than Galvani the scientist, however, is Galvani the man. As one of his biographers said of him, he joined to the most eminent intellectual genius a group of very precious qualities of the heart. Utterly unselfish in his relationship to others, he was known to be extremely sympathetic and had a large number of friends. His friends, too, he bound to him by even more than the proverbial hoops of steel, so that when they passed out of life they left him unconsolable. While it was very hard to get him to take part in social functions at which numbers of people were gathered, he was by no means a recluse, and liked to be in the company of a few friends. He seemed to care very little for the renown that his discoveries gave him, and refused, as far as possible, to be made the object of public congratulations and testimonials.

His relations with his patients—for during all of his long career he continued to practise, especially surgery and obstetrics—were of the friendliest character. While his distinction as a professor at the university gave him many opportunities for practice among the rich, he was always ready and willing to help the poor, and, indeed, seemed to feel more at home among poor patients than in the society of the wealthy and noble. Even towards the end of his life, when the loss of many friends, and especially his wife, made him retire within himself much more than before, he continued to exercise his professional skill for the benefit of the poor, though he often refused to take cases that might have proved sources of considerable gain to him. Early in life, when he was very busy between his professional work and his practice, he remarked more than once, on refusing to take the cases of wealthy patients, that they had the money with which to obtain other physicians, while the poor did not, and he would prefer to keep some time for his services for them.

Toward the end of his life Galvani was not a little perturbed by the course of events around him and by the sweeping away of faith in old beliefs, consequent upon the French Revolution and the philosophic movement that had led up to it. Seeing around him, too, the abuses to which this supposed liberty and assertion of the rights of man led, it used to be a favorite expression of Galvani that "A little philosophy led men away from God, but a good deal of it led them back to Him again." Especially did he consider this true with regard to younger men, whose lack of wisdom in the difficult phases of life made them think their philosophy of things was complete, until sad experience had taught them the necessity for lifting men's minds above any mere religion of humanity, any mere stoic resignation to the inevitable, if what was best in them was to be brought out.

A very interesting phase of the Italian university life of that time is revealed in two important incidents of Galvani's university career. One of his professors, one, by the way, for whom he seems to have had a great deal of respect, and to whose lectures he devoted much attention, was Laura Caterina Maria Bassi, the distinguished woman professor of philosophy at the University of Bologna, about the middle of the eighteenth century. It is doubtless to her teaching that Galvani owes some of his thoroughgoing conservatism in philosophic speculation, a conservatism that was of great service to him later on in life, in the midst of the ultra-radical principles which became fashionable just before and during the French Revolution. Madame Bassi seems to have had her influence on him for good not only during his student

career, but also later in life, for she was the wife of a
prominent physician in Bologna, and Galvani was often in
social contact with her during his years of connection with
the university.

As might, perhaps, be expected, seeing that his own happy
domestic life showed him that an educated woman might
be the centre of intellectual influence, Galvani seems to
have had no spirit of opposition to even the highest education
for women. This is very well illustrated by the first formal
lecture in his course on anatomy at the university, which had
for its subject the models for the teaching of anatomy that
had been made by Madame Manzolini. In the early part
of the eighteenth century Madame Manzolini had been the
professor of anatomy at the University of Bologna, and in
order to make the teaching of this difficult subject easier and
more definite she modelled with great care and delicate attention to every detail, so that they imitated actual dissections of the human body very closely, a set of wax figures
which replaced the human body for demonstration purposes
at least at the beginning of the anatomical course.

Galvani, in taking up the work of lecturer on anatomy,
appreciated how much such a set of models would help in
making the introduction to anatomical study easy, yet at the
same time without detracting from its exactness, and, accordingly, introduced his students to Madame Manzolini's
set of models in his very first lecture. At the time there were
those connected with the teaching of anatomy who considered
the use of these models as rather an effeminate proceeding.
Galvani's lack of prejudice in the matter shows the readiness
of the man to accept the best wherever he found it without
regard to persons or feelings.

He was one of the most popular professors that the University of Bologna has ever had. He was not in the ordinary

sense of the word an orator, but he was a born teacher. The source of the enthusiasm which he aroused in his hearers was undoubtedly his own love for teaching and the power it gave him to express even intricate problems in simple, straightforward language. More than any of his predecessors he understood that experiments and demonstrations must be the real groundwork of the teaching of science. Accordingly, very few of his lectures were given without the aid of these material helps to attract attention. Besides he was known to be one who delighted to answer questions and was perfectly frank about the limitations of his knowledge whenever there was no real answer to be given to a question that had been proposed. Though an original discoverer of the first rank, he was extremely modest, particularly when talking about the details of his discoveries, or subjects relating to them.

The most striking proof of the thorough conscientiousness with which he faced the duties of life is to be found in his conduct after the establishment of the so-called Cis-Alpine Republic in Italy. This was a government established merely by force of arms without the consent of the people and a plain usurpation of the rights of the previous government. He considered himself bound in duty to the authority under which he had lived all his previous life and to which he had sworn fealty. When the University of Bologna was reorganized under the new government the first requirement of all those who were made professors was that they should take the oath of allegiance to the new government. This he refused to do. His motives can be readily understood, and though practically all the other professors of the university had taken the oath he did not consider that this freed him from his conscientious obligations in the matter.

Accordingly, he was dropped from the roll of professors

and deprived of the never very large salary which he had obtained from this chair. On this sum he had practically depended for his existence and he soon began to suffer from want. While he had been a successful practitioner of medicine, especially of surgery, he had always been very liberal and had spent large sums of money in demonstrations for his lectures and personal experimentation and in materials for the museums of the university. He began to suffer from actual want and friends had to come to his assistance. He refused, however, to give up his scruples in the matter and accept the professorship which was still open for him. Finally, at the end of two years, influence was brought to bear on the new government and Galvani was allowed to accept his chair in the university without taking the oath of allegiance. This tribute came too late, however, and within a short time after his restoration to his professorship he died.

That his action in this matter was very properly appreciated by his contemporaries, and that the moral influence of his example was not lost, can be realized from the expressions used by Alibert, the Secretary-general of the Medical Society of Emulation, in the historical address on Galvani which he delivered before that society in 1801:

"Galvani constantly refused to take the civil oath demanded by the decrees of the Cis-Alpine Republic. Who can blame him for having followed the voice of his conscience, that sacred, interior voice, which alone prescribes the duties of man and which has preceded all human laws? Who could not praise him for having sacrificed with such exemplary resignation all the emoluments of his professorship rather than violate the solemn engagements made under religious sanction?"

In the same penegyric there is a very curiously interesting passage with regard to Galvani's habit of frequently closing his

lectures by calling attention to the complexity yet the purpose-
fulness of natural things and the inevitable conclusion that they
must have been created with a definite purpose by a Supreme
Being possessed of intelligence. At the time that Alibert
wrote his memoir it was the fashion to consider, at least in
France, that Christianity was a thing of the past, and that
while theism might remain, that would be all that could be
expected to survive the crumbling effect of the emancipation
of man.

He says: "We have seen already what was Galvani's
zeal and his love for the religion which he professed. We
may add that in his public demonstration he never finished
his lectures without exhorting his pupils to a renewal of
their faith by leading them always back to the idea of the
eternal Providence which develops, preserves and causes
life to flow among so many different kinds of things. I write
now," he continues, "in the age of reason, of tolerance and
of light. Must I then defend Galvani in the eyes of posterity
for one of the most beautiful sentiments that can spring
from the nature of man? No, and they are but little initiated
in the saner mechanism of philosophy who refused to recognize the truths established on evidence so strong and so
authentic. *Breves haustus in philosophiâ ad atheismum
ducunt, longiores autem reducunt ad deum*, small draughts
of philosophy lead to atheism, but longer draughts bring
one back to God"—(which may perhaps be better translated
by Pope's well-known lines, "A little learning (in philosophy)
is a dangerous thing; drink deep or touch not the Pierian
spring").

Galvani has been honored by his fellow-citizens of Bologna
as one of their greatest townsmen and by the university as
one of her worthiest sons. In 1804 a medal was struck in his
honor, on the reverse of which, surrounding a figure of the

genius of science, were the two legends: "*Mors mihi vita*," "Death is life for me," and "*Spiritus intus alit*," "The spirit works within," which were favorite expressions of the great scientist while living and are lively symbols of the spirit which animated him. In 1814 a monument was erected to him in the courtyard of the University of Bologna. It is surmounted by his bust, made by the most distinguished Bolognian sculptor of the time, De Maria. On the pedestal there are two figures in bas-relief executed by the same sculptor, which represent religion and philosophy, the inspiring geniuses of Galvani's life.

Before he died, he asked, as had Dante, whose work was his favorite reading, to be buried in the humble habit of a member of the Third Order of St. Francis. He is said to have valued his fellowship with the sons of the "poor little man of Assisi" more than the many honorary fellowships of various kinds which had been conferred upon him by the scientific societies all over Europe.

LAENNEC, MARTYR TO SCIENCE

The knowledge which a man can use is the only real knowledge, the only knowledge which has life and growth in it and converts itself into practical power. The rest hangs like dust about the brain, or dries like rain-drops off the stones.—FROUDE.

LAENNEC, MARTYR TO SCIENCE.

On August 13, 1826, there died at Quimper in Brittany at the early age of forty-five, one of the greatest physicians of all time. His name, René Theodore Laennec, was destined to be forever associated with one of the most fruitful advances in medicine that has ever been made, and one which practically introduced the modern era of scientific diagnosis. At the present time the most interesting phase of medical development is concerned with the early recognition and the prevention of tuberculosis. To Laennec more than to any other is due all the data which enable the physician of the twentieth century to make the diagnosis of tuberculosis with assurance, and to treat it with more confidence than before, and so prevent its spread as far as that is possible.

The history of pulmonary consumption in its most modern phase is centred around the names of three men, Laennec, Villemin, and Koch. To Laennec will forever belong the honor of having fixed definitely the clinical picture of the disease, and of having separated it by means of auscultation and his pathological studies from all similar affections of the lungs. Villemin showed that it was an infectious disease, absolutely specific in character, and capable of transmission by inoculation from man to the animal. To Koch the world owes the knowledge of the exact cause of the disease and consequently of the practical method for preventing its spread. The isolation of the bacillus of tuberculosis is the great triumph of the end of the nineteenth century, as the separation of the disease from all others by Laennec was the triumph of the beginning of that century. There is

(135)

still room for a fourth name in the list, that of the man who will discover a specific remedy for the disease. It is to be hoped that his coming will not be long delayed.

The estimation in which Laennec was held by the most distinguished among his contemporaries, may be very well appreciated from the opinions expressed with regard to him and his work by the best-known Irish and English clinical observers of the period. Dr. William Stokes, who was himself, as we shall see, one of the most important contributors to our clinical knowledge of diseases of the heart and lungs in the nineteenth century, said with regard to the great French clinician whom he considered his master:

"Time has shown that the introduction of auscultation and its subsidiary physical signs has been one of the greatest boons ever conferred by the genius of man on the world.

"A new era in medicine has been marked by a new science, depending on the immutable laws of physical phenomena, and, like the discoveries founded on such a basis, simple in its application and easily understood—a gift of science to a favored son; one by which the ear is converted into the eye, the hidden recesses of visceral disease open to view; a new guide to the treatment, and a new help to the ready detection, prevention and cure of the most widely spread diseases which affect mankind."

Dr. Addison, who is best known by the disease which since his original description has been called by his name, was no less enthusiastic in praise of Laennec's work. He said:

"Were I to affirm that Laennec contributed more toward the advancement of the medical art than any other single individual, either of ancient or of modern times, I should probably be advancing a proposition which, in the estimation of many, is neither extravagant nor unjust. His work,

De l'Auscultation Mediate, will ever remain a monument
of genius, industry, modesty and truth. It is a work in
perusing which every succeeding page only tends to increase
our admiration of the man, to captivate our attention, and
to command our confidence. We are led insensibly to the
bedside of his patients; we are startled by the originality
of his system; we can hardly persuade ourselves that any
means so simple can accomplish so much, can overcome
and reduce to order the chaotic confusion of thoracic pathology; and hesitate not in the end to acknowledge our unqualified wonder at the triumphant confirmation of all he
professed to accomplish."

These tributes to Laennec, however, from men who were
his contemporaries across the channel, have been more than
equalled by distinguished physicians on both sides of the
Atlantic at the end of the nineteenth and the beginning of
the twentieth century. While we might hesitate to accept
the opinions of those who had been so close to him at the
beginning of the new era of physical diagnosis, there can
be no doubt now, after the lapse of three-quarters of a century, of what Laennec's influence really was, and the tributes
of the twentieth century place him among the few great
geniuses to whom scientific medicine owes its most important
advance.

At the annual meeting of the State Medical Society of New
York held in Albany at the end of January, 1903, the president
of the society, Doctor Henry L. Elsner, of Syracuse, in his
annual address devoted some paragraphs to a panegyric of
Laennec. He wished to call attention to what had been
accomplished for scientific medicine at the beginning of the
last century by a simple observant practitioner. In the
course of his references to Laennec and his work he said:

"It is by no means to be considered an accident that,

among the greatest advances in medicine made during the century just closed, the introduction of pathological anatomy and auscultation into the practice of medicine at the bedside were both effected by the same clear mind, Laennec. He is one of the greatest physicians of all time."

He then quoted the opinion of a distinguished English clinician, Professor T. Clifford Allbutt, who is well known, especially for his knowledge of the history of medicine. Professor Allbutt is the Regius Professor of Physic (a term about equivalent to our practice of medicine) of Cambridge University, England, and was invited to this country some years ago as the representative of English medicine to deliver the Lane lectures in San Francisco. During his stay in this country he delivered a lecture at Johns Hopkins University on "Medicine in the Nineteenth Century," in which he said, "Laennec gives me the impression of being one of the greatest physicians in history; one who deserves to stand by the side of Hippocrates and Galen, Harvey and Sydenham. Without the advances of pathology Laennec's work could not have been done; it was a revelation of the anatomy of the internal organs during the life of the patient."

René Theodore Hyacinthe Laennec, who is thus conceded by twentieth century medicine a place among the world's greatest medical discoverers, was born February 17, 1781, at Quimper in Bretagne, that rocky province at the north of France which has been the sturdy nursing mother of so many pure Celtic Frenchmen who have so mightily influenced the thought not only of their own country but of all the world. The names of such Bretons as Renan and Lamennais have a universal reputation and the province was even more distinguished for its scientists.

There was published[1] a few years ago in France a detailed

[1] Les Médecins Bretons par Dr. Jules Roger. Paris, J. B. Baillière, 1900.

history of Breton physicians. This work sketches the lives of the physicians of Breton birth from the sixteenth to the twentieth century. Only those of the nineteenth century concern us, but the list even for this single century includes such distinguished names as Broussais, whose ideas in physiology dominated medicine for nearly the whole of the first half of the nineteenth century; Jobert, the famous French surgeon whose reputation was world-wide; Alphonse Guerin, another distinguished surgeon, whose work in the protection of wounds in some respects anticipated that of Lister; Chassaignac, to whose inventive genius surgery owes new means of preventing hemorrhage and purulent infection, and who introduced the great principle of surgical drainage; finally Maisonneuve, almost a contemporary, whose name is a household word to the surgeons of the present generation; without mentioning for the moment the subject of this sketch, Laennec, the greatest of them all. Six greater men never came from one province in the same limited space of time.

Bretagne, "the land of granite covered with oaks" as the Bretons love to call it, may well be proud of its illustrious sons in the century just past. Taken altogether they form a striking example of how much the world owes to the children of the countryside who, born far from the hurrying bustle of city life, do not have their energies sapped before the proper time for their display comes. These Bretagne physicians, illustrious discoverers and ever faithful workers, are at the same time a generous tribute to the influence of the simple, honest sincerity of well-meaning parents whose religious faith was the well-spring of humble, model lives that formed a striking example for their descendants. The foundations of many a great reputation were laid in the simple village homes, far from the turmoil and the excitement of the fuller

life of great cities. The Bretons are but further examples
of the fact that for genuine success in life the most precious
preparation is residence in the country in childhood and
adolescent years. The country districts of Normandy, the
province lying just next to Bretagne, have furnished even
more than their share of the Paris successes of the century,
and have seen the Norman country boys the leaders of
thought at the capital.

Laennec's father was a man of culture and intelligence,
who, though a lawyer, devoted himself more to literature
than his case books. His poetry is said to recall one of
his better known compatriots, Deforges-Maillard. Laennec
was but six years old when his mother died. His father
seems to have felt himself too much preoccupied with his
own work to assume the education of his son, and so the boy
Laennec was placed under the guardianship of his grand-
uncle, the Abbé Laennec, and lived with him for some years
in the parish house at Elliant.

A relative writing of Laennec after his death says that the
boy had the good fortune to be thus happily started on his
path in life by a hand that was at once firm and sure. The
training given him at this time was calculated to initiate him
in the best possible way into those habits of application
that made it possible for him to make great discoveries in
after life. The boy was delicate besides, and the house of
the good old rector-uncle was an excellent place for him,
because of its large and airy rooms and the thoroughly
hygienic condition in which it was kept. Household hygiene
was not as common in those days as in our own and child
mortality was higher, but the delicate boy thrived under the
favorable conditions.

Besides the parish house was situated in the midst of a
beautiful country. The perfectly regular and rather serious

life of the place was singularly well adapted to develop gradually and with due progression the precious faculties of a young, active mind and observant intelligence. This development was accomplished besides without any excitement or worry and without any of the violent contrasts or precocious disillusions of city life.

The boy passed some four or five years with his grand-uncle the priest and then went to finish his studies with a brother of his father, Dr. Laennec, a physician who has left a deservedly honored name. At this time Dr. Laennec was a member of the Faculty of Medicine at the University of Nantes. The growing lad seems to have been wonderfully successful in his studies, and a number of prizes gained at school show how deeply he was interested in his work. During this time he learned English and German and became really ready to begin the study of the higher sciences. Besides working at his academic studies, Laennec paid some attention to his uncle in his professional work, and by careful observation laid the foundation of his medical studies. His character as an observer, rather than a student of books, showed itself very early. He devoted himself to the clinical investigation of cases in the military hospital and was especially interested in the study of anatomy.

In 1800, at the age of nineteen, he went to Paris. It was typical of the man and his careful thoroughness all through life that the first impulse, when he found himself free to work for himself, was to try to make up for what he considered defects in his elementary studies. It must not be forgotten that the ten years of Laennec's life, from his tenth to his twentieth year, came in the stormy time of the French Revolution, and that school regularity was very much disturbed. His first care then was to take up the study of Latin again. He learned to read and write the language with elegance and

purity. Later on, occasionally, he delivered his clinical
lectures, especially when foreigners were present, in Latin.
We shall have the occasion to see before the end of this article,
with what easy grace he learned to use it from some passages
of the preface of his book written in that language.

He did not allow his accessory studies, however, to inter-
fere with his application to his professional work. He was
one of those rare men who knew how to rest his mind by
turning it from one occupation to another. When scarcely
more than a year in Paris, Laennec secured the two first
prizes for medicine and surgery in the medical department
of the University of Paris. In 1804 he wrote two medical
theses, one of them in Latin, the other in French. The
subject of both was Hippocrates, the great Greek father of
medicine, whom Laennec admired very much and whose
method of clinical observation was to prove the key-note of
the success of Laennec's own medical career.

At this time the Paris school of medicine had two great
rival teachers. One of them was Corvisart, who endeavored
to keep up the traditions of Hippocrates and taught especially
the necessity for careful observation of disease. The other
was Pinel, famous in our time mainly for having stricken the
manacles from the insane in the asylums of Paris, but who
was known to his contemporaries as a great exponent of what
may be called "Philosophic Medicine." Corvisart taught
principally practical medicine at the bedside; Pinel mainly
the theory of medicine by the analysis of diseased conditions
and their probable origin.

Needless to say, Laennec's sympathies were all with
Corvisart. He became a favorite pupil of this great master,
who did so much for scientific medicine by introducing the
method of percussion, invented nearly half a century before
by Auenbrugger, but forgotten and neglected, so that it

would surely have been lost but for the distinguished Frenchman's rehabilitation of its practice. Corvisart was a man
of great influence. He had caught Napoleon's eye. The
great Emperor of the French had the knack for choosing
men worthy of the confidence he wished to place in them.
His unerring judgment in this matter led him to select
Corvisart as his personal physician at a moment when his
selection was of the greatest service to practical medicine,
for no one was doing better scientific work at the time, and
this quasi-court position at once gave Corvisart's ideas a
vogue they would not otherwise have had.

Corvisart's most notable characteristic was a sympathetic
encouragement of the work of others, especially in what
concerned actual bedside observation. Laennec was at once
put in most favorable circumstances, then, for his favorite
occupation of studying the actualities of disease on the living
patient and at the autopsy. For nearly ten years he devoted
himself almost exclusively to the care and study of hospital
patients. In 1812 he was made physician to the Beaujon
Hospital, Paris. Four years later he was transferred to the
Necker Hospital, where he was destined to bring his great
researches to a successful issue. To the Necker Hospital,
before long, students from all over the world flocked to his
clinical lectures, to keep themselves in touch with the great
discoveries the youthful master was making. In spite of
rather delicate health Laennec fulfilled his duties of physician and professor with scrupulous exactitude and with a
self-sacrificing devotion that was, unfortunately, to prove
detrimental to his health before very long.

One of his contemporaries says of him:

"Laennec was almost an ideal teacher. He talked very
easily and his lesson was always arranged with logical
method, clearness and simplicity. He disdained utterly

all the artifices of oratory.   He knew, however, how to give
his lectures a charm of their own.   It was as if he were
holding a conversation with those who heard him and they
were interested every moment of the time that he talked, so
full were his lectures of practical instruction."

Another of his contemporaries says, naïvely: "At the end
of the lesson we did not applaud, because it was not the
custom.   Very few, however, who heard him once, failed
to promise themselves the pleasure of assisting at others of
his lectures."

The work on which Laennec's fame depended and the
discovery with which his name, in the words of our great
American diagnostician, Austin Flint, the elder, will live to the
end of time was concerned with the practice of auscultation.
This is the method of listening to the sounds produced in the
chest when air is inspired and expired in health and disease,
and also to the sound produced by the heart and its valves
in health and disease.   Nearly two centuries ago, in 1705,
an old medical writer quoted by Walshe, in his "Treatise
on the Disease of the Lungs and Heart " said very quaintly
but very shrewdly: "Who knows but that one may discover
the works performed in the several offices and shops of a
man's body by the sounds they make and thereby discover
what instrument or engine is out of order!"

It was just this that Laennec did.   He solved the riddle
of the sounds within the human workshop, to continue the
quaint old figure, and pointed out which were the results
of health and which of disease.   Not only this, but he showed
the difference between the sounds produced in health and
disease by those different engines, the lungs and the heart.
The way in which he was led to devote his attention originally
to the subject of auscultation is described by Laennec himself
with a simplicity and directness so charmingly characteristic

of the man, of his thoroughly Christian modesty, of his solicitude for even the slightest susceptibility of others and of his prompt inventive readiness, that none of his biographers has been able to resist the temptation to quote his own words with regard to the interesting incident, and so we feel that we must give them here.

He says: "In 1816 I was consulted by a young person who was laboring under the general symptoms of a diseased heart. In her case percussion and the application of the hand (what modern doctors call palpation) were of little service because of a considerable degree of stoutness. The other method, that namely of listening to the sounds within the chest by the direct application of the ear to the chest wall, being rendered inadmissible by the age and sex of the patient, I happened to recollect a simple and well-known fact in acoustics and fancied it might be turned to some use on the present occasion. The fact I allude to is the great distinctness with which we hear the scratch of a pin at one end of a piece of wood on applying our ear to the other.

"Immediately on the occurrence of this idea I rolled a quire of paper into a kind of cylinder and applied one end of it to the region of the heart and the other to my ear. I was not a little surprised and pleased to find that I could thereby perceive the action of the heart in a manner much more clear and distinct than I had ever been able to do by the immediate application of the ear.

"From this moment I imagined that the circumstance might furnish means for enabling us to ascertain the character not only of the action of the heart, but of every species of sound produced by the motion of all the thoracic viscera, and consequently for the exploration of the respiration, the voice, the *râles* and perhaps even the fluctuation of fluid effused in the pleura or pericardium. With this conviction I forthwith

10

commenced at the Necker Hospital a series of observations from which I have been able to deduce a set of new signs of the diseases of the chest.   These are for the most part certain, simple and prominent, and calculated perhaps, to render the diagnosis of the diseases of the lungs, heart and pleura as decided and circumstantial as the indications furnished to the surgeons by the finger or sound, in the complaints wherein these are of use."

This is the unassuming way in which Laennec announces his great discovery. He did not in modern fashion immediately cry "Eureka!" and announce the far-reaching importance of his method of diagnosis. For two years he devoted himself to the patient study of the application of his method and the appreciation of its possibilities and its limitations.   Then he presented a simple memoir to the French Academy of Sciences on the subject.   A committee of three, then distinguished members of the Academy, Doctors Portal, Pelletan and Percy were named to investigate the new discovery.

It is rather interesting to notice, though almost needless to say, that the names of these men would be now absolutely unremembered in medical history but for the fortuitous circumstance that made them Laennec's investigators.   Such is too often the ephemeralness of contemporary reputation. Fortunately for the committee, they reported favorably upon Laennec's discoveries.   It is not always true of new and really great advances in medicine that they are received with proper appreciation upon their first announcement.   Even Harvey said of his discovery of the circulation of the blood that he expected no one of any reputation in his own generation to accept it.   It is not very surprising to find then in the matter of the Laennec investigators that there is a cautious reserve in their report, showing that they were not too ready to commit themselves to a decided opinion on the importance of the new discovery, nor to any irretrievable commendation.

The important part of the discovery was supposed to consist in the use of the wooden cylinder which Laennec came to employ instead of the roll of paper originally used. This wooden cylinder, now familiar to us under the excellent name invented for it by Laennec himself is the modern single stethoscope. This instrument is of great service. The really important part of Laennec's work, however, was not the invention of the stethoscope, but the exact observation of the changes of the breath sounds that could be noted with it in various forms of chest diseases.

Laennec succeeded in pointing out how each one of the various diseases of the heart and lungs might be recognized from every other. Before his time, most of the diseases of the lungs, if accompanied with any tendency to fever particularly, were called lung fever. He showed the difference between bronchitis and pneumonia, pneumonia and pleurisy, and the various forms of tuberculosis and even the rarer pathological conditions of the lung, such as cancer, or the more familiar conditions usually not associated with fever, emphysema, and some of the forms of retraction.

With regard to heart disease, it was before Laennec's discovery almost a sealed chapter in practical medicine. It was known that people died from heart disease often and, not infrequently, without much warning. The possibility that heart conditions could be separated one from another, and that some of them could be proved to be comparatively harmless, some of them liable to cause lingering illness, while others were surely associated with the probability of sudden fatal termination, was scarcely dreamed of. It is to Laennec's introduction of auscultation that modern medicine owes all its exacter knowledge of heart lesions and their significance. He himself did not solve all the mysteries of sound here as he did in the lungs; indeed, he made some mistakes that render him more sympathetic because they bring him down to the level of our humanity. He did make important discoveries with regard to heart disease, and his method of diagnosis during his own life was, in the hands of the Irish school of medicine, to prove the key to the problems of disease he failed to unlock.

Almost at once Laennec's method of auscultation attracted widespread attention. From Germany, from Italy, from England, even from the United States, in those days when our medical men had so few opportunities to go abroad, medical students and physicians went to Paris to study the method under the direction of the master himself and to learn from him his admirable technique of auscultation. Those who came found that the main thing to be seen was the patient observation given to every case and Laennec's admirably complete examination of each condition. The services to diagnosis rendered by the method were worthy of the enthusiasm it aroused. Only the work of Pasteur has attracted corresponding attention during the nineteenth century. Physicians practice auscultation so much as a matter of course now that it is hard to understand what an extreme novelty it was in 1820, and how much it added to the confidence of practitioners in their diagnosis of chest diseases.

Bouilland said, with an enthusiasm that does not go beyond literal truth, "A sense was lacking in medicine and I would say, if I dared, that Laennec the creator, by a sort of divine delegation of a new sense, supplied the long-felt want. The sense which medicine lacked was hearing. Sight and touch had already been developed in the service of medical diagnosis. Hearing was more important than the other two senses, and in giving it to scientific medicine Laennec disclosed a new world of knowledge destined to complete the rising science of diagnosis."

Henri Roger said: "Laennec in placing his ear on the chest of his patient heard for the first time in the history of human disease the cry of suffering organs. First of all, he learned to know the variations in their cries and the expressive modulations of the air-carrying tubes and the orifices of the heart that indicate the points where all is not well. He was the first to understand and to make others realize the significance of this pathological language, which, until then, had been misunderstood or, rather, scarcely listened to. Henceforth, the practitioner of medicine, endowed with one sense more than before and with his power of investigation materially increased, could read for himself the alterations hidden in the depths of the organism. His ear opened to the mind a new world in medical science."

The freely expressed opinions of distinguished German, English and American physicians show that these enthusiastic praises from his French compatriots are well deserved by Laennec for the beautifully simple, yet wonderfully fecund method that he placed before the medical profession in all its completeness.

The first employment of the stethoscope by rolling up sheets of paper is of itself a sign of his readiness of invention. He made his own stethoscopes by hand and liked to spend his leisure time fashioning them carefully and even ornately. One of the stethoscopes certainly used by him and probably made by himself is to be seen at the Museum of the College of Physicians of Philadelphia.

After three years of study and patient investigation of the use of auscultation in pulmonary and cardiac diagnosis, Laennec wrote his book on the subject. This is an immortal work—a true classic in its complete treatment of the subject.

We have had thousands of books written on the subject since Laennec's time, and yet no physician could do better at the present moment than study Laennec's two comparatively small volumes to learn the art of physical diagnosis.

It is a characteristic of genius to give a completeness to work that endows it with an enduring independent vitality. Almost innumerable disciples follow in the footsteps of a teacher, and each thinks that he adds something to the fulness of the revelation made by the master. At the end of a century the fourth generation finds that scarcely anything has been added and that the master's work alone stands out, not merely as the great central fact of the new theory or doctrine, but as the absolute vital entity to which the other supposed discoveries are only adventitious and not entirely indispensable accessories.

Dr. Austin Flint, the elder, admittedly one of the greatest diagnosticians in pulmonary and heart diseases that we have ever had in America, said on this subject: "Suffice it to say here that, although during the forty years that have elapsed since the publication of Laennec's works the application of physical exploration has been considerably extended and rendered more complete in many of its details, the fundamental truths presented by the discoverer of auscultation not only remain as a basis of the new science, but for a large portion of the existing superstructure. Let the student become familiar with all that is now known on this subject, and he will then read the writings of Laennec with amazement that there remained so little to be altered or added."

Laennec's unremitting devotion to his hospital work finally impaired his health. He was never robust and strangers who came to Paris and saw him for the first time wondered that he should be able to stand the labor he required of himself. The portraits of him give a good impression of his ascetic delicacy; they convey besides a certain wistfulness, the look of one close to human suffering, and unable to do all that he would wish to relieve it. Long before his discovery of the mysteries of auscultation, he had accomplished results that of themselves, and without his subsequent master discovery, would have given him an enduring name in medical literature. Laennec's genius enabled him to make a really great discovery, but Laennec's talent, the principal part of which was an inexhaustible faculty for untiring labor, an infinite capacity for taking pains with all that he did, enabled him to make a number of smaller discoveries any one of which would have given a great reputation to a lesser man.

Some idea of the amount of work that he did in preparing himself for the observations that were to result in his discovery may be gathered from details of his earlier career. During the first three years of his attendance at La Charité Hospital in Paris he drew up a minute history of nearly four hundred cases of disease. As early as 1805 he read a paper on hydatid cysts. These cysts were formerly thought to be hollow tumors formed within the tissues themselves somewhat as other cystic tumors are formed. Laennec showed conclusively that their origin was entirely due to certain worms that had become parasites in human beings. The cysts instead of being tumors were really one stage of the worm's existence, and had an organization and an independent existence of their own. He gave an exact description of them and even showed that there were several types of the parasite, and described the different changes that various forms produced in the human tissues. This study of the hydatid parasites remains a remarkable contribution to medicine down even to our own day.

During these early years Laennec devoted himself particularly to the study of pathology. Like all the men who have made great discoveries in medicine he understood that all true medical advance must be founded on actual observation of the changes caused by disease in the tissues, and that this knowledge can only be obtained in the autopsy room. For years he devoted himself to the faithful study of the tissues of patients dead from various forms of disease. He wrote as the result of this work a treatise on peritonitis that was a distinct advance over anything known before his time and which, in the words of Benjamin Ward Richardson, "as a pathological study was shrewdly in anticipation of the later work of one who became his most formidable rival, the famous Broussais."

From the peritoneum his attention was attracted to the liver. As early as 1804 he wrote a description of the membranes of the liver. Pathological changes in the liver continued to occupy his attention for some time, and it is to him we owe the name cirrhosis of the liver, as a term for the changes which are produced by alcohol in this gland. Alcoholic cirrhosis is often spoken of as Laennec's cirrhosis of the liver, and he was the first to point out the significance of the changes in the organ, their etiology and the reason for the symptoms that usually accompany this condition. This work alone would have been sufficient to have made Laennec's name a permanent fixture in medical literature.

During the early years of Laennec's career at Paris, the French Anatomical Society was founded and Laennec became a prominent member of it. Corvisart, who was the moving spirit in the society, was at this time—the early years of the nineteenth century—doing his great teaching at the medical school of the University of Paris. He was Laennec's master, and was at the height of his glory. It was a constant source of surprise to his students to note how well the master's diagnosis agreed with postmortem findings. This is, after all, the only true criterion of scientific diagnosis. It is not surprising that the strict application of this practical method of control of medical theory soon gave rise to a series of distinct advances in medical knowledge of the greatest importance.

Discussions of cases were frequent and Laennec took a prominent part in them. His knowledge of medicine was broadening in this great field of practice, and he was chosen as one of the contributors to the *Dictionnaire des Sciences Médicales*. His articles for this work contained much original matter of great value and suggestive views of notable importance. Laennec was the first to give a description of carcinoma encephaloides and certain especially malignant forms of cancers. He showed the distinction between pigmented spots of benignant character and those that were due to malignant disease.

"After all, however," says Benjamin Ward Richardson, "the grand reputation of Laennec must rest on his one immortal work. It is not too much to say that any man of good intelligence could have written the other memoirs. No one less than Laennec could have written the 'Treatise on Mediate Auscultation and the Use of the Stethoscope.' The true student of medicine, who never wears out, reads this original work of Laennec once in two years at least, so long as he is in practice and takes a living interest in the subject of which it treats. It ranks equally with the original works of Vesalius, Harvey and Bichat and as a section of medical literature is quite equal to any section of Hippocrates."[1]

[1] The full title of this work of Laennec's is " De l'auscultation médi-ate ou traité du diagnostic des maladies des poumons et du cœur par R. T. H. Laennec." Its modest motto is the Greek sentence: Μέγα δὲ μερός ἡγευμαί τῆς τεχνῆς εἶναι τὸ δύνάσθαι σκοπεῖν. (The most important part of an art is to be able to observe properly.) The book was pub-lished in Paris by J. A. Brosson et J. S. Chandé, rue Pierre-Sarrazin, No. 9, 1819.

Some quotations from the Latin preface to the book will serve to show that Laennec appreciated the value of the discovery he had made for the diagnosis of chest diseases, yet that he did not expect it to be taken up enthusiastically at once, and in his modest way he adds that he shall be satisfied if it should serve to save but one human being from suffering and death.[1]

Unfortunately, as we have said, Laennec's untiring devotion for nearly twenty years to medical investigation caused his health to give way. It is painful to think that in the full tide of the success of his great labors, when the value of his work was only just beginning to be properly appreciated and when he had attained a position which would satisfy even lofty ambitions, his nerves gave way and he had many

---

[1] " Imo neminem hanc methodum expertum deinceps cum Baglivio dicturum esse spero: O quantum difficile est diagnoscere morbos pulmonum."

" Nostra enim *aetas incuriosa* quoque *suorum* (the italics are Laennec's own); et si quid novi ab homine coaevo in medio ponitur, risu ut plurimum ineptisque cavillationibus excipiunt ; quippe facilius est aspernari quam experiri."

" Hoc mihi satis est quod bonis doctisque viris nonnullis acceptam aegrotisque multis utilem, hanc methodum fore confidere possim ; hominem unum ereptum orco dulce dignumque meae atque etiam majoris operae pretium praemium fore existimem."

" I may say that no one who has made himself expert with this method will after this have occasion to say with Baglivi, Oh! how difficult it is to diagnose disease of the lungs."

" For our generation is not inquisitive as to what is being accomplished by its sons. Claims of new discoveries made by contemporaries are likely for the most part to be met by smiles and mocking remarks. It is always easier to condemn than to test by actual experience."

" It suffices for me if I can only feel sure that this method will commend itself to a few worthy and learned men who will make it of use to many patients. I shall consider it ample, yea, more than sufficient reward for my labor, if it should prove the means by which a single human being is snatched from untimely death."

of the typical melancholic symptoms that disturb the modern neurasthenic. Fortunately, his habits of life, always extremely abstemious, and his liking for outdoor sports had been a safeguard for him. He retired to the country and for nearly two years spent most of his time in the open air.

It was not long before surcease from intellectual labor and indulgence in field sport restored him to health and to activity. He foresaw, however, that to go back to the city and to his scientific work would almost surely lead to another breakdown. One of his biographers states that it was the great regard which he had for his family and the powerful influence of his religious principles which alone had sufficient weight to make him leave his retreat in the country. After an absence of two years, he returned to Paris and once more took up his hospital duties.

Soon after his return he received the appointment of physician to the Duchesse de Berri. One of the main objections to this position in Laennec's mind seems to have been the necessity for occasionally wearing court dress with a sword and regalia. Ordinarily he went dressed very plainly, and it was noted that, when men of much less authority and much less practice used their own carriages, he usually took a hired cab. His position at court gave him enough influence to bring about the proper recognition of his merit as a teacher. At this time his lectures on auscultation, though he held no regular professorship, were crowded by students from all nations. The year after his return to Paris he was appointed Professor of Medicine in the College of France, and afterward of clinical medicine at the Hospital La Charité where he had made his own studies as a medical student.

About this time he was offered a position of importance as a member of the Royal Council of Public Instruction. This he refused, however, because it would deprive him of some of the precious time that he wished to devote to the further investigation of important subjects in clinical medicine and especially to the elaboration of his method of auscultation.

One of the most striking features of Laennec's character was his absolute placidity and lack of personal ambition. His life was passed in the most complete calm. He devoted himself to his work, and had the supreme joy of duty accomplished, seeming to look for no other enjoyment in life. Those who knew him best said that they had never seen him angry or even impatient. In the midst of his discussion with Broussais, it might have been expected that there would occasionally have been some flashes of impatience, for the great protagonist of medical theory was a man of satiric character, and his supposedly scientific discussion was stained by some very bitter personalities. In spite of all Broussais' sarcasm, Laennec remained absolutely unmoved. Occasionally his friends saw a smile at some of Broussais' emphatic asseverations, but Laennec simply continued at his work, and looked straight ahead, convinced that what he was doing was for the cause of truth, and the truth would finally prevail.

He was known for the kindness of his disposition, and his readiness to help his friends whenever it was possible. He was never known to injure anyone, and a certain quiet elevation of spirit preserved him from all conceit. One of his most intimate Breton friends, Kergaradec, said, "I have never heard Laennec express by a single word, or even by the slightest insinuation, anything that might seem to indicate pride in what he had accomplished or that might provoke a listener to say something in praise of him." The friends he made were bound to him with hoops of steel. They were not many, for he had not the time to waste on many friends. He was too devoted to his work, and too deeply interested in the great problem whose solution he fore-saw meant so much for the good of humanity, to have much time for anything but his studies and his patients.

With regard to Laennec's personal character, his most recent biographer Dr. Henri Saintignon, has said:[1]

"I have shown in the course of this life just what was the character of Laennec and his intellectual and moral qualities, so that it will not be necessary for me to dwell at length on this subject, in concluding. His great piety, which had never been abandoned from his earliest infancy, was his main guide during all his life. Without ostentation, yet without any weakness, absolutely ignoring human respect, he obeyed with utter simplicity the prescriptions of his faith. While he did not conceal his convictions when during the first empire they might have proved a source of lessened esteem, or positive prejudice, he made no noise about them when under the Restoration they might have proved the means of advancement and of fortune. He had not in the slightest degree what is so often objected to, in devoted persons, namely, the love of making proselytes. The words of Prof. Desgenettes might very well have been applied to him: as he did not believe himself to have any mission to lead others to his opinions, he limited himself to preaching by example. The reproach of being rabidly clerical or propagandist, which was urged against him, when he first became a member of the faculty of medicine, was absolutely unjustified. Laennec never occupied himself with politics nor with religion in public. As a physician he devoted himself exclusively to his profession, receiving at his clinic all those who desired to follow his teaching, whatever might be their opinions or their beliefs."

[1] Laennec, Sa vie et son oeuvre. Par Dr. Henri Saintignon. Paris, J. B. Baillière et Fils, 1904.

It was not long, however, before Laennec's many labors
in Paris began to tell on his health once more. His practice
after his return to health and his attachment to the court
became large and lucrative. It is characteristic of the man
and his ways that he frequently refused, owing to lack of
time, to go to see wealthy patients, from whom he would
have received large fees, but it is said that he never refused
to go to see a poor patient. His hospital patients always
received the most solicitous attention, and his time was almost
entirely at their disposal. It was not long before Laennec
himself, who had taught modern physicians so much about
the diagnosis of pulmonary diseases, began evidently to suffer
from pulmonary disease himself. There seems no doubt
now that almost constant association with tuberculous patients
in an overworked subject inclined naturally to be of under-
weight, and therefore especially susceptible, led to the contraction of the disease.

After about four years in Paris, a dry, hard cough developed
insidiously, gradually increased in annoyance, and finally
grew so serious as to demand a return once more to his
native Bretagne. He lost flesh, became subject to inter-
mittent attacks of fever and suffered from some pleuritic and
pulmonic pains. For some time after his return to his native
air he improved. He was treated by the usual method
employed at the time whenever fever accompanied any ailment. Venesection was the main part of what was then called
the antiphlogistic treatment. It is needless to say he did
not improve. He was suffering from exhausting disease
and the treatment became really an accessory to further
exhaustion.

At last there could be no longer any doubt that the end
was approaching. The old curé of the village came often
to visit him, and brought him all the consolations of religion.

With his sincere Christian faith and firm conviction, it was not hard for Laennec to find the moral force and the calm necessary to secure an easy death. Finally one day, on August 13th, his wife saw him take off his fingers one after another the rings he wore, and place them softly upon the table. When she asked him why he did so, he replied, "It will not be long now before someone else would have to do this service for me, and I do not wish that they should have the trouble." Even in death he was thinking of others rather than of himself, and he was calmly facing the inevitable, thoroughly prepared for it. Two hours afterward, at five o'clock in the afternoon, without there having been at any time the slightest loss of consciousness, Laennec passed away.

How faithfully his family had watched over him, and how simple was the feeling of Christian confidence in all of them, may very well be gathered from the letter of his cousin Ambrose to Laennec's brother Meriadec in Paris.

"MY DEAR MERIADEC:—Poor Renè is no more. His life was passed in the midst of labor and of benevolence. While he had all the virtues of the true Christian, and a wisdom far beyond what was usually granted to men, they have not sufficed to obtain for him the grace of a longer life. Somehow it was ordained that this glory and ornament of our family was not to remain with us. What a sad reflection it is on our restless eagerness in this life, and on the vanity of our hopes, that a genius like this must perish just when it was about to receive the fruit of its labors! He leaves to us a name, a name difficult to sustain and the example of virtues that it will not be easy to imitate. Let us hope that he will watch over us in the future as he has done in the past, and that he will still continue to aid us after his death. Although I have been prepared for this sad event, I could not suspect how much grief I was to experience in losing my second master, my friend from earliest infancy, and him whom I had become accustomed to consider as my eldest brother. I must confess that for some years now we have all had to pay dear for the short intervals of happiness that it has pleased heaven to accord to us."

Laennec's burial took place in the cemetery of Ploare. The attendance at the funeral was very large. Practically the entire population of the countryside came to mourn for the benefactor that they loved so much. He had made friends even among the simplest of the country people and knew most of them by name. After his return to the country, he had improved somewhat in appearance, and the neighbors had been very glad to express their feelings of gratitude for his apparent improvement in health. Undoubtedly not a little of this state of better spirits was due to the fact that he liked Brittany and the peasants of the neighborhood so well, and always felt so much at home among them.

He was mild and agreeable in his manners, and of a quiet and even temper. His conversation was lively and full of quiet humor, and his friends often said that they never came away from a conversation with him without having learned something. Toward the end of his life, when his great reputation caused him to be honored by medical men from all over the world, and when his reputation made him the lion of the hour, he lost none of his natural affability and kindness of heart. He was remarkable, especially, for his great kindness and courtesy to foreigners, and he is said to have taken special care to make himself understood by English-speaking medical visitors.

It must be confessed that he was somewhat less popular with his contemporaries who did not belong to his immediate circle of friends and students. One of the reasons for this was his genius, which no generation seems ready to acknowl-

edge in any of its members. Another reason was his continued misunderstanding with Broussais. Broussais was the
medical theorist of the hour, and medical theories have always
been popular, while medical observation has had to wait
for due recognition. There were undoubtedly good points
in Broussais' theories that Laennec failed to appreciate. This
is the only blot on a perfect career, taking it all in all,
whether as man or as physician. It can easily be understood
with what impatience Laennec, entirely devoted himself to
observation, would take up the study of what he considered
mere theory, and it is easy to forgive him his lack of
appreciation.

Benjamin Ward Richardson says: "It was a common saying regarding Laennec by his compeers that, while he was
without a rival in diagnosis, he was not a good practitioner;
which means that he was not a good practitioner, according
to their ideas of practice, heroic and fearful. To us, Laennec
would now be a practitioner very heroic; so much so, that I
doubt if any medical man living would, for the life of him,
take some of his prescriptions. But in his own time, when
so little was known of the great system of natural cure, he
would be easily out of court. It was amply sufficient against
him that he had a glimmering of the truth as to the existence
of a considerable run of cases of organic disease, for which
the so-called practice of remedial cure by drugs, bloodlettings
and other heroic plans, could do no good but was likely to
do grievous harm." We are reminded of Morgagni's refusal
to permit bloodletting in his own case, though he practised
it himself on others. Like Laennec, Morgagni seems to
have doubted the efficacy of bloodletting at a time when
unfortunately all medical men were agreed that it was the
sovereign remedy.

If Laennec was not popular with his immediate contem-

11

poraries, succeeding generations have more than made up for the seeming neglect. Less than twenty-five years after his death, Austin Flint, here in America, hailed him as one of the five or six greatest medical men of all times. Forty years after his death, Professor Chauffard, himself one of the distinguished medical men of the nineteenth century, said:

"Without exaggeration we can call the glory which has come to French medicine because of the great discovery of auscultation a national honor. It must be conceded that for a long time before Laennec, the great man of medicine, those to whom medical science owed its ground-breaking work did not belong to France. Harvey, Haller and Morgagni had made the investigations on which are founded the circulation of the blood, experimental physiology, and pathological anatomy, in other lands than ours. It almost seemed that we were lacking in the fecund possibilities of daring and successful initiative. Auscultation, however, as it came to us perfect from the hands of Laennec, has given us a striking revenge for any objections foreigners might make to our apathy. This discovery has rendered the scientific medicine of the world our tributary for all time. It was an immortal creation, and its effects will never fail to be felt. More than this, it will never be merely an historical reminiscence, because of the fact that it guided men aright, but it will in its actuality remain as an aid and diagnostic auxiliary. Auscultation will not disappear but with medical science itself, and with this stage of our civilization which guides, directs and enlightens it."

Laennec was known for his simple Bretagne faith, for his humble piety, and for uniformly consistent devotion to the Catholic Church, of which he was so faithful a member. His charity was well known, and while his purse was very ready to assist the needy, he did not hesitate to give to the poor what was so much more precious to him, and it may be said to the world also, than money—his time. After his death, and only then, the extent of his charity became known.

Dr. Austin Flint said of him: "Laennec's life affords an instance among many others disproving the vulgar error that the pursuits of science are unfavorable to religious faith. He lived and died a firm believer in the truths of Christianity. He was a truly moral and a sincerely religious man."

Of his death, his contemporary, Bayle, who is one of his biographers, and who had been his friend from early youth, said:

"His death was that of a true Christian, supported by the hope of a better life, prepared by the constant practice of virtue; he saw his end approach with composure and resignation. His religious principles, imbibed with his earliest knowledge, were strengthened by the conviction of his maturer reason. He took no pains to conceal his religious sentiments when they were disadvantageous to his worldly interests, and he made no display of them when their avowal might have contributed to favor and advancement." Surely in these few lines is sketched a picture of ideal Christian manhood. There are those who think it wonderful to find it in a man of genius as great as Laennec. It should not be surprising, however, for surely genius can bow in acknowledgment to its Creator.

Shortly after the death of Pasteur it was well said that two of the greatest medical scientists of the nineteenth century have given to the physicians of France a magnificent, encouraging and comforting example. It is almost needless to say these two were Laennec and Pasteur, and their example is not for France alone, but for the whole medical world. They were living nineteenth century answers to the advocates of free thought, who would say that religious belief and

especially Catholic faith make men sterile in the realm
of scientific thought.

No better ending to this sketch of Laennec's life seems
possible than the conclusion of Dr. Flint's address to his
students in New Orleans, already so often quoted from. It
has about it the ring of the true metal of sincere Christian
manhood and unselfish devotion to a humanitarian profession:

"The career of the distinguished man whose biography
has been our theme on this occasion is preëminently worthy
of admiration. In his character were beautifully blended
the finest intellectual and moral qualities of our nature.
With mental powers of the highest order were combined
simplicity, modesty, purity and disinterestedness in such
measure that we feel he was a man to be loved not less than
admired. His zeal and industry in scientific pursuits were
based on the love of truth for its own sake and a desire to be
useful to his fellow-men. To these motives to exertion much
of his success is to be attributed. Mere intellectual ability
and acquirements do not qualify either to make or to appreciate important scientific discoveries. The mind must rise
above the obstructions of self-love, jealousy and selfish aims.
Hence it is that most of those who have attained to true eminence in the various paths of scientific research have been
distinguished for excellencies of the heart as well as of the
head. The example of Laennec is worthy of our imitation.
His superior natural gifts we can only admire, but we can
imitate the industry without which his genius would have
been fruitless. Let us show our reverence to the memory
of Laennec by endeavoring to follow humbly in his footsteps."
Quod faustum vertat !

THE IRISH SCHOOL OF MEDICINE

There are men and classes of men that stand above the common herd: the soldier, the sailor, and the shepherd not infrequently; the artist rarely; rarelier still, the clergyman; the physician almost as a rule. He is the flower (such as it is) of our civilization; and when that stage of man is done with, and only to be marvelled at in history, he will be thought to have shared as little as any in the defects of the period, and most notably exhibited the virtues of the race.—ROBERT LOUIS STEVENSON, Preface to *Underwoods*.

The physician who is not also a scholar may be a more or less successful practitioner, but his influence will be confined, his methods mechanical and his interests narrow. The doctor, the lawyer and the minister of religion can do but inferior work, unless to a knowledge of their several sciences they bring the insight, the wide outlook, and the confidence which nothing but intimate acquaintance with the best that has been thought and said can confer. The more accomplished the specialist, the greater the need of the control which philosophic culture gives.—BISHOP SPALDING.

THE IRISH SCHOOL OF MEDICINE.[1]

ROBERT GRAVES, M.D.

IT has been always generally recognized that a very important portion of what is called English literature is really due to the native genius of the English-speaking writers of Irish birth and parentage, whose Celtic qualities of mind and heart have proved the sources of some of the most significant developments in the language of their adoption. What a large lacuna would be created in English literature by the removal from it of the work of such men as Dean Swift, Goldsmith, Burke, Sheridan, and Moore! It is not so generally known, however, that if the work of the distinguished Irish physicians and surgeons of the last century were to be blotted out of English medical literature there would be left quite as striking and as wide a gap. It is, indeed, to what is known as the Dublin School of Medicine, for medical schools have very properly been named usually after the cities rather than the countries in which they were situated, that we owe not a little of our modern progress in practical medicine, and especially the advance in the clinical teaching of the medical sciences. Now that the Gaelic movement is calling attention more than ever before to things Irish, it

[1] For much of the material embodied in this series I am indebted to Sir Charles Cameron, the Historian of the Royal College of Surgeons in Ireland, whose courtesy to me while on a visit to Dublin in 1904 is one of the precious memories I shall always cherish. At the same time Sir Christopher Nixon and Sir John Moore, for letters of introduction to whom I was indebted to Prof. Osler, not only gave me valuable suggestions, but demonstrated how kind is the Celtic nature at its best.

seems only proper that this feature of the national life should be given its due prominence and that the great members of the Irish School of Medicine should not be without honor in their own and other English-speaking countries.

There are three great names in the history of Irish medicine recognized by all the world as well deserving of enduring fame. These three names are Robert James Graves, William Stokes, and Dominic Corrigan. Graves' name is indelibly attached to the disease known as exophthalmic goitre, which he described and separated from other affections before anyone else had realized its individuality. William Stokes was, perhaps, the best authority on diseases of the heart and lungs in his time. His name will be preserved in the designation of the peculiar form of breathing which occurs in certain comatose conditions and has received the name Cheyne-Stokes respiration, in honor of the men who first called attention to it. Corrigan was in his time one of the greatest authorities on the heart, and especially on the pulse. His name is preserved in the term Corrigan pulse, which is applied to a peculiar condition that occurs very characteristically in disease of the aortic valves of the heart.

The lives of these men deserve to be better known, for they can scarcely fail to be an inspiration to others to do work of a high order in medicine—work that will represent not alone present success and emolument but will stand for medical progress for all time.

Dr. Robert Graves was the youngest son of the Rev. Richard Graves, D.D., Senior Fellow of Trinity College and Regius Professor of Divinity in the University of Dublin, and of Elizabeth, daughter of James Drought, also a fellow of Trinity College, whose family had been long settled in King's County. His father, as a tribute to his distinguished learning, was later promoted to the deanery of Armagh. There were two other sons in the family, Richard and Hercules. All three of the boys passed through Trinity College with high honors and, in fact, established a record there that has since been unequalled, for at the degree examinations of three successive years the gold medal in classics and in science, then the highest distinctions attainable by students of Trinity, was conferred upon one of the brothers.

Dr. Graves received his degree of Bachelor of Medicine at the University of Dublin in 1818. After this he studied for some time in London, and then spent three years on the continent, at Berlin, Göttingen, Vienna and Copenhagen, as well as in Paris and certain Italian schools, finally studying also for some months in Edinburgh before his return to Dublin. As Dr. Stokes very well says: "In this large and truly liberal education, which embraced the training of the school, the university and the world, we can discover in part the foundations of his subsequent eminence. He did not content himself, as is so commonly the case, with commending —to use his own words—'the life of a practitioner without practice,' but he made himself intimate with the recent discoveries and modes of thinking in every great school of medicine, whether abroad or at home, and formed friendships with the leading physiologists and physicians of Europe, with many of whom he kept up a correspondence during his life."

An interesting incident in his travels serves to illustrate very well his facility for the acquisition of languages. Once while on a pedestrian journey in Austria he neglected to carry his passport, and was arrested as a spy. He was thrown into prison and for a time his condition seemed serious enough. He insisted that he was a British subject, but his assertions in this matter were immediately repudiated by the Austrian authorities in the little town, who insisted that no

Englishman could possibly speak German as well as he did. He was kept in prison for some ten days until authentic information could be obtained with regard to him, and, during this time, such was the state of the prison that he suffered many privations. Later in life this gave him a sympathy with the prisoners of Ireland and led to his making suggestions for the amelioration of their condition.

Like practically all the great medical men who have proved to be original workers, Graves' interest was not confined alone to medicine. During his sojourn in Italy he became acquainted with Turner, the celebrated English landscape painter, and was his companion in many journeys. Graves himself was possessed of no mean artistic powers, as his friend Stokes tells us, and his sketches are characterized by natural vigor and truth. His thorough appreciation of his companion, however, and the breadth of his sympathy and admiration for the great painter of nature can perhaps best be understood from some candid expressions of his with regard to their work in common: "I used to work away," he said, "for an hour or more and put down as well as I could every object in the scene before me, copying form and color as faithfully as was possible in the time. When our work was done and we compared drawings the difference was strange. I assure you there was not a single stroke in Turner's drawing that I could see like nature, not a line nor an object, and yet my work was worthless in comparison with his. The whole glory of the scene was there."

After wandering for some three years in Europe, Graves returned to Dublin and at once took a leading position in his profession as well as in society. He came back at a very fortunate period for him. In 1807, Dr. Cheyne, who had been educated in Edinburgh, made the first step toward the foundation of a new school of medical observation, by the publication of the first volume of the Dublin Hospital Reports. Dr. Stokes says that the best proof of the value of these reports is that they appear to have given the tone to the subsequent labors of the Irish school which inherited their practical nature and truthfulness. Within a year after Graves' return he appeared as one of the founders of the new school of medicine in Park Street, and was also elected physician to the Meath Hospital, where he commenced to put into effect that system of clinical observation and instruction which has done so much to establish the lasting reputation of the Dublin School of Medicine.

For the next thirty years Graves' life is full of the teaching and the practice of medicine. He was noted for his tenderness toward the poor, but the rich soon came to appreciate his skill. Nothing ever made him neglect his poor patients. Meantime he left his mark on every subject that he handled in medicine. Fevers, nervous diseases of many kinds besides that named after him, tuberculosis, and other forms of pulmonary disease, were all illuminated by his practical genius in a way that has made them clear for succeeding generations in medicine.

With regard to fevers especially Graves' work will count for all time, because he set their treatment on so practical a basis. The trained nurse is quite a modern acquisition, yet seventy-five years ago Dr. Graves insisted that the services of a properly qualified nurse in severe, continued fever are inestimable. He emphasized the necessity for moral management in fever, and friends and relatives are seldom capable of discharging this office. "If they chance to discover from the physician's remarks or questions the weak points of the patient's case they generally contrive to let him know them in some way or another. If the patient is restless, for instance, the ill-judged anxiety of his friends

will most certainly keep him from sleeping. If he happens
to take an opiate and they are aware of the nature of his
medicine they will surely inform him of it in some way or
another, though it may be only by a hint and his anxiety for
sleep conjoined with their disturbing inquiries prevents its
due operation."

We are apt to think that the modern aphorism, nursing
(meaning trained care) is more important than medicine
in the treatment of fever, is the result of observations in our
own day. Dr. Graves, however, felt very deeply that the
most important element in the treatment is the conservation of the patient's strength with the preservation of his
morale, and this can be best accomplished when the patient
is constantly under the care of an experienced nurse, noting
every symptom and averting every possible source of worry
and every form of exhaustion of energy.

With regard to fever treatment, however, Graves' name is
immortal in medicine because of his insistence on the doctrine
that fever patients must be fed. A century ago the presence
of fever was supposed definitely to indicate that the patient
should have no food. Any contribution to his nutrition was
supposed to feed the fever rather than the patient. Graves
pointed out, however, that at the end of a long-continued
fever the most serious condition is the emaciation and
weakness of the patient. He insisted that, appetite or no
appetite, fever patients should be fed regularly. The result
was at once noteworthy. Only the very hardy individuals
had recovered before this; now even weaker patients had
a good chance for life. The mortality from fever fell very
strikingly, and in his time Dublin was overrun with typhoid
and typhus fever and the saving of life produced by the new
method of treatment was very considerable. Graves himself, when he saw how much he had accomplished by his

new doctrine, said that he wanted no better epitaph on his
tombstone than the words, "He fed fevers."

Some of Dr. Graves' very particular hints with regard to
treatment of fever show how careful he was in clinical observation. He deprecates the allowance of very much fluid
for patients, since their thirst cannot be assuaged in that way,
and the amount of liquid taken may be harmful by causing
depression. He suggests, therefore, the use of acidulated
water made by means of a little currant jelly or raspberry
vinegar, given in small portions and at regular intervals.
Much better than plain water he considers water to which
some light bitter has been added, such as cascarilla. Small
quantities of this will appease the morbid thirst of fever
more effectually and for a much longer period than large
draughts of water.

Even more interesting in these modern times, however,
than Graves' attitude toward the treatment of fever is the
position he took with regard to the habits of life that were
best for the consumptive. At that time tuberculosis of the
lungs was considered to be an inflammatory disease requiring
the patient to be in the house most of the time, carefully
protected from cold, and during any rise of temperature to
be kept in warm rooms, without any special encouragement
to take food. Graves and Stokes changed all that, and for
the time completely revolutionized the principles of treatment
for this serious ailment. Alas! their work, notwithstanding
the good results shown in a certain number of cases, failed
to attract widespread attention, and not until our own
time did the principles that they laid down as the rational
basis of successful therapeutics for tuberculosis come to be
generally adopted.

Graves insisted that his patients when suffering from
beginning tuberculosis should not be confined to the house,

but on the contrary should be out of doors most of the time. He emphasized what he called the taking of exercise, but in such a way that he agrees much more than might be thought with modern ideas on this subject. Now, it is insisted that tuberculous patients must not overtire themselves by taking exercise, though they must be in the open air a large part of the time. Graves explains the exercise that he would like to have them take by saying that they should spend four or five hours every day riding in a carriage, or, as he seems to prefer, in an open jaunting-car. And that they should spend at least as much time sitting outside in quiet.

Besides this the most important element in treatment he considers to be the encouragement of the appetite—as might be expected from the man who first fed fevers. His directions in this matter are very explicit, and he suggests various methods by which patients can be tempted to eat more and more food, and emphasizes the use of cereals and of milk and eggs as likely to be of most service in helping these patients to gain in weight and strength so as to be able to resist the further advance of the disease. This, it may be said in passing, is just the ideal treatment for the consumptive at the present time.

Others of Graves' opinions in regard to tuberculosis are in general surprisingly modern. He insists, for instance, that the main causes of the disease are overcrowding in towns, the long hours of hard work in factories, and abuse of alcohol. He thought that the population of country places, though fed no better as a rule than in the city, do not develop the disease so frequently because of their opportunity for fresh air. He placed very little confidence in the opinion that cold has anything to do with tuberculosis, though he disputed Laennec's dictum that bronchitis was never the beginning of tuberculosis. Graves advises his students not to try to protect their throats by means of mufflers, for this will only render them more liable to cold. His advice is rather to harden themselves against cold. For this he suggests the use of water plentifully on the chest and throat, to be employed not too cold during the winter time, unless one is used to it. He also suggests the use of vinegar and alcohol as hardening fluids. They should be applied freely, and in his experience were effective.

Another interesting anticipation of modern methods was with regard to child feeding in summer diarrhoea. It is often thought that only in recent years, with the development of the science of bacteriology, the danger of continuing milk feeding when infants are already ill in the summer has come to be recognized. Milk is now known to be an excellent culture medium for various forms of bacteria, that is, it is a substance on which microbes grow plentifully, and it is often used in the laboratory to raise microbes. Dr. Graves, however, without any knowledge of modern bacteriology, but from clinical observation alone, pointed out that the only way to avoid summer diarrhoea is to stop all milk feeding.

"Let the infant," he says, "abstain from milk in any shape for twenty-four hours, sometimes for the space of two or even three days. It is incredible how small a portion of milk, even in the most diluted state, will keep up this disease, acting like a species of poison on the intestinal mucous surface."

Here, of course, was scientific intuition running far beyond medical knowledge, and pointing out a serious danger and the best means of avoiding it. There is scarcely a subject touched upon in Dr. Graves' clinical lectures, however, which is not illuminated in this way by precious sidelights, many of which unfortunately were obscured by medical theories, and conclusions founded on them without due experience.

We have already said that his careful clinical observations led him to separate the type of disease which has since come to be known as Graves' disease from a number of other forms of nervous disturbances of the heart rhythm. There is at least one other class of disease usually considered to be much more modern, the type of affection known as Raynaud's disease, or a tendency to spontaneous stoppage of the circulation in the extremities, and also the other type now known as Weir Mitchell's disease, or erythromelalgia, in which there is suffused redness and pain in the extremities, examples of which Graves picked out from his hospital service and described in such a way that it is easy to recognize them even at this distance of time. His two volumes of clinical lectures on the practice of medicine are much more than an index of the medical teaching of his time. They contain anticipations of many a supposed after-discovery, besides an immense amount of very practical observations made at the bedside, and valuable hints for treatment, the result of his personal experience.

One of the best proofs of the greatness of the work accomplished by Graves is to be found in the tribute to his character, and what he achieved, by Professor Trousseau, who was at the time the acknowledged leader of the clinicians of Europe. He said:

"For many years I have spoken of Graves in my clinical lectures; I recommend the perusal of his work; I entreat those of my pupils who understand English to consider it as their breviary; I say and repeat that, of all the practical works published in our time, I am acquainted with none more useful, more intellectual; and I have always regretted that the clinical lectures of the great Dublin practitioner have not been translated into our language."

A little later in the same lecture he said:

"And nevertheless, when he inculcated the necessity of giving nourishment in long-continued fevers, the Dublin physician, single-handed, assailed an opinion which appeared to be justified by the practice of all ages; for low diet was then regarded as an indispensable condition in the treatment of fevers. Had he rendered no other services than that of completely reversing the medical practice upon this point, Graves would, by that act alone, have acquired an indefeasible claim to our gratitude."

His tribute closes with the following very striking passage:

"I freely confess that I had some difficulty in accepting, notwithstanding the imposing authority of Graves, what he states of the influence of certain remedies, such as mercurials, essence of turpentine, spirituous preparations, nitrate of silver, etc.; but the Dublin professor speaks with so much conviction that I ventured to follow his precepts, and I must say that my early trials very soon encouraged me to adopt unreservedly what I at first accepted only with misgivings. There is not a day that I do not in my practice employ some of the modes of treatment which Graves excels in describing with the minuteness of the true practitioner, and not a day that I do not, from the bottom of my heart, thank the Dublin physician for the information he has given me.

"Graves is, in my acceptation of the term, a perfect clinical teacher. An attentive observer, a profound philosopher, an ingenious artist, an able therapeutist, he commends to our admiration the art whose domain he enlarges, and the practice which he renders more useful and more fertile."

After this tribute from one who was himself one of the greatest medical teachers of his generation, it will be very interesting to find how much Graves anticipated nearly three-quarters of a century ago the principles of the bedside

12

teaching of medicine which have come to be acknowledged
as the only sure basis of a genuine, practical medical education.
For him the only possible way to learn medicine practically
was to study it at the bedside, and he insisted over and over
again that while the theoretical sciences allied to medicine
were eminently fascinating, they were of little actual value
in teaching the student how to solve the all-important problem of treating patients.   In his address before the Dublin
Medico-Chirurgical Society, an association of students in
connection with the Dublin hospitals, he said in 1836:

"Many causes contribute to prevent students from at-
taining what after all should be the great object of their
wishes—practical knowledge. The different sciences to
which you are required to turn your attention successively
possess so many fascinations that you may attach to some
an undue degree of importance; but be assured of this, that
however accurate be your knowledge of anatomy, healthy
and morbid, however skilful you may be in the chemical
theories and manipulations, however extensively you may
have mastered the necessary properties of botany, however
well you are acquainted with the nature and properties of
drugs—be assured, I say, that you have acquired all this
knowledge in vain unless you have diligently studied symptoms at the bedside of the patient and have observed the
consequences and causes of disease in the dead room.   In
fact, in whatever other pursuits you may employ your afternoon hours, the morning should always be dedicated with
earnestness to the hospital; from its wards all appearance
of levity and inattention must be banished, for your neglect
of the opportunities there presented for observation loads
you with a serious amount of responsibility, I had almost
said of guilt.   It is no light thing to have life entrusted into
your hands; we are all liable to err, we all commit mistakes;

the rules of our art are not invariably precise and certain; but they only are guilty who have not used every opportunity of acquiring practical knowledge; he is doubly guilty who, conscious of his neglect, embarks in practice and commences with the decision and boldness true experience alone can confer."

At a comparatively early age Graves realized more than most men that medicine is an art and not a science, and that each individual case presents problems that have to be studied out for themselves and for which no general principles of diagnosis, prognosis or therapeutics serve. He appreciated that there was no royal road to medical wisdom, in the sense of a scientific shortcut by means of which manifestations of disease and their indications for treatment might be grouped together and easily learned. Nor, may we add, has any such road been found since. Each physician must train himself by patient, repeated observation, and without this discipline and training there can be no real success. Accordingly he said to his students in Dublin:

"The chief object of medical science is to relieve suffering and to save life: you must, therefore, anxiously watch the action of remedies and, by constantly noting down the effects of treatment, learn to appreciate its merits and apply it when required. Nor is this an easy task; some indeed have vainly imagined that the method of treating or curing disease could be compressed within the limits of a few short directions made easily deducible from some general principles and easily applicable in any particular case; but it is not so. Gentlemen, we have as yet discovered no such general principles to serve as guides. This discovery presupposes a knowledge of the laws and relations of the vital powers far beyond what we now possess: no, we must toil onward by a much more laborious and circuitous route and must commence by making ourselves thoroughly masters of a vast number of individual cases, assisted by the observations and the writings of practical men; we may afterward proceed to arrange our knowledge, to classify it so as to render it more available; analogy and induction are here our only or at least our most valuable guides, and they will seldom fail to instruct us how to act when properly consulted."

While recognizing all the difficulties of medical practice and the essential individualization of all its problems, Dr. Graves had little or no patience with the skeptic who thought that medicine could accomplish but little for the cure of many ailments. He said once before the Medico-Chirurgical Society:

"Many, indeed, aiming at acquiring the character of medical skeptics, think they exhibit proofs of superior discrimination when they, with apparent candor, make the confession that the more they see the less confidence they have in the resources of medicine. This confession should be interpreted not as a reproof of our art, but as a testimony of the want of skill of the would-be philosophical asserter of so false a proposition. No, God be praised, our predecessors have not toiled in vain; the anxious experience of ages has not been recorded to no purpose; our art is in truth boundless in resources and, when applied with ability, most successful. There are, indeed, some acute and many chronic diseases which baffle our powers of diagnosis, and defy our modes of treatment; such appear to be, however, not numerous when compared with the great mass of cases capable of cure or alleviation. The medical skeptic, however acute his powers of reasoning may be, and however he may labor to render plain subjects obscure and direct facts ambiguous, can never rob the good practitioner of the pure, the inward joy he feels when conscious that he has snatched a patient from the jaws of death."

Knowing that such were his ideas with regard to the practice of medicine, it is all the more interesting to review the system of teaching that Graves considered most likely to produce genuine practitioners of medicine. Those who have been mainly concerned with the reform of medical education here in America in recent years can scarcely fail to be struck with the appropriateness of Graves' ideas on this subject nearly a century ago. When a very young man he did not hesitate to express his deprecation of the conventional and artificial methods of medical instruction in his own time, and he anticipated what is best in the methods that have gradually come into vogue at the end of the nineteenth and the beginning of the twentieth centuries. His views will always remain a suggestive storehouse of thought for those who have the higher medical education at heart.

In his introductory lecture at the opening of the Medical course at the Meath Hospital in Dublin in 1821, he declared very definitely what he considered to be the principal aim of the medical student:

"Students should aim not at seeing many diseases every day; no, their object should be constantly to study a few cases with diligence and attention; they should anxiously cultivate the habit of making accurate observations. This cannot be done at once; this habit can be only gradually acquired. It is never the result of ability alone; it never fails to reward the labors of patient industry. You should also endeavor to render your observations not only accurate but complete. You should follow when it is possible every case from its commencement to its termination; for the latter often affords the best explanation of previous symptoms and the best commentary on the treatment."

Graves was inculcating in principle what Corrigan and himself and Stokes were to exemplify so thoroughly in practice in the next few years. Before the end of the decade in which this address was delivered at the Meath Hospital, Corrigan at the little Jervis Street Hospital, where there were only beds for six medical patients altogether, was to make his great discoveries with regard to aortic disease, and to lay the sound basis of the diagnosis of affections of the heart for all time. There are many passages in this address of Graves that might well serve for warnings to the present day and generation as regards methods of medical education which do not include sufficient practical teaching. He said, for instance:

"The chief objection to our present mode of teaching is that, however well inclined the student may be, he is never obliged to exercise his own judgment in distinguishing diseases and has no opportunity of trying his skill in their cure, and consequently at the end of his studies he is perhaps well grounded in the accessory sciences—is a perfect medical logician—able to arrange the names of diseases in their classes, orders and different subdivisions; he may be master of the most difficult theories of modern physiologists; he may have heard, seen and, if a member of the medical society, he may also have talked a great deal; but at the end of all this preparation what is he when he becomes a full doctor?—a practitioner who has never practised!"

These words have quite as suggestive applications to most phases of our modern education as they had to that of Graves' time. There are other passages that bear so significant a meaning in this regard that one can scarcely refrain from quoting:

"Our present method of instruction is indeed very useful and nothing better can be devised for a beginner; but for the more advanced student it is by no means sufficient, nor is it calculated to give him practical experience, without which all other acquirements are of no avail. I say it does not give him experience, because he has at no time been charged with the responsibility of investigating a case for himself, and by himself; because at no time has he been called on to make a diagnosis, unassisted by others; and above all because he has never been obliged to act upon that diagnosis and prescribe the method of treatment. If those who had been thus educated, and who had been made doctors upon so slender a foundation, were to confess the truth, we should be presented with a picture calculated to excite dismay if not a stronger feeling. How many doubts and distracting anxieties attend such a man at his first patient's bedside. If the disease be acute and life in imminent danger, and if he shrink under this sudden and unusual load of responsibility, he gains little credit for professional ability. If, on the contrary, inexperienced as he is, he assumes that decision of judgment, that energy of practice which experience alone can confer, is it not probable that the result will be still more disastrous?"

Graves' last days and the circumstances of his death and burial are given by Professor Stokes, his great personal friend, and himself one of the most distinguished physicians of his time. We quote the concluding paragraph of Professor Stokes' biographical notice:

"It was in the autumn of 1852, he being then in his fifty-seventh year, that the symptoms of the malady which was to prove fatal first showed themselves. In the following February he began to succumb to the disease. Although at times his sufferings were great, yet he had many intervals of freedom from pain. And he then showed all his old cheerfulness and energy. To the very last he continued to take pleasure in hearing of any advance of knowledge that tended to ameliorate the condition of man, or to throw light on his relations to a future state. In this latter point of view, the discoveries of Layard greatly interested him, as illustrative of the Sacred History; and thus he was permitted to fill up the intervals of his sufferings, even to the last; for his mental faculties never failed or flagged,—a mercy for which he often expressed a fervent gratitude; and so he was providentially enabled to review the past, and to form a calm and deliberate judgment on the religious convictions of his earlier years. And once the truthfulness of these were ascertained, he adhered to them with that earnestness which characterized all his decisions.

"It was after the attainment of this state of patient expectation that one who was dear to him expressed a prayerful wish for his recovery. 'Do not ask for that,' he replied; 'it might prove a fatal trial.'

"His mind having become thus satisfied he made few remarks on these subjects, except in reply to the inquiries of others. Thus, when referred to the prophetic illustration of purifying and redeeming love, 'A fountain shall be opened for sin and for uncleanness,' 'No,' he said, 'not a fountain, but an ocean.'

"On the day before his death he desired (a second time) to partake of the Holy Communion, with his family. When some explanations were commenced, he answered, 'I know all that; I do not regard this as a charm, but I wish to die under the banner of Christ.' Feeling himself sinking, he asked for prayer, and a petition was offered suitable to his condition; but he seemed to long for something more and, when questioned, replied, 'I want some prayer that I know, some of the prayers of my youth, some of my father's prayers.' The Litany was commenced, he immediately took up the

well-known words, and when the speaker's voice faltered he
continued them alone, and distinctly, to the end of the strain,
'Whom thou hast redeemed with thy most precious blood.'

"On the twentieth day of March, 1853, and without renewed suffering, he ceased to breathe.

"His tomb is in the cemetery of Mount Jerome. It bears
the following inscription dictated by himself:

"ROBERT JAMES GRAVES,
Son of Richard Graves, Prof. of Divinity,
Who,
After a Protracted and Painful Disease,
Died in the Love of God, and
In the
Faith of Jesus Christ."

WILLIAM STOKES.

Very closely associated with the name of Robert Graves
in all that made the Irish School of Medicine influential for
good, about the beginning of the second quarter of the nineteenth century, is that of William Stokes. Stokes' work on
Diseases of the Chest and, later in life, his treatise on Diseases
of the Heart and Aorta stamp him as one of the great physicians of all time. His name is assured of immortality in
medicine, because with that of the well-known Scotch physician, Cheyne, who came to Dublin late in the second decade
of the nineteenth century, it is associated in the term most
commonly used for a form of breathing, having special
diagnostic and prognostic significance in certain serious
diseases, and which is known as Cheyne-Stokes respiration.
Even more interesting, however, than Stokes the physician,
is, as we shall see, Stokes the man, and all that he stood for
in his generation in Dublin, during a long life.

William Stokes was of a family that had long been distinguished in Dublin for scholarship. While his ancestors came originally from England, five generations occupied more or less prominent positions in the public life of Ireland, and they had lived in Dublin for more than one hundred and fifty years before Stokes began to be prominent in Irish medicine. His father, Whitley Stokes, had been a scholar and Senior Fellow of Trinity College, and was prominent in the scientific, political, and literary circles of the Irish capital at the end of the eighteenth and the beginning of the nineteenth century. He had been a member of the United Irishmen, but fearing that the revolutionary principles that were being propagated would only bring about an ineffectual rebellion, he separated himself from them, though years after when the United Irishmen came under the ban of the English government his previous connection with them cost him suspension from the fellowship. Later on, however, Whitley Stokes became the Regius Professor of the Practice of Medicine at Trinity College, a chair which he held until succeeded in the early forties of the nineteenth century by his son, William, the subject of this sketch. Something of the character of the man can be judged from the fact that though he was a distinguished physician and interested in every branch of science, taking an active part in the foundation of Trinity College Botanical Gardens, and being one of the founders of the Zoological Garden in Phœnix Park, he was also the author of a prize essay in reply to Tom Paine's Age of Reason, which was then attracting so much attention.

Our William Stokes was the second son of Whitley Stokes, and was born in Dublin in 1804. Like many another distinguished investigator in science, he was not looked upon as a bright student as a boy, and indeed could be prevailed upon to interest himself only very slightly in what is usually considered to be the absolutely necessary fundamental work in education. He had a great love for poetry and romance, which indeed he carried with him all his life. The Scottish Border Ballads were his favorite reading, and he spent days in committing them to memory. Almost needless to say his apparent indolence and disinclination to any steady, methodical system of study were, as his son, the late Sir William Stokes, records in his biography of his father, sources of real concern to his parents, and caused his mother specially much anxious thought. One day while reading his favorite author, Sir Walter Scott, he fell asleep—to be awakened shortly after by some warm drops falling on his face. He started up to find his mother bending over him. It was her tears that had awakened him. Stung with remorse at having been the cause of so much sorrow to the mother whom he loved very dearly, his nature underwent an immediate and salutary change, and the dreamy, indolent boy became thereafter the ardent and enthusiastic student.

Stokes amply made up for any neglect of study there might have been in his boyhood days as soon as he entered upon the medical course to which he felt called. Here he came to be looked upon as one of the most ardent and painstaking of students.

His preliminary medical studies were begun in Dublin at the Meath Hospital. Chemistry he learned in the laboratory of Trinity College and anatomy in the Royal College of Surgeons. After spending several years thus he went to Glasgow, where for two years more he was occupied mainly at chemistry in the laboratory of Professor Thompson. Like most of the young Irishmen of his time, he next proceeded to Edinburgh in order to complete his education in clinical medicine and, if possible, obtain his medical degree from that famous institution. It was at Edinburgh, under the magnetic influence of that great teacher, Allison, that Stokes began to develop the rare powers of original observation which at an early age placed him in the front rank of the best medical men of the time.

It is interesting to note that before he left Edinburgh he published his first medical work, a treatise on the use of the stethoscope, which was undoubtedly the means of bringing that instrument—and with it Laennec's fruitful system of physical diagnosis by means of auscultation—to the general notice of the English-speaking medical profession. Even after all that has been written on the subject, it remains a very valuable little book. It was dedicated to the famous Cullen, who had already published a series of cases which had been illustrated by the use of the stethoscope, and to whom Stokes probably owed the idea of the need for a formal little treatise on the subject. It is typical of the slow adoption of medical novelties even when they are of great importance that more than ten years afterward, old-time, though distinguished, physicians not infrequently made fun of Stokes for spending so much time in the study of cases with the stethoscope, since in their opinion it was little more than a toy. This was done in no bitter, carping spirit, but with the most friendly complacency and condescension. Stokes, however, intensely practical in his way, realized the value of the instrument, and as the result of his teaching it soon began to be more generally used; thus introducing into English-speaking medical circles that exact knowledge of diseases of the chest which can only be obtained by means of this little instrument and the methods of auscultation which are associated with it.

Immediately after graduation, Stokes settled down in his native city to practise. In 1826, when Stokes was only twenty-two, Dublin was visited by one of those epidemics of typhus fever which were so common in the first half of the

THE IRISH SCHOOL OF MEDICINE 189

nineteenth century, and which consisted evidently, at least
to a great degree, of what we now call typhoid fever, but inter-
mixed with many cases of the real, dread typhus. The mortality in such epidemics, as we have reason to know from
statistics here in New York, was always over twenty-five per
cent. and often reached far above fifty per cent. The manner
of contagion was unknown, only it was very well understood
that those much in contact with the patients were likely to
contract the disease. Among the poorer classes in Dublin
the fever raged with virulence, but young Stokes devoted
himself to the care of patients to an extent that severely
taxed his physical powers of endurance. He devoted himself
especially to the poorer classes. He did not contract the
fever during the height of the epidemic in 1826, but he did
in 1827, when it recurred, but fortunately he suffered in the
mild form.

An epidemic of another disease, Asiatic cholera, the danger
from which has been almost entirely removed by the progress
of scientific medicine in modern times, followed not long
after. It showed itself in Dublin, when Stokes was about
twenty-five. He it was who recognized the first case of the
disease, and sounded the note of warning that probably
saved many lives by calling attention to the danger that was
just beginning. Once more he devoted himself to the care
of the patients, and, as with regard to typhus fever, wrote
an account of his experiences, which is in itself a valuable
medical document that shows the powers of observation of
the young medical man.

Stokes spent himself in labor for the poor, and his deep
interest in their welfare led him to sacrifice much time in
order to organize medical charities for his unfortunate countrymen during the sad years of that awful fifth decade of the
nineteenth century. His interest in this matter of organiza-

tion led him also to realize how much might be accomplished by public hygiene and efficient government sanitation. He recognized too how much would be accomplished along these lines if men were given proper training to make them specialists in these subjects. To Stokes then, almost more than to any other man, is due the development of public sanitation as a special science, and its organization for the proper safeguarding of public hygiene.

His efforts, especially with regard to the physicians of Ireland, who so nobly sacrificed, not unfrequently at the expense of other practice, their time, health, and often even their lives, in order to aid their stricken countrymen, form one of the best monuments to his tender sympathy and his goodness of heart as a man. His testimony before the Parliamentary Committee was at this time of the utmost value in securing due recognition of their services.

In 1843, when the Medical Charities Bill was brought forward, Stokes and Cusack united in the effort to procure for these devoted men an amelioration of the conditions under which they labored. They repaired to London to give evidence on the subject before the House of Commons. Both these friends had had to deplore the loss of many of their dearest and most promising pupils, who, after a short experience of country practice, had fallen victims to fever contracted in the discharge of their duties. They pleaded that in all justice the remuneration for attendance on fever hospitals and dispensaries should be fixed at a liberal scale, and that some provision ought to be made for the widows and children of gentlemen who had lost their lives in the public service. They collected statistics which proved that during a period of twenty-five years the mortality of the medical practitioners of Ireland was twenty-four per cent., while in most instances the cause of death was typhus fever. They showed that, on the authority of Inspector-General Marshall, the comparative mortality of combatant officers in the army was less than half that, amounting to only ten and a quarter per cent. It was little to be wondered at that William Stokes should say, in answer to the chairman's question regarding the existence of any special risk to the medical officer in Ireland: "Such a number of my pupils have been cut off by typhus fever as to make me feel very uneasy when any of them take a dispensary office in Ireland. I look upon it almost as going into battle." Again he observes: "The medical practitioners in Ireland are placed in a position very different from and far more serious than that of their brethren in Great Britain. . . . . The Irish physician is often exposed to contagion in its most concentrated force when himself under the influence of cold, wet, fatigue, and hunger, as he labors among the poor, passing from hovel to hovel in wild and thinly-populated but extensive districts. He has often to ride for many hours in the worst weather, and at night, enduring great fatigue, while himself a prey to mental as well as physical suffering; for if we add to such labor the injurious influence which the knowledge of danger must have on the system of a man feeling that he is struck down by the disease under which he has seen so many sink, and tortured by the thought of leaving a young family unprovided for, we can understand how it happens that the country is so often deprived by death of so many of its best educated and most devoted servants."

Perhaps the most interesting phases of Stokes' purely medical work during the first part of his career is his treatment of the subject of consumption. When not quite thirty-three he wrote a treatise on the diagnosis and treatment of diseases of the chest. His familiarity with the work of Graves and of Auenbrugger gave him command of all the

modern methods of physical diagnosis, so that he was able
to study tuberculosis to the best possible advantage and with
the least possible chance of too favorable judgment with
regard to its cure. Notwithstanding the accuracy of his
knowledge, however, he insisted that the disease was curable,
and that the important point with regard to it was the recognition of it as early as possible, in order that the patient might
be given the best chance for life.

At that time most physicians considered tuberculosis to
be an hereditary disease, without any idea of its being possibly contagious. Acceptance of heredity seemed to set the
stamp of inevitable fatality on the heads of victims of the
disease. To announce the curability of tuberculosis then
was to run counter to all the medical traditions of the time,
and Stokes in doing so must have had in support of his teaching many observations of patients who had been cured notwithstanding the fact that they were assured sufferers from
this supposedly fatal disease. We know that Stokes was
surely correct in his judgment in this matter, and realize too
that his method of treatment, which included abundant feeding and long hours each day in the outdoor air, comprised
the best elements of the modern treatment of tuberculosis.

Perhaps one of the most striking anticipations of what
is apt to be considered quite modern in medicine is Dr.
Stokes' descriptions of the methods by which he considers
certain forms of heart weakness, especially that incident
to incipient fatty disease, should be treated. His directions
are almost exactly those which have made the names of the
Schott Brothers known throughout the world during the
last twenty-five years. To have anticipated our modern
views with regard to tuberculosis, its curability, and the best
methods of treatment shows how thoroughly Stokes had
studied his cases of consumption. That the same man

should also have been able to work out the details of treatment for heart weakness is a triumph that indicates better than anything else perhaps the genius of the physician not only in the observation of disease, but above all in that more important part of medicine—the proper application of therapeutic principles.

Stokes observes, "In the present state of our knowledge the adoption of the following principles in the management of a case of incipient fatty disease seems justifiable:

"We must train the patient gradually but steadily to the giving up of all luxurious habits. He must adopt early hours, and pursue a system of graduated muscular exercises; and it will often happen that, after perseverance in this system, the patient will be enabled to take an amount of exercise with pleasure and advantage which at first was totally impossible owing to the difficulty of breathing which followed exertion. The treatment by muscular exercise is obviously more proper in younger persons than in those advanced in life. The symptoms of debility of the heart are often removable by a regulated course of gymnastics or by pedestrian exercise, even in mountainous countries, such as Switzerland, or the Highlands of Scotland or of Ireland. We may often observe in such persons the occurrence of what is commonly known as 'getting the second wind;' that is to say, during the first period of the day the patient suffers from dyspnœa and palpitation to an extreme degree, but by persevering, without overexertion, or after a short rest, he can finish his day's work and even ascend high mountains with facility. In those advanced in life, however, as has been remarked, the frequent complications with atheromatous disease of the aorta and affections of the liver and lungs must make us more cautious in recommending the course now specified."

13

If any proof of Stokes' ability as an observer and a teacher were needed it would be readily found in his original description of the form of respiratory disturbance since known as Cheyne-Stokes respiration. The passage is besides a model of succinct completeness of description that would well deserve to be in the commonplace book of physicians who write, for so many of them need to imitate his conciseness and clarity. It is to be found in his book *Diseases of the Heart and the Aorta,* p 336.

"A form of respiratory distress, peculiar to this affection (fatty degeneration of the heart), consisting of a period of apparently perfect apnœa, succeeded by feeble and short inspirations, which gradually increase in strength and depth until the respiratory act is carried to the highest pitch of which it seems capable, when the respirations, pursuing a descendant scale, regularly diminished until the commencement of another apnœal period. During the height of the paroxysm the vesicular murmur becomes intensely puerile."

It is curiously interesting to find that a favorite subject of discussion in the Irish medical societies of nearly fifty years ago was a topic which is still frequently on the tapis in medical society meetings. In one of his public addresses Dr. Stokes bewailed the fact that medicine did not have its proper place in the estimation of the people and was not able to assert its dignity as a profession in its proper sphere. He discussed also the remedies for this state of affairs, and as he was a man of eminently broad views, of very large experience, and of sane, conservative judgment, they are worth while pondering at the beginning of the twentieth century, for the practical problems of professional life which he sets forth are still with us. It is for this reason that it has seemed worth while to give a rather lengthy quotation that would adequately represent his conclusions in the matter.

"Is it by public agitation and remonstrances addressed to deaf or unwilling ears that these medical abuses are to be corrected? Is it by the demand for class legislation? or is it, by the efforts of one and all, to place medicine in the hierarchy of the sciences—in the vanguard of human progress; eliminating every influence that can lower it, every day more and more developing the professional principle, while we foster all things that relate to its moral, literary, and scientific character? When this becomes our rule of action, then begins the real reform of all those things at which we fret and chafe. Then will medicine have its due weight in the councils of the country. There is no royal road to this consummation. On the one hand, the liberal education of the public must advance, and the introduction of the physical sciences in the arts courses of the universities must give the death-blow to empiricism; and, on the other, education of ourselves must extend its foundations, and we should trust far less to the special than to the general training of the mind. When medicine is in a position to command respect, be sure that its reward will be proportionally increased and its status elevated. In the history of the human race, three objects of man's solicitude may be indicated: first, his future state; next, his worldly interests; and lastly, his health. And so the professions which deal with these considerations have been relatively placed: first, that of divinity; next, that of law or government; and, as man loves gold more than life, the last is medicine. But, with the progress of society, a juster balance will obtain, conditionally that we work in the right direction, and make ourselves worthy to take a share in its government, not by coercive curricula of education; not by overloaded examinations in special knowledge, which are, in comparison to a large mental training, almost valueless; but by seeing to the moral and religious cultivation, and the general intellectual advancement of the student."

From this, it is to be feared that Dr. Stokes would have very little sympathy with the specializing trend of modern medical education   Certain it is that not thus were the medical giants of the old days developed; but the times have changed; perhaps we should change with them, only the danger of the change must be ever kept in mind so as to avert, if possible, its most serious consequences at the first warning.

While Stokes felt deeply for the Irish people, and the sad conditions under which they were laboring, unfortunately, like many another educated Irishman, he had very little active sympathy in any of the movements for their relief. He was a man in early middle life when O'Connell's agitation began, but he had no part in the movement.   Later on, when his personal friend, Isaac Butt, was engaged in his great political work for Ireland, Stokes tried to dissuade him from it, feeling that the arousing of the people to a realization of their rights only led to a tighter riveting of their chains. Better judgment has prevailed and now practically all classes are united in the Gaelic movement, making it harder to understand Stokes' position, yet his is a case for sympathy rather than blame.   His heart was touched, but his head could not see a happy issue for his countrymen, and so he preferred to have them endure in patience rather than suffer further ills through coercive measures.

Dr. Stokes realized, however, all the iniquity of the union of the Irish and English parliaments, and a favorite story of his was told with regard to one of the members of the Irish Parliament who sold themselves to England.   This member, finding that he was unnoticed in the distribution of rewards after the passage of the Union, though eighteen of his fellow-members were raised to the peerage, waited on the Secretary of State and in an injured tone complained of having been neglected. The Secretary answered in the blandest manner: "The government, sir, is most anxious to do all it can to assist those who supported it. What is the object of your ambition?"

"Make me aqual to the rest of the blackguards," was the prompt reply of this conscientious legislator.

Stokes used to add: "History does not tell if his quite reasonable request was granted."

In the midst of Stokes' sympathy for his compatriots there was always a counter-current of reactionary feeling, as if he feared the Celtic enthusiasm for reform would overstep the mark and bring evils in its train, even worse than the good it might entail. The following letter to a friend, as representing one phase of this feeling on the part of a true-hearted Irishman, seems worth reproducing, because it suggests thoughts with regard to the present movement which warn of possible dangers from the commercial spirit that must be avoided at all hazards, if Irishmen are to retain the influence their idealism has ever given them in whatever part of the world they might be:

"October 27, 1836.—You will be sorry to hear that I have been for two days down to Connemara, to see poor Macnamara. He is dying. Oh, what a tragedy it will be! We expect him up to town this week. I never saw the glorious Lough Corrib look so beautiful. I was entertained by Miss Blake; she is a perfect specimen of the old Irish aristocracy. Tall, distinguished, elegantly formed, with dark hair and exquisitely fair complexion; she looked, as she stood in her tapestried hall, a lady of romance; her youth, her mourning dress, her classic head, and the symbols of her loved religion all combined to form a picture not easily to be forgotten.

The castle, grey and worn, stands on a green platform over the clear and rapid river through which the whole waters of Lough Mask and Lough Corrib rush to the sea. It reverses Byron's simile, 'All green and wildly fresh without,' etc., etc. You will say I am raving; but in truth a little time will level these ancient castles, and their highborn and honorable inhabitants and the feelings which their communion creates, and then 'utility' will have its reign, and 'common sense,' laughing at the past and the beautiful, will build factories with the remains of history, make money, and die."

Dr. Stokes' interest in Irish historical matters can be best judged from the fact that toward the close of his life, when he was extremely busy with his practice and medical work of all kinds, he took the time to write a life of his friend, George Petrie, the distinguished Irish antiquary. It will be recalled by those who are interested in Irish antiquities that Petrie's work eminently deserved this tribute, and that Stokes' life is worthy of Petrie's merit. Dr. Stokes' daughter Margaret, as the result of association with Petrie and her father's interest in Irish antiquities, became a deep student of the same subject and wrote a little volume, *Early Christian Art in Ireland*, which has come to be the standard handbook on this subject for those who want sure and definite information, yet are not specializing in antiquities.

On March 17, 1874, as a recognition of his interest in Irish antiquities, Stokes was nominated to the presidency of the Royal Irish Academy. "It was a new departure for the members of that society," says Stokes' biographer, "which is mainly representative of literature and abstract science, to choose a physician as their head, but it was felt that the time had now come when medicine had obtained, owing to the labors of Stokes and others, such a position in the estimation of literary and scientific men that the election of the Regius Professor of that art in Trinity College (to the presidency of the Royal Irish Academy) would be welcomed by the majority." Certainly no member of the medical profession could have been found more deserving of the tribute because of all that he had done for Irish medicine, and besides his broad, sympathetic, liberal interest in Irish antiquities eminently fitted him for this honorable position.

When Stokes' death was announced at the beginning of January, 1878, the medical world thought that it had lost one of its most representative men. For some years before his death many honors had come, all unsought, to this worthy protagonist of Irish medicine. He had been made a member of the Prussian order of Merit, and an honorary Fellow of many scientific societies on the Continent. He had received the rare distinction of the degree of LL.D. from Cambridge, and had been similarly honored by many other universities. Perhaps the honor that Stokes himself would have appreciated most came after his death, when the country people who had learned to know and love him asked to be allowed to carry his remains from Carrig Breac to the church of St. Fintan—the "grassy churchyard grave," where he was to be laid beside his beloved wife and children. They laid him in the same grave and beneath the same stone with her who was the beloved companion of his life, and on whose tomb he had engraved these words:

> "When the ear heard her, then it blessed her;
>   When the eye saw her it rejoiced;
> When the poor and suffering came unto her
>   They were comforted."

Surely a union like theirs was not destined to be but passing.

Stokes' beautiful domestic affection was but another index of one of the most beautifully rounded types of man that ever lived. The affective side of his being, profoundly tender, deeply sympathetic, thoughtful always of others first, and humanely devoted to the poor and the helpless above all others, was typical of the best side of the Irish character. For this even more than for all he did for practical medicine (yet the absence of his work would make a large lacuna in nineteenth century medical progress) the race may well be proud of him. His example still lives to animate his professional brethren, one of whom (Sir John Moore) said of him: "Those who have seen Dr. Stokes at the bedside of the sick know how gentle, how refined, how kindly was his bearing toward the patient. Amid all the ardor of clinical observation and research he never for one moment forgot the sufferer before him—no thoughtless word from his lips, no rough or unkind action ever ruffled the calm confidence reposed in him by those who sought his skill and care. In many eloquent lectures delivered in the Meath Hospital he inculcated those Christian lessons of charity and thoughtfulness; and so by precept and example he strove to teach the duties of a true and God-fearing physician."

Dominic Corrigan.

The third of the great trio of the founders of the Irish School of Medicine is Sir Dominic John Corrigan, whose name will be forever associated with the form of pulse which occurs in aortic heart disease. It was his supreme merit to have been the first to describe in all its details this type of heart disease, and the distinguished French clinician, Trousseau, declared that aortic regurgitation should be called Corrigan's Disease. At this time Trousseau was deservedly looked up to as the leading spirit among the clinicians of Europe. He was never tired of commending to his students Corrigan's acute clinical observations, and insisted that it was work of this kind which assured real progress in medicine. Trousseau's suggestion as to nomenclature was not adopted in its entirety, but Corrigan's pulse is well-known all over the medical world, and there is no doubt now that it will continue for many generations to confer deserved honor on the man who first appreciated its full significance though he was not the first to recognize it—and indeed it could scarcely escape notice—but who showed just what diagnostic conclusions might be reached from it.

Corrigan's career should prove a stimulating example to the young physician just taking up that real post-graduate work in medicine which comes after he has received his degree, finished, perhaps, his hospital work, and is beginning his practice. Corrigan was only twenty-seven when he began the series of observations on which was founded his paper on aortic heart disease, which was published when he was about thirty. In this matter of youthful accomplishment, Corrigan is not alone among his distinguished Irish contemporaries. Stokes, it will be remembered, wrote his little book on the stethoscope when he was only twenty-one and had made some very important observations on disease of the chest before he had reached the age of thirty. Graves had showed very clearly the sound metal of his intelligence before he was twenty-five, and had described the cases of the nervous disease which have since come to be called after his name, Graves' disease, before his fourth decade had run more than a year or two. In fact these young men accomplished so much by their careful observation and dependence on their own resources that the medical writer of the modern times is tempted to wonder if perhaps that most precious

202 MAKERS OF MODERN MEDICINE

quality of the human mind in the young adult, its originality, is not obscured by the amount of information that it is expected to absorb before it is tempted to do any thinking for itself.

There is another remarkable feature of Corrigan's achievement, in the recognition and description of this form of heart disease. At the time he was the physician to a hospital which had only room for six medical patients. This appointment to the little Jervis Street Hospital in Dublin had been secured only after competition, and Corrigan had to pay for the privilege of being the attending physician. This he could ill afford to do at the time, and so he resolved, as he told a friend, to make all his opportunities for the study of patients count to the greatest possible extent. He did not visit his hospital merely to see patients, but to study the cases carefully. His success is only another example of the necessity for seeing much, and not many things, if there is to be any real progress. In our day, physicians scarcely consider that they have any hospital experience unless they are the attending physicians to several hospitals, seeing at least one hundred patients a week. The result is that patients do not receive the skilled care they should, and that advance in medicine suffers because of the wasted opportunities for clinical observations while a busy attending physician rushes through a ward and the resident physician has only time for the routine work that enables him to keep just sufficiently in touch with the progress of his cases to satisfy the hurrying chief.

Before publishing his classic paper on the *Permanent Patency of the Aortic Valves*, on which his reputation as a wonderful clinical observer in medicine rests, Corrigan had called attention to some mistakes in the classification of heart murmurs as made by Laennec in Paris. At this time Laennec was considered to be the best authority in Europe on diseases within the thorax. As regards diseases of the lungs, he well deserved the reputation. To him the medical world owes all that it knows about diseases of the chest, as far as these can be detected by means of the ear. His young contemporary in Ireland, however, was able to show that in diseases of the heart some of the ideas acquired in long years of study of the lungs were leading Laennec into false conclusions as regards the significance of murmurs of the heart. Even genius does not succeed in doing more than one thing well, and especially in the matter of taking a second step into the unknown. While the distinguished Frenchman might have been thought just the one to complete the work he began so well on the heart, and while his experience with the lungs might have been expected to help him in the recognition of the significance of heart murmur, this did not prove to be the case. The privilege of solving the mystery of heart diseases was to be left for his Irish contemporaries, one of the most successful of whom in this matter was Corrigan.

Anyone who wishes to see how little subsequent study has added to our knowledge of aortic disease should read Corrigan's original paper on this subject. He describes all the varying forms of affections of the aortic valve, with their various clinical manifestations. His paper is illustrated by a set of plates that would still be valuable for demonstrative purposes, and which serve to show how painstaking were his pathological studies. He illustrated experimentally his ideas of how the murmurs and thrills occur by means of an apparatus consisting of rubber tubes through which water might be allowed to flow under pressure, and varying calibre. Some of his conclusions, derived from experimental observations, will not stand the test of our modern knowledge, but they are very suggestive. Perhaps the best idea of the clinical

value of Corrigan's observations can be given by a quotation
from his original paper, in which he discusses the interesting
and difficult question of the relationship between aneurism
of the aorta and inadequacy of the aortic valve. He said:

"The two diseases, aneurism of the aorta and inadequacy
of the valves, may, however, be combined. Aneurism of the
ascending aorta may, by extending to the mouth of this
vessel, dilate it so that the valves are unable to meet, and
there is then a combination of the two diseases; there is
aneurism and there is permanent patency of the aortic opening. The first cases that came under my observations pre-
senting the signs of inadequacy of the aortic valves were
cases in which the valves were rendered useless in this way,
namely, by the mouth of the aorta sharing in the aneurismal
dilatation. These cases led me into an error; for, meeting
the signs of permanent patency of the aortic orifice in conjunction with aneurism, I erroneously attributed to the
aneurism the signs which arose from the permanent patency.
Aneurism of the aorta of itself does not produce the signs
arising from permanent patency of the mouth of the aorta.
It can only produce them in the way already described, by
involving in the dilatation the mouth of the aorta; and
hence, when in conjunction with an aneurismal tumor of the
arteria innominata or aorta, there are found visible pul-
sation, *bruit de soufflet*, and *frémissement* in the ascending
aorta, and the trunks arising from it, we may be certain that,
in addition to the aneurism, there is a defect in the aortic
valves, or that the aneurism has extended downward, involving the mouth of the aorta. On the other hand, if these
signs be absent, the valves are sound and the mouth of the
aorta is not included in the disease. The propriety of performing Mr. Wardrop's or indeed the common operation
for aneurism about the neck might depend on the information

thus obtained of the state of the aortic valves. To perform either in a case where the aneurismal dilatation was so extensive as to involve the mouth of the aorta, or where the aortic valves were diseased, would only bring the surgical treatment of the disease into unmerited discredit."

Another very distinct contribution of Corrigan to the medicine of his time was his insistence on the distinction that exists between typhoid and typhus fever. This is one of the most interesting features of his little book on the *Nature and Treatment of Fever*. With our present knowledge, it seems hard to understand that these two fevers should have been so long confounded, but as a matter of fact it was not until the middle of the nineteenth century that the distinction between them was recognized even by the most acute observers. In this matter the French and Americans anticipated most of the rest of the world, though Corrigan's teaching in the matter had been correct for many years before others in the British Isles came to the true position.

It was his work among the poor particularly that enabled Corrigan to recognize the differences between these two diseases. He came to have one of the largest practices that any practitioner in Dublin, or for that matter in any city of the world, has ever enjoyed, if enjoyment it can be called. His office used to be crowded with patients who would occupy all his time if he allowed them to do so. In order to secure opportunities for his other work, for his lectures, for his hospital visitation, and for his pathological investigation, he had a back entrance to his house through which he could steal out—even though there were many patients waiting for him—when he felt that it was time for him to fill another engagement.

Late in life, after his return from Parliament when he took up his practice again, it was only a very short time before the same state of affairs developed once more. It almost seemed as though every sick Irishman and Irish woman wanted to have the opinion of Dr. Corrigan. He had also a large consultant practice, though he was known for being a very different man from the ordinary type of the medical consultant. As one of his younger colleagues said, "he never wore the supreme air of a consultant." He was always simple and easy in his manner, was always congenial and ready to listen to what had developed and had been found in the case before consultation with him, and had none of that superciliousness that was supposed to characterize the true high-grade consultant physician in the British Isles a half a century ago.

Within a few years after his essay on aortic heart disease, Corrigan published a paper on chronic pneumonia or, as he called it, cirrhosis of the lungs. Corrigan's successful achievements in medicine depended mainly on the fact that he studied the pathological anatomy of fatal cases with the greatest care. He had detected that in certain cases of chronic pneumonia the process seemed to be quite different from tuberculosis. Observations made postmortem showed that his clinical observations were justified by the differences observed in the organ. As a result he formulated his opinions on the subject. He called particular attention to the fact that what he found corresponded very closely with the pathological process which had been observed by Laennec in the liver, and to which the French medical pathologist had given the name of cirrhosis. It would seem as though the pathology of the time was so crude that Corrigan must surely fall into serious errors in his account of what he saw. Twenty years later, Virchow was to revolutionize pathology by the publication of his "Cellular Pathology." Notwithstanding the progress made since his time, however, Corrigan's description of the condition of the lungs that he noted and of the pathological process observed is so true that even to the present day this paper remains of distinct value in medicine and represents the beginning of correct ideas on the subject.

After Corrigan's death in 1881 the London *Lancet* said: "In the light of recent pathology Corrigan's speculations on cirrhosis of the lungs are more meritorious than ever and continue to be regarded as in the main sound. They anticipated by forty years much of the present pathology." Needless to say it is only a genius of a very high order that is thus capable of rising above the limitations of environment, and in spite of the defective knowledge of his times observing correctly and drawing proper conclusions, though all the usual accepted principles would seem to be sure to lead him from the truth. The principal lesions of chronic pneumonia, after having been the subject of much disputation, with conclusions now one way and now another in the intervening years, are at the present time recognized as being essentially due to the pathological processes Corrigan originally pointed out.

The man who thus made a permanent place for himself in the history of medicine was the son of a poor shopkeeper in one of the outlying districts of Dublin. His early education was obtained at Maynooth College, which had at that time a department for the training of youth for secular vocations, though it has since become an exclusively clerical institution. It is needless to say he acquired an excellent knowledge of the classics, of which he made abundant use later in life, and of which he was always very proud. The physician in attendance at Maynooth in his time took quite a liking to him, and it was the result of his suggestion that Corrigan took up medicine as his profession. For a time he was under the tutelage of this Doctor O'Kelley, who seems to have been a very intelligent man, and a rather painstaking clinical observer. Most of his medical studies were made in Dublin and he attended the practice at Sir Patrick Dun's Hospital. It was the fashion at this time, however, for Irish students of medicine to finish their medical education at Edinburgh, whenever possible, and Corrigan spent several years there, receiving his degree of Doctor in Medicine in 1825.

He had attracted considerable attention in Edinburgh for his acute powers of observation, and received an appointment to the Meath Street Dispensary shortly after his return. From the service here he was appointed to the Jervis Street Hospital. He had to pay, however, for the privilege of being attending physician here, and this, as he said, made him more careful in endeavoring to secure all the advantages possible from his service.

After his publication of the article on "The Permanent Patency of the Mouth of the Aorta," or "Inadequacy of the Aortic Valves," he at once became recognized as one of the best clinicians in the city. This article appeared, in April, 1832, in the *Edinburgh Medical and Surgical Journal*, at a time when, as has been said, its author was not yet thirty years of age. As soon as he began his work at the Jervis Street Hospital, he gave a course of lectures, and as he was an excellent talker and a good demonstrator, he at once attracted a large class. In 1834 he joined Hargrave's School, in Digges Street, Dublin, as lecturer on the practice of medicine, and continued to hold the position for more than ten years. His success as a lecturer attracted many students from the other medical schools. Corrigan's class was often three times as large as that of other medical lecturers in the city. It not infrequently happened that as a result of his popularity the medical class was two or even three times as large as the surgical and anatomical classes at the same institution. This was very unusual, for Dublin was famous for its anatomical instruction, and there were often five times as many pupils enrolled in the anatomy classes as in the medical classes.

It was not long before honors began to be showered upon Corrigan. When he was about forty the diploma of the London College of Surgeons was conferred upon him, and, as according to the by-laws of the institution the diploma can only be conferred after examination, Corrigan's examination was made to consist of the reading of the thesis, "Inadequacy of the Aortic Valves," before the faculty and the other members of the college. In 1849 the University of Dublin conferred upon him the degree of M.D., *honoris causa.*

There was only one setback in Corrigan's medical career in Dublin. When first proposed for honorary fellowship in the Irish College of Physicians, he was rejected. The reason was entirely apart from medical matters. Corrigan was the most active member of the Irish Board of Health, which had charge of the famine cases in Ireland, during the awful years between 1845 and 1850. This Board proposed to allow about five shillings per day to physicians who would be sent to the country to attend famine fever cases. It is easy to understand that this remuneration was considered inadequate and the Board's decision in the matter raised a storm of protest. Graves wrote very bitterly with regard to it, and blamed Corrigan for any part he might have had in it. The result was that for some time Dr. Corrigan was the most popularly hated physician in the medical profession of Dublin.

Corrigan made up for any lack of tact he might have had

14

in this matter, however, before long, and in 1855 he obtained the licence of the college. Two years later he was elected a Fellow. Before another two years had passed he was elected President of the College, and had the unprecedented honor of being re-elected four years in succession. The college further made up for its offense by having a statue of Dr. Corrigan, by the famous Irish sculptor Foley, made for its hall while he was still alive.

His own self-sacrificing work during the famine fever years was well known. After he had achieved nearly every distinction that his brother physicians could confer upon him, he was created a baronet. It was understood that this distinction was mainly meant as a reward for his services during the famine, though also for the time which he had so unstintedly given to the improvement of national education in Ireland, in the capacity of a Commissioner of Education.

Not long after his creation as a baronet, Sir Dominic stood, in Dublin, for a seat in Parliament in the Liberal interests. At first he was unsuccessful. In 1869, however, he was returned as one of the members of the government and sat in Parliament for five years. As he was a very eloquent speaker, it was thought that he would produce a very distinct impression in Parliament. His type of eloquence, however, did not prove to have any special influence in the cold British House of Commons, though Sir Dominic was always looked upon as one of the men to be counted on whenever there was under consideration legislation that affected Irish interests.

He was defeated for re-election in 1874, but it is rather to his credit than otherwise, since he had been approached by the vintners of Dublin, who were at that time all-powerful in municipal politics, and offered the membership, provided he would agree not to actively support the Sunday Closing

Bill, which was to come up at the next session of Parliament. Such an agreement Sir Dominic absolutely refused to consider as consistent with his legislative honor, and the result was the close of his Parliamentary career.

His years in Parliament, however, did not separate him from his interests either in medicine or in general science. He continued to be especially interested in zoology and made liberal contributions to the Dublin Zoological Garden. His residence at Dalkey, the grounds of which ran down to a rocky coast line, enabled him to obtain many specimens for his aquarium, and these were often transferred to the Dublin Zoological Gardens, for which he was one of the most active collectors. It was his custom during his Parliamentary career, though he was more than seventy, to leave London on Friday night and reach Dublin about eight o'clock on Saturday morning. From the station he went directly to the Zoological Gardens and took part in the pleasant breakfast which the Council of Officers of the Zoological Society, with some invited guests, had there every Saturday morning. He was noted for his humor, and his presence at these breakfasts was always appreciated, because in spite of his advancing years he was sure to add to the pleasure of the occasion.

His friends feared that his Parliamentary career might prove a serious drawback to his health at his time of life, and their fears were not without foundation. He suffered severely from gout, which left its marks upon his feet and made it very difficult for him to walk for a time, and maimed him for all his after-life. Though a man who had worked very hard all his life and who, at the age of seventy, practically took up another career, that of politics, Sir Dominic lived to be nearly eighty years of age; thus illustrating the old aphorism that "it is not work but worry that kills," and furnishing another example of the fact that great men are great also in their superabundant vitality, and are able to spend their lives in the hardest kind of work, yet, barring accident, live on to an age beyond even that which is considered the average term of human existence.

Few men have had happier lives than Corrigan, if the high esteem of contemporaries can ever confer happiness. There was no honor in the gift of his Dublin professional brethren or of scientific bodies in which he was interested which was not conferred upon him. He was the president of the Royal Zoological Society, the president of the Dublin Pathological Society, of which he was one of the founders, and the first president of the Dublin Pharmaceutical Society. When not yet fifty years of age he was made physician in ordinary to the Queen in Ireland, and had the unapproached record of five elections to the presidency of the King and Queen's College of Physicians in Dublin— more than enough to make up for the one serious setback in his medical career, his black-balling by the college only a few years before. Foreign medical societies invited him to honorary, membership and foreign universities conferred many degrees on him.

It is easy to understand then that his death was followed by tributes of the loftiest character to his professional work, to his standing as an influential member of the community and as a man of the highest intelligence and thoroughly conservative patriotism. The London *Lancet* said in its obituary: "By the death of Sir Dominic Corrigan, the medical profession loses one of its most conspicuous members, the University at Edinburgh one of its most illustrious graduates, and the Irish race one of its finest specimens. Though a perfect Irishman, Sir Dominic was as much at home in London, and though a sincere Catholic in religion, he had

too much humor and too much humanity in his constitution
to be a bigot. It were well for Ireland if all her public men
displayed so much moderation, sense, and good humor as
Sir Dominic habitually displayed in dealing with difficult
and delicate questions."

About the same time the *British Medical Journal* said,
after calling attention to the distinguished contemporaries
with whom Corrigan had been associated, that he was
"*haud minimus inter magnos*—not the least among the
great ones." "Indeed," his biographer added, "in originality of conception which, confirmed by later and independent
observation, is the true test of genius, in a correct appreciation
of the operation of natural laws, in producing and modifying
the phenomena of disease, in a rare aptitude for testing his
hypotheses by actual experience, and in a forcible exposition
of them, he probably had no equal among his contemporaries."

In the midst of all his honors and political influence,
including association with the highest English officials in
Ireland, Sir Dominic Corrigan had remained a consistent
and faithful Catholic. Educated at Maynooth as a boy, he
was proud to remain the physician to the college during many
of the busiest years of his life when he must have often found
it very difficult to spare the time to fulfil the duties attached
to the position. He was the consultant physician till the end
of his life. He is not even yet, after a quarter of a century,
forgotten by the poor of Dublin, who recall his kindly help
in affliction and his generous aid often given in ways that
would be arranged with studied care so as not to hurt delicate Irish susceptibilities.

The Irish School of Medicine has in Graves and Stokes
and Corrigan a greater group of contemporaries than has
been given to any other nation at one time. If we were to
eliminate from nineteenth century medicine all the in-

spiration derived from their work there would be much of value lacking from the history of medical progress. These men were deeply imbued with the professional side of their work as physicians, and were not, in any sense of the word, money-makers. Another very interesting phase in all their careers is that no one of them occupied himself exclusively with medical studies. All of them had hobbies followed faithfully and successfully together with medicine, and all of them were deeply interested in the uplifting of the medical profession, especially in securing the rights of its members and saving poor sick people from exploitation by quacks and charlatans. All of them gave of their time, their most precious possession, for the political and social interests of their fellow-men, and felt in so doing that they were only accomplishing their duty in helping their generation to solve the problem that lay immediately before it.

JOHANN MÜLLER, FATHER OF GERMAN MEDICINE

I say, then, that the personal influence of the teacher is able in some sort to dispense with an academical system, but that system cannot in any way dispense with personal influence. With influence there is life, without it there is none; if influence is deprived of its due position, it will not by those means be got rid of, it will only break out irregularly, dangerously. An academical system without the personal influence of teachers upon pupils is an Arctic winter; it will create an ice-bound, petrified, cast-iron university, and nothing else.—NEWMAN, *Idea of a University*.

JOHANN MÜLLER, FATHER OF GERMAN MEDICINE.

GERMANY has come to occupy so large a place in progressive medicine during the last half-century that it is rather hard to conceive of a time when the Teutonic race was not the head and front of modern medical progress. The leadership that had existed in Italy for over five centuries only passed to Germany at the beginning of the nineteenth century. The first great leader in German medical thought was Johann Müller, and to the wonderful group of students that gathered around him German medicine owes the initiative which gradually forced it into the prominent place it still holds in the world of medicine. The great institutions of learning that have since come in Germany did not exist with anything like their modern systematic arrangement when Müller began his work. It was the marvellous influence of the man as a teacher, and not the scientific aids afforded by institutional methods, that brought forth the great generation of teachers which followed immediately on Müller's footsteps. Nowhere more than in the life of Müller can it be recognized with absolute certainty that the system and the institution count for little in education, as compared to the man and his methods.

The keynote of Müller's career, even more than what he did for biology, and for all the biological sciences related to medicine, is the wonderful conservatism of thought which characterizes his scientific conclusions, while at the same time he began the application of the experimental methods to medicine as they had never been applied before. At a time when physiologists, because of Woehler's recent discoveries of the possibility of the artificial manufacture of urea, might easily have been led to the thought that life counted for little in the scheme of the universe, Müller continued to teach consistently that vital energy may direct chemical or physical forces, but must not be confounded with them. It looked as if in the development of the chemistry of the carbon compounds, all of which are the result of life action, that materialistic views must be expected to prevail. Müller insisted, however, that life ever remains the guiding principle which rules and coördinates all the physical and chemical forces at play, within living organisms; and that the vital principle is entirely independent of these forces so closely attached to matter.

All Müller's disciples, and they were the representative biological scientists in Germany during the nineteenth century, followed closely in his footsteps in this matter, and the result was a conservatism of thought in biology in Germany that is the more surprising when we realize how much German philosophers in their systems emphasized the necessity for absolute independence from all previous systems of philosophical speculation. It is so much more interesting, then, to find what was the method of education that made of Johann Müller so conservative a thinker, while not injuring his genius for experimental observations. The influences that were at work in his earlier years were evidently those that made him subsequently the bulwark against materialistic tendencies in biology, and yet did not impair his originality. His early education was obtained under influences that are usually considered to be distinctly harmful to independence of thought, and yet they seemed to have helped him to the fulfilment of his destiny, as a great thinker and investigator.

Müller is undoubtedly one of the very great men of modern science, and is the recognized founder of the system and methods of investigation which have given German medicine its present prominence and prestige.

In recent years there have been many tributes to Müller, because as Virchow's teacher it was considered that some of the praise for the work done by Virchow must naturally reflect on the man to whom the great German pathologist acknowledged that he owed so much of his inspiration and his training in methods of investigation. Virchow's death too very naturally led to the recall of what had been accomplished in German medicine during the nineteenth century, and for much of this Johann Müller must be considered as at least indirectly responsible, since to him so many of the great German medical scientists owed their early training. These men, all of them, did not hesitate to attribute the progress of German medicine to the methods introduced by Müller. At the beginning of the twentieth century something of the estimation in which he was held in a land far distant from the German Fatherland may be gathered from the following tribute paid to him in a recent meeting of the Medical Society of the State of New York by Dr. C. A. L. Read, of Cincinnati, former President of the American Medical Association. In the midst of his panegyric of Virchow Dr. Read described in some detail the medical faculty of Berlin at the time when Virchow was beginning his work as a student at that University. He said:

"In the faculty there were Dieffenbach, the foremost surgeon of his day; Schoenlein, the great physician who had come from Zurich the same year to join, not only the teaching body, but to act as a reporting counsellor for the ministry and to serve as physician-in-ordinary to the King; Froriep, who was in charge of the Pathological Institute; Caspar, who

was also medical counsellor, with a seat in the special deputa-
tion for medical affairs in the ministry; but towering above
them all was the intellectual figure of Johann Müller, the
Professor of Physiology. He was an original genius with
daring, actually engaged in winnowing the wheat of demonstrated truth from the prevailing chaff of egoistic opinion
which divorced physical science from speculative philosophy. Prompted by the inspiration which he had derived in
turn from Bichat and the French school, the Professor of
Physiology was busily retesting in the laboratory truths
previously elaborated by Haller, Whytt, Spalanzani, Cullen,
Prochaska, John Hunter, the Bells, Magendie, Berzelius
and Bichat himself."

This is the tribute to Johann Müller, nearly fifty years
after his death. That of Virchow, at his obsequies in Berlin,
is even more enthusiastic. Virchow, then at the age of
thirty-seven, at the height of his powers, already acknowledged the greatest of living pathologists, just recalled to
Berlin to become Professor of Pathology in the University
which he had left more or less in disgrace because of his
political opinions, could not say too much of the teacher
whom he respected and honored so highly and whose inspiration he felt stood for so much in his own career.

He said: "My feeble powers have been invoked to honor
this great man whom we all, representatives of the great
medical family, teachers and taught, practitioners and investigators, mutually lament and whose memory is still so
vividly with us. Neither cares by day nor labors by night
can efface from our mind the sorrow which we feel for his
loss. If the will made the deed, how gladly would I attempt
the hopeless task of proper appreciation. Few have been
privileged, like myself, to have this great master beside them
in every stage of development. It was his hand which guided

my first steps as a medical student. His words proclaimed my doctorate and from that spot, whence now his cold image looks down upon us, his kindly eyes beamed warmly upon me, as I delivered my first public lecture as Privat-Docent under his deanship. And, in after years, I was the one out of the large number of his pupils who, by his own choice, was selected to sit beside him within the narrow circle of the faculty.

"But how can one tongue adequately praise a man who presided over the whole domain of the science of natural life; or how can one tongue depict the master mind, which extended the limits of his great kingdom until it became too large for his own undivided government? Is it possible in a few short minutes to sketch the history of a conqueror who, in restless campaigns, through more than one generation, only made use of each new victory as a standpoint whereon he might set his feet and boldly look out for fresh triumphs?

"Yet such is the task to which we are called. We have to inquire what it was that raised Müller to so high a place in the estimation of his contemporaries; by what magic it was that envy became dumb before him, and by what mysterious means he contrived to enchain to himself the hearts of beginners and to keep them captive through many long years? Some have said—and not without reason—that there was something supernatural about Müller, that his whole appearance bore the stamp of the uncommon. That this commanding influence did not wholly depend on his extraordinary original endowments is certain, from what we know of the history of his mental greatness."

Virchow's tribute could not well be more enthusiastic or more ample. His appreciation has been the standard for all other medical opinions of the man. How much Müller is honored at the present time in Germany can be best appreciated from the number of times that his name is mentioned with respect and often with laudation in the proceedings of German medical societies. Scarcely a meeting passes in which more than once Johann Müller is not referred to as the founder of the scientific method in medicine which has given Germany her present position in the very forefront of medical scientific progress. It is a common expression, said half in jest it is true, but surely more than half in earnest, that the proceedings of no medical society would be really successful within the bounds of the German fatherland unless they were hallowed by an invocation of the great name of Johann Müller, the revered patron of modern German medicine. This is no witticism by exaggeration, after the American fashion, but a sincere Teutonic expression of feeling that occupies German medical minds with regard to the man who founded the most progressive school of modern medicine, and in doing so brought honor to his native country.

Johann Müller was born at Coblentz, on July 14, 1801. About six months before, the Emperor of Austria by the treaty of Luneville, signed February 9, 1801, ceded to the French Republic all the Austrian possessions on the left bank of the Rhine. The electors of Treves, who were archbishops and reigning princes and who had resided for centuries at Coblentz, by this treaty disappeared forever from the list of German rulers. When Johann Müller was born, French prefects of the Departments of the Rhine and Moselle took up their residence in the old town which had been, since the beginning of the French Revolution, a favorite dwelling place for the French nobility driven from their homes by fear of persecution.

Müller's father was a shoemaker and lived in a small house in the street of the Jesuits, so called because the fathers had had a school in it for many years. Johann was not destined to receive his education from the Jesuits, however, for the order had been suppressed nearly thirty years before his birth, and did not re-establish itself in the Rhineland for many years afterward. The circumstances of the Müller family were not such as to encourage hopes of a broad education, though his father seems to have taken every possible means to secure as much school training as could be obtained for his son. The early death of his father promised to deprive Müller of whatever advantages might have accrued from family sacrifices, but his mother was one of these wonderful women who somehow succeed in raising their families well and affording their children an education in spite of untoward circumstances.

Johann was the eldest of five children, with two sisters. He was very proud himself of the fact, that while he took from his father a large, strong, healthy frame and a dignified carriage, he had his mother's skill for putting things in order, her constancy of enterprise and her tireless faculty for hard work. After his father's death, his mother's energy and good sense enabled her to carry on the business established by the elder Müller by means of assistants, and as Coblentz was the centre of a district that during the Napoleonic wars was constantly overrun with soldiery, the shoe-making trade was profitable.

Johann seems to have learned the trade, but his mother succeeded in enabling him to begin his education seriously at the age of eleven or twelve. About this time, Joseph Görres, who was afterward the great leader of Catholic thought in Germany, and after whom is named the famous Görres Gesellschaft which stands for so much in German Catholic life and progress, was a professor in the Sekunden Schule, or secondary school, in Coblentz, and had recently published treatises on natural philosophy with special refer-

ence to physiology. Müller entered this school in 1810 and
Görres did not resign his professorship until 1814, when
owing to the publication of a political work he was obliged
to flee from the country. It is not known how much influence Görres exercised over young Müller, but some at
least of his precious love for the natural sciences, which even
in his student days led to the making of natural collections
of various kinds, seems to have been imbibed under the influence of the philosopher physiologist. The touching of
the orbits of the two men, who were destined, more than
any of their fellow-citizens of Coblentz, to influence Germany's future, must always remain an interesting consideration in the lives of both.

Johann's parents were, as might have been expected,
down in the old Catholic Rhineland in the capital of the
spiritual principality of Treves, faithful members of the
Roman Catholic Church. Very early in life, Johann con-
ceived the wish to become a priest. His mother, rejoiced
at her son's idea, was ready to make every possible sacrifice
to secure his education. It was with the intention of
education for the priesthood, then, that Johann entered the
Sekunden Schule, an old college of the Jesuits, in which Jesuit
tradition and methods of education still survived, and in which
some of the old Jesuit pupils seem still to have held positions
even during Müller's time as a student (1810 to 1817).

It would appear probable that because of the traditions
of Jesuit teachings that held over at the school in Coblentz,
and perhaps, too, because of the presence of some of the old
masters and teachers trained by them, Müller knew the
ancient languages so well. He made his own translations
of Plato and Aristotle, and consulted the latter especially
always in the original and had a lifelong reverence for the
great Greek philosophic naturalist's work. Latin he used

so well as to speak it readily, and practice in the disputations of the University at Bonn made the language still more familiar to him. It was said that he wrote Latin better than German. After the fall of Napoleon the Prussian government took up the reorganization of the schools in this part of the Rhineland, and Müller became more interested in scientific studies. At this time he became devoted to mathematics, which he studied under the old pupil of Pestalozzi, Professor Leutzinger, to whom Müller, in the sketch of his life prefixed to his thesis at the university, expressed the feeling that he owed a special debt of gratitude.

During his school days Müller became a collector, as we have said, of natural objects. He was especially interested in butterflies for a time, and collected all the species in the country around. He had a curious dislike for spiders which remained with him all his life. He was able to overcome this, however, and made important studies of that insect's eyes, and of its changing expressions under the influence of fear or when about to fall upon its prey.

His feeling with regard to the insect is an index of a certain feminine quality of mind that had a characteristic expression in later life in his dislike for vivisection. He could not bring himself to the conclusion that animals must be sacrificed in the midst of horrible pain unless there was some very definite scientific point to be determined, and unless every precaution was taken to avoid inflicting needless suffering. Even then he preferred that others should do this work and more than once took occasion to point out the fallacy of physiological observations founded on animal experimentation under such anomalous circumstances, and insisted that very frequently the results gave conclusions only by analogy and not by any strict logic of animal similarity or absolute physiological nexus.

15

In a sketch of Müller's life, by Professor Brücke, of Vienna, himself one of the most distinguished physiologists of the nineteenth century, to whom the University of Vienna has paid the tribute of a marble bust and tablet in its courtyard, the great Austrian physiologist sums up very well the reasons for Müller's fame. Professor Brücke's tribute may be found in the *Medical Times and Gazette*, of London, July 17, 1858. "If we inquire," he says, "what were the circumstances to which Müller, independently of his high intellectual endowment, his gigantic power for work, the energy and massiveness of his character, and his active and vigorous bodily constitution, owed the commanding position he incontestably held among men of science in our day, we must admit that before all things this was due to the breadth and depth of the foundations upon which his intellectual cultivation had been built." Professor Brücke then dilates on the variety of scientific interests which occupied Müller's earlier years and the thoroughness with which he accomplished everything that he set himself to.

A very curious reflection on our modern methods of education, and especially the tendency to specialization and the formation of specialists from their very early years, is to be found in Brücke's account of the extent and variety of Müller's studies in all lines. Far from considering that these diverse intellectual interests hindered the development of his genius, he seems to consider that they rather aided in the evolution of that largeness of mind characteristic of the great genius. He says:

"In his schooldays Müller's attention was directed to subjects of study far beyond the mere medical curriculum, for we find him attending the lectures of celebrated professors on poetry and rhetoric, on the German language and literature, on Shakespeare and Dante." As a matter of fact, Brücke seems to have understood that no one is so little likely to make scientific discoveries as he whose mind has been directed without diversion along the narrow lines of a specialty in science. Constantly trained to see only what lies in the sphere of this short-sighted interest, the mind never raises itself to a view beyond the horizon of the already known.

The old classical training, supposed to be so useless in this matter-of-fact, practical age, trained the minds of the men who have given us all the great discoveries in science. The evolution of intellectual power consequent upon the serious study of many things proved an aid rather than a hindrance to future original work. Not one of these great scientific investigators had at the beginning any hint of the work that he was to do. It seems almost an accident that their researches should have been conducted along certain lines which led to important discoveries. What was needed for them was not special training, but that mental development which puts them on a plane of high thinking above the already known, to look for progress in science.

Müller continued for many years to entertain the idea of eventually becoming a priest. At about the age of sixteen, however, he became deeply interested in Goethe's work, and was especially attracted by the great poet's studies of scientific subjects. About this time he became interested in the collection of plants and animals and took up seriously the study of physiology. Lavater's work was, at that time, still sufficiently recent to have little of the novelty worn off, for young students, at least. At the age of eighteen Müller went to Bonn and, when about to begin his university career, hesitated as to whether he should study theology or not. His natural liking for nature study, however, finally caused him to decide in favor of a scientific career, and he began the study of medicine.

He took up his medical studies with the greatest enthusiasm. Under the special guidance of Mayer, who besides being his teacher was a personal friend, he applied himseif zealously to the study of anatomy. One of his expressions in his early student days that has often been repeated, but which Müller took the greatest care in later life to correct and deny as a lasting impression, was the famous "Whatever cannot be demonstrated by the scalpel, does not exist." The professor of physiology at the time at Bonn was the famous Fredrich Nasse, especially known for the wonderful attractiveness of his lessons and his power of arousing enthusiasm in others, and it is not surprising that Müller, naturally so enthusiastic in scientific studies, should have acquired a liking for the study that he never afterward lost.

During Müller's second year of medical study the University of Bonn announced its first prize, which was to be given for an investigation of the subject of respiration in the fœtus. Although Müller was only in his first year as a medical student at the time, he grappled with the difficult subject and devoted all his spare time to arranging experiments for the demonstration and investigation of doubtful points. He received the prize, and Virchow, surely a good judge in the matter, says that this work of his student days is distinguished alike by the extent of its learning and by the number and boldness of the experiments detailed. At the moment of his graduation, the young doctor, in his twenty-first year, was already a marked man. From this time on everything that he did attracted attention and had a ready audience.

Müller's mind was constantly occupied after this time with the arranging of experiments to demonstrate natural principles. How far he carried this habit of experimenting can be understood from some of the habits of control over his muscles which he had acquired by continual practice and intense attention. He had thorough control over the muscles of his ears and used often to amuse his fellow-students by their movements. The anterior and posterior muscular portions of this occipito-frontalis muscle were able readily to move his scalp and produce curious disturbances in his hair. These habits of muscular control many people have acquired. Other acquisitions of Müller's are, however, much rarer. He could, at will, contract or dilate his pupils, having secured control over his iris by practice before a mirror, and he could use the little muscles that connect the bones within the ear, the hammer, anvil and stirrup, so as to make them produce an audible click at will.

His habits of experimentation on one occasion at least placed him in a rather ridiculous position. While making his military service, it happened one day that when the command "Order arms" was given, Müller amused himself by inserting one finger after another into the muzzle of his firelock. At last his middle finger got fairly wedged into the weapon. When the order attention was given, Müller could not withdraw his finger. His predicament at once attracted notice, and he was ordered to the front to be reprimanded by the major, to the no small amusement of his comrades, who laughed heartily at his ridiculous predicament. He was sent to his quarters in disgrace and the regimental surgeon had no little trouble in liberating the thickly swollen finger.

While everything thus seemed to promise a life of experimentation, Müller's imagination had a powerful hold on him, and he gave himself up for some time to certain mystical theoretical questions and problems of introspection which, for a time, threatened to take him away from his real calling of an experimental physiologist. Fortunately for Müller, as we shall see, though at the moment he doubtless thought it a serious misfortune, these excursions into a too introspective psychology were followed by nervous troubles, what we could now call neurasthenia, and he was consequently led back to the study of external nature.

Just after Müller's promotion to the doctorate in medicine, the Rhenish universities came once more under the authority of the Prussian government, and Berlin became a Mecca for students, who looked upon it in a way as the mother university. After his graduation at Bonn, then, Müller was attracted to Berlin, and came especially under the influence of Rudolphi, who recognized his talents and gave him special opportunities for original investigation. Rudolphi's private library and his collection were placed at the command of this young original worker, who had already proved his power of investigation and his capacity for following a subject to its ultimate conclusions, even though those were not yet extrinsically known. While at Berlin, too, Müller came under the influence of the younger Meckel, whom he learned to respect very much. After Meckel's death the *Archives of Physiology*, previously edited by Meckel, fell into Müller's hands, who successfully continued it for many years.

At Müller's departure from Berlin he was presented by Rudolphi with an English microscope, as a testimonial of the old professor's appreciation of the young man's labors while under his observation. As Müller's pecuniary resources were very limited, this must have been an especially acceptable gift, since it enabled him to continue his researches in embryology, and it was not long before these began to bear fruit. At Bonn, to which Müller returned, he set up as a Privat-Docent in the University, and for several years eked out by teaching the allowance his mother could give him, and even by the practice of medicine.

Bonn, at this time, had a population of perhaps 30,000,

and had some eighteen regular practitioners of medicine. It is easy to understand, then, that Müller's practice did not add materially to his pecuniary resources. It was not long before he gave up the practice of medicine entirely, led to the step by the sad death of a friend, who, while under his care, suffered from perforation of the intestines, followed by peritonitis. Notwithstanding the rather precarious state of his finances, at the age of twenty-six, Müller married Anna Zeiler, the daughter of a landholder in the Rhineland, not far from Bonn. He had previously dedicated to her a poem, in which he promised her, in lieu of more material advantages as a marriage settlement, an immortal name. The young man seems to have felt something of the genius that was in him, but, then, so have others, and their presages have not always been confirmed by the issue. Shortly before and after his marriage, he applied himself so hard to his investigations of many kinds that within a few months he broke down. The government allowed him a furlough, and for several months he wandered with his bride along the Rhine, in what has been described by a biographer as a "one-horse shay," and came back to his work renewed in mind and body.

As a matter of fact, Müller's breakdown was what would be called at the present time a neurasthenic attack, induced by overwork and too great introspection. He had been experimenting upon himself in many apparently harmless ways, but by methods which often cause serious trouble. It was not an unusual thing for him to fast, in order to note the physiological effect on his mind and senses of the absence of proper nutrition. He would often lie awake for hours at night in the darkness, experimenting upon himself and noting the phenomena induced, especially in his sight, by the total absence of light. He devoted himself, too, to the investigation of the curiosities of second sight; those interesting reminders of things seen long ago, though without producing much impression, and which recur at unexpected moments, to make us think that we are seeing again when we are really only unconsciously remembering. He used to exercise a good deal the faculty of bringing up objects into his vision with all the physical peculiarities of actual sight. In this his master was Goethe, who had written extensively on this subject in treating of the phenomena of vision, and who was able himself to recall to his imagination with great vividness the many shades of colors of objects with the sensory satisfaction of actual vision. Müller had this imaginative power only for the reds.

It is not surprising that a young man, engaged too exclusively at this sort of investigation, should have impaired his nervous equilibrium to some degree, and made symptoms, otherwise unimportant, appear to him as the index of serious illness. For a time Müller despaired of ever being himself again. When he had regained his health, however, he realized what had been the essential cause of his nervous condition; and so he never went back to his introspective observations, considering their results somewhat in the nature of a series of illusions.

After this, Müller devoted himself for ten years strictly to his physiological investigations. The best knowledge of what Müller accomplished for scientific medicine, during these early years, can be obtained from Virchow's summation of the discoveries of this period made shortly after his great teacher's death.

Virchow says: "It was Müller who introduced to the knowledge of physiologists and physicians the doctrine of reflex actions, which had been already indicated by Prochaska, and simultaneously discovered by Marshall Hall and himself. Just before this Müller succeeded in showing an easy mode of performing experiments on the anterior and posterior roots of the spinal nerve in corroboration of Bell's teaching of their diverse functions. Thus he had the privilege of establishing for all time two of the greatest practical discoveries of the physiology of the nervous system.

"Next to the nerves the blood became the subject of his researches and he not only naturalized in German medicine the accurate knowledge of the fibrin and blood-corpuscles, which Hewson had cultivated with such fertility in English literature, but he also managed by simple experiment to demonstrate the peculiar composition of the vital fluid. The discernment of right methods of investigation lay ever open to his clear and cultivated intellect, and he knew well that there were cases in which the scalpel and experiments could not determine a question, and where the truth was only to be elicited by means of chemical agents and physical instruments. It was thus he discovered the peculiar gelatinous substance found in cartilage, called chondrin; thus he proved the existence of lymphatic hearts in the amphibia, and thus that he determined not only the organs but all the laws which are concerned in the production of the human voice.

"The special researches of the Bonn epoch are those of the minute structure and anatomy of the glands. They put an end to the controversy which had existed so long between adherents of Malpighi and Ruysch, concerning the sacculated extremities of the glandular follicles, and obtained for us a correct knowledge of these important organs throughout the whole animal kingdom. Perhaps his most important work is that of the Ducts of Müller, the structures (named after him) which form so important a part of the genito-urinary system in the embryo."

Practically all this had been accomplished before he was

quite thirty-two years of age. In the autumn of 1832, Rudolphi, the professor of physiology at Berlin, died. As Virchow says, candidates sprung up on every side, and some who were the least qualified considered themselves best fitted for the position. Müller took an unusual step which illustrated his decision in character, though in any other it would have seemed an evidence of conceit. He declared, in an open letter, laid before the Minister of Prussia, that his claims were superior to those of any other living physiologist, except John Frederick Meckel. So powerful was the impression produced upon the minister by this letter that he immediately appointed Müller to the vacant chair.

Not long after his appointment to the chair of physiology at the University of Berlin Müller completed the well-known "Hand-book of Physiology," which established his reputation. The book is sometimes spoken of as an experimental physiology, but this is not correct. Müller was no more a mere experimentalist than Haller, and he, himself, heartily detested the tendency which experimental physiology had assumed in France, especially under the influence of Magendie. Part of Müller's aversion to experimental physiology was æsthetic. He could not bear the idea of inflicting so much pain as many of his colleagues inflicted without a thought. In his panegyric of Rudolphi, Müller says: "Rudolphi looked upon physiological experiments as having no relation to anatomical accuracy, and it is no wonder that this admirable man, who had at every opportunity expressed his abhorrence of vivisection, took up a hostile position against all hypotheses and conclusions insufficiently established upon physiological experiments." Müller adds: "We could not have failed to share his righteous indignation, had we seen how many physiologists were using every effort to reduce physiology to an experimental science by the live dissection and agonies of innumerable animals, undertaken without any definite plan, and yielding often only insignificant and imperfect results."

Müller shared these views of Rudolphi with regard to vivisection. The uncertainty of the conclusions, the amount of suffering inflicted, and the indefiniteness of the conditions of experiment, so that the conclusions could not have any very great weight, or any special accuracy of information, made him consider such experiments, unless very carefully conducted by trained investigators, as largely a waste of time and infliction of unnecessary pain and a leading astray of physiological advance because of the uncertainty involved.

The qualities in Müller's "Hand-book of Physiology," which gave it its greatest value, are the thorough review of all of the physiological literature of the world which it contains, and the greatest number of original observations it details as the basis of the principles enunciated. Müller himself said, in the preface to his "Hand-book": "I need scarcely remark that it is the duty of a scholar to make himself acquainted with the progress of science among all nations; and this is now possible and, moreover, quite indispensable in these days of progress. A purely German, French, or English school of medical science is barbarism; and in Germany we would consider the idea of an isolated English or French system of natural history, physiology or medicine just as barbarous as the notion of Prussian, Bavarian, or Austrian medicine or physiology."

How valuable the book was as the corner-stone of modern German medicine, may best be judged from Virchow's opinion of it. He says in his panegyric of Müller:

"There are two qualities in his 'Hand-book of Physiology' which have particularly enhanced my estimation of its value—its strictly philosophical method and its completeness

in facts. Since the time of Haller no one has so thoroughly
mastered the entire literature of natural history or collected
in all directions so many original experiences, and no one
has been at the same time familiar with medical practice,
as well as with the remotest provinces of zoology. It has
been well said that while Haller often, in doubtful questions,
espoused a side which must eventually be forced to succumb,
Müller always had the luck (if we may call that luck which
was preceded by so much intelligent activity), sooner or
later, to discern the opinion that was sure, eventually, of the
victory. He was wonderfully fitted for the office of critic by
his comprehensive knowledge. He knew how to discriminate
the healthy from the unsound, the essential or real from the
adventitious or accidental. And, in surveying the whole
series of forms—often widely different—among which a well-
determined plan of nature seemed to be realized, he knew
the changes which not infrequently altered considerably the
arrangement and composition of the substances within these
forms. In Müller, as a physiologist, it is not the genius of
the discoverer, nor the ground-breaking nature of his observations we admire, but rather the methodical exactness of investigation in calculating judgment, the confident tranquility
and the perfect consummation of his knowledge."

In a word, Müller owed the success of his career to the
perfect poise of his intellect and the admirable critical faculty
that guided him in the thorny path of knowledge at a time
when there were so few landmarks of real scientific significance to show the investigator what the probable course and
progress of real science must be. It was for this reason that,
as Virchow has said, the reform of newer views became
embodied in him, and in spite of the almost monastical retirement of the scholar, the influence of the method introduced
by Müller was not limited to physiology, but continues to

spread beyond that science in ever-widening circles into the domain of all the biological sciences.

Virchow concludes: "Müller vanquished mysticism and phantasms in the organic kingdom and he was most distinctly opposed to every dangerous tendency, whether it was pursued under the pretext of physiology or belief, or merely in accordance with conjectures. Müller did not discover, but he firmly established the exact method of investigating natural sciences: Hence, he did not found a school in the sense of dogmas—for he taught none, but only in the sense of methods. The school of natural science which Müller created knew no community of doctrine, but only of facts and still more of methods."

He did not confine himself in his studies, however, to the physiology and pathology, nor even to the anatomy and embryology of man. After 1840 he devoted himself to the study of invertebrates and investigated the starfish and the pentacrinites. While engaged in his work on the invertebrates he found that the fossil remains of animals had not been carefully explored, so for a time he devoted himself to paleontology. While his salary as professor was ample for his own support, it was not what would be called generous at the present time, yet Müller became so devoted to his science that he paid certain of the workmen to be on the lookout for fossil remains for him in the quarries of the Eifel. He became deeply interested, too, in life in the sea and made his vacations times of specially hard work, investigating the conditions of low life among marine organisms. He passed from one class of life to another. From sea-urchins and starfish to infusoria and polycystina, whose varieties he was himself the first to recognize and describe.

Müller was one of the first to point out that certain of the lower animals could propagate similar and dissimilar generations, that is, reproduce by alternate generations. He studied and demonstrated especially the metamorphoses in the echinodermata, and his broad vision and careful observation in this new and surprising scientific field cleared up many things that had been mysteries before.

In paleontology Müller worked with our own Agassiz, then a young man, or perhaps it should rather be said that Agassiz worked with Müller. A paper, for whose compilation they made a series of observations together, appeared at Neufchatel, in 1834. It was a note on the vertebræ of living and fossil dog fishes. At this time Müller was interested in fossil fishes of many kinds and wrote several articles in later years on this subject. Toward the end of Müller's life he studied especially the polycystina, certain of the radiolaria, and some of the many chambered specimens, fossil and living, that were attracting much attention at that time. As a matter of fact he went the day before his death to the zoological museum of Professor Peters in Berlin, in order to obtain some polythalamacea.

How open to advance in science and how ready to encourage the work of others Müller was, may be gathered from his attitude to parasites as the cause of disease, when these began to be discovered. After Professor Schoenlien's discovery of the parasite of favus, Müller became interested in it, confirmed Schoenlein's observations and added something to our knowledge of it. About this time, also, he discovered the psorosperm as a parasite of animals and possibly of man, and devoted considerable attention to it. His work was afterward greatly extended by one of his pupils, Lieberkühn, whose researches with regard to these minute organisms attracted the attention of the medical world.

It is not a little surprising how many of the investigations that afterward were to give fame to Virchow were initiated

by his great teacher, Müller. It was Müller whose study
of tumors led Virchow to devote himself to this subject and
give us the best pathological work on it that has ever been
written. Virchow himself notes with regret that Müller
turned aside from pathology and never finished the promised
work which was to have contained his theory of the origin
of tumors. Another work in which Virchow followed in
Müller's footsteps was the development of craniometry and,
in general, the scientific investigations of skulls. Müller had
interested himself very much in microcephalic skulls and
Virchow assisted him in the investigations of them. Many
years afterward Virchow established the science of craniology
in the department of anthropology, and succeeded in throwing
not a little light on the origins of races by his discoveries in
this matter.

After Schoenlien's discovery of the parasite of favus, Müller
became interested in the parasitology of human beings, and
with Retzius, the famous Swedish anatomist, investigated
certain molds which occur in the respiratory passages of
birds. They succeeded in demonstrating that these vegetable parasitic growths were a form of Aspergillus. Their
studies in the white owl particularly called general attention
to the possibility of such molds occurring as parasites of
animals. Later on, Virchow showed that these same molds
occur occasionally in the respiratory passages of men. Virchow found them in three bodies at autopsy, all of them
being run down individuals, two of them old subjects, and
all sufferers from chronic bronchitis. Usually, when the
parasites were found, there was a distinct tendency to very
low resistive vitality in the tissues, sometimes proceeding
even to the extent of beginning pulmonary gangrene. In
reviewing the subject Virchow[1] said that the light thrown

[1] Virchow's Archiv, Bd. ix.

upon it by the investigations of Müller and Retzius was of the greatest possible assistance in enabling him to identify the parasite when he found it in human subjects.

The number of positive facts which Müller brought to light in the most diverse departments of science is almost beyond calculation, and yet it is astonishing how seldom the slightest error, or even an incomplete observation, can be found in his work. On the other hand, it has happened, over and over again, that when the correctness of his observations in the beginning seemed according to other investigators to be dubious, they have come eventually to be acknowledged as representing the truth. As a rule, he went over every set of observations three times. During the second series he wrote about them. He always repeated the experiments on which his observations were founded while his material was going through the press. His manuscripts were a mass of corrections; notwithstanding this, his proof sheets were the despair of the printers.

Müller accomplished all this only by the most careful husbanding of his time. He knew how to make use even of the ends of hours and brief intervals which others waste without a thought about them. He used to call these periods of short duration between the duties "the gold-dust of time," and said that he did not wish to lose a particle of it. In the quarter of an hour between two lectures it was not an unusual thing to find that he took up some dissection at which he was engaged, or continued his work sketching the observations that he had been making during the previous day.

How thorough was Müller's work in everything that he devoted himself to can be gathered from certain excursions into pathology, which was, after all, only a side issue in his work, and to which he gave very little serious attention. Müller's assistant in the Museum of Berlin, and one of his

favorite pupils, Schwann, made a series of what Virchow
calls comprehensive and magnificent investigations on the
cell structures of the animal tissues, on which progress in
pathology so essentially depends. Müller followed up these
discoveries, and, to quote Virchow once more, he was in this
matter the authority of authorities; for the medical world
owes to him practically all its knowledge of tumors. Müller
first demonstrated the harmony which existed between the
pathological and the embryonic development of tumors.

This physiological observation is of the highest importance.
It came at a time when tumors were considered to have
nothing of the physiological about them, but to be entirely
manifestations of morbid processes foreign to all natural
functions of the body. Müller's observation of the identity of
the pathological and the embryonic development of tumors is
really the key to the whole doctrine of morbid formations.
Virchow assures us that Müller's labors gave the strongest
impulse to the employment of the microscope in pathological
investigations. Undoubtedly this was his most important contribution to scientific medicine. With this he laid the foundation of the explanations of tumors—a work that his great
pupil was destined to carry on. Some of Müller's work in this
line, his study of enchondromata for instance, Virchow con-
fesses to have been part of the inspiration that led to his own
later work. Müller was occupied, however, with too many
things to devote himself to the study of pathology in the way
that would have been necessary to make great discoveries
in the science. He promised that he would sometime settle
down to make a classification of tumors, and that the principle of such a classification would not be based either on
their fineness of structure or on their chemical composition,
but that their physiological nature and tendency to grow
must be taken into account. When he died, however, he

16

left behind him nothing unfinished except the long-expected
conclusion of his book on tumors.

Müller's most important work in physiology, and his most
far-reaching influence on the biological sciences, which were
just then beginning their modern development, came from
his assertion of vital force as a thing entirely different from
and absolutely independent of the physical or chemical forces
which it directs and makes use of. Vital force for Müller
was the ultimate cause and supreme ruler of vital phenomena,
so that all the energies of an organism follow a definite plan.
It was for him the complete explanation of all the physical
manifestations of life. It disappears in death without producing any corresponding effect. Without losing anything
of itself it hands over in multiplication or reproduction a
force equal to itself to the new being that is born from it.
This vital force that is thus handed over need not necessarily
manifest itself at once, but may lie dormant for a long time
to be awakened to manifestations of life by the concurrence
of proper conditions in its environment.

In a word, Müller appreciated fully the mystery of life, faced
the problem of it directly, stated it in unequivocal terms, and
by so doing saved the rising science of biology from wandering
off into speculations which were seductive enough at that time,
but which would have proved vain and wasteful of time and
investigative energy. Müller's influence on his students
was sufficient in this matter to set the seal of vitalism, as it
is called, on most of the biological work done in Germany
about the middle of the century, and it was a recurrence to
his observations and his methods which led the reaction to
vitalistic theories that characterized the concluding years of
the nineteenth century.

With regard to the significance of Müller's work, Professor
Du Bois-Reymond, himself a pupil of Müller, in his memorial

address delivered before the Royal Academy of Sciences of Berlin in 1859,[1] says: "It has been objected by those who insist on the greatness of Müller's reputation that he himself made no discovery that can be said to be of the first rank. Müller's fame is great enough for us to allow that there is something true in this objection. He accomplished more in developing the ideas of others than in original research of his own. That he did not make any great discovery is, however, rather due to the fact that he came at a time when great discoveries were no longer lying around loose as they had been in the preceding century, waiting to be made, as it were; and what he accomplished was of more value than one or two single discoveries of primary importance. He made the original ideas of other men so clear that they were at once accepted by all the medical and scientific world. In this way he furthered the progress of medicine better than any devotion, however successful, to one single feature could possibly have accomplished.

"Müller made mistakes, but then who ever fails to make mistakes in the face of nature? As a rule, however, he hit the nail on the head. There are many suggestive thoughts from him that the investigators of later times have proved to be true. He suggested, for instance, that there must necessarily be some connection between the ganglionic bodies and the nerve stems. He suggested, also, that there must be a special nerve system for the intestinal tract. Later discoveries in physiology have established both of these thoughts and have shown that Müller had so entered into the spirit of nature and her processes as to be able to think her thoughts. There is no doubt that there are suggestions in

[1] Gedächtnissrede auf Johannes Müller, von Emil Du Bois-Reymond, Berlin, Buckdruckerei der Königlichen Akademie der Wissenschaften (Dummler), 1860.

his writings, especially those of the later years of his life, which will give a series of triumphal substantiations of the same kind."

Du Bois–Reymond's final judgment is of special interest, because it tries to point out the comparative place that will be occupied by three great men in the biological sciences of a century ago:

"Haller and Müller must be considered as giants of earlier days, though when future generations compare them with Cuvier they will occupy somewhat of the position that Galileo and Newton hold in comparison to La Place and Gauss, or Lavoisier in comparison to Berzelius. The first of these men had the opportunity to do great things while it was yet possible to do them, and left to their successors only the possibility of developing their thoughts."[1]

[1] Some idea of the estimation in which Müller was held by his contemporaries, German and foreign, may be gathered from the number of scientific bodies of which he was a member. He was an associate in practically every serious scientific body in Germany. He was, besides, foreign member of the scientific academies at Stockholm, Munich, Brussels, Amsterdam; the scientific societies of Göttingen, London, Edinburgh, Copenhagen; foreign honorary member of the Academy of Sciences of Vienna; corresponding member of the Academies of St. Petersburg, Turin, Bologna, Paris and Messina; of the Society for Science at Upsala, of the Mecklenburg Naturalist Society of Rostock, of the Senkenberg Institute of Frankfort-on-Main, of the Academy of Natural Sciences of Philadelphia, of the Society of the Museum of Natural History at Strasbourg, of the Naturalists' Association of Dutch East India; member of the Holland Society of Sciences, Haarlem; of the Naturalist Society of Frieburg in Breisgau, Halle, Dantzig and Mainz; of the American Philosophical Society of Philadelphia, of the Society of Biology of Paris; honorary member of the Cambridge Philosophical Society, of the Natural Science Union of Hamburg, and the Natural Science Association of the Prussian Rheinland and Westphalia, of the American Academy of Arts and Sciences in Boston, of the Ethnological Society of London, of the Microscopic Association of Giessan, member of the Society for Science and Medicine at Heidelburg, of the

It is as a teacher that Müller did his best work. He was
not by nature a good talker and never said much, but he was
very direct; and, as he spoke from the largest possible and
most progressive knowledge of the subject, his lectures were
always interesting to serious students. There seems to be
a more or less general agreement that for the mass of his
students he was uninteresting because likely to be above their
heads. For the talented members of his class, however, he
was an ideal teacher—always suggestive, always to the point,
and eminently complete. Du Bois–Reymond says that he
never was confused, never repeated himself, and never contradicted himself.

He was able to illustrate his lectures by sketches on the
board in a way that enabled students to follow every step of

Naturalists' Society at Dresden; corresponding member of the Scientific and Medical Association of Erlangen and Moscow; member of
the Academy of Medicine of Paris; honorary member of the Academy of Medicine of Prague and of Dorpat, of the Medico-Chirurgical
Academies of Wilna and of St Petersburg, of the Medical Society
of Guy's Hospital in London, of the Medical Society of Edinburgh
and of the Hunterian Society of the same city, and of the Medico-
Chirurgical Societies of London and of Zurich, of the Medical Societies of Budapest, of Lisbon, of Algiers and Constantinople; corresponding member of the Medico-Chirurgical Academy of Turin and
of the Medical Society of Vienna.

Even this long list does not include all his various honorary and
active memberships in scientific and medical societies. He was, besides, the laureate, that is, a prize winner, of the Medical Faculty
of the University of Bonn, of the Sömmering Prize of the Senkenberg Institution, of the Copley Medal of the Royal Society of London,
of the Culver Prize Monthyon of the same institution, as well as
laureate of the Academy of Sciences of Vienna for Experimental
Physiology. He had been honored by the King of Prussia by the
conferment of the knighthood of the Order of the Red Eagle, by
the King of Sweden by the Royal Swedish Order of the North Star,
by the King of Bavaria by the Royal Bavarian Maximilian Order,
and by the King of Sardinia by a knighthood in the Order of SS.
Mauritius and Lazarus.

even a complex, embryological developmental process. He
could trace, step by step, with the chalk, every stage of evolution in the organism and bring it clearly before his students.
To a narrow circle of the best men within his class he
became a personal friend, whose inspiration led them on
to the deepest original researches. Among his students
were some of the men who made German medicine and
German science known all over the world in the last fifty
years. Chief among them may be mentioned Virchow,
Helmholtz, Du Bois–Reymond, Schwann, Lieberkuhn, the
discoverer of the follicles in the intestines; Max Schultze,
whose work in histology and physiology are well known;
Claparede, Remak, Guido, Wagener, Lachmann and Reichert.

What he demanded of his students above all was that they
should learn to help themselves. He set them tasks, gave
them suggestions, directed their work, corrected their errors,
but he wanted them to do work for themselves. His very
presence was an inspiration. Both Virchow and Du Bois–
Reymond speak of the power of his eye. Du Bois–Reymond
says that there was in him an almost demoniac magic, and that
students looked to him as the soldiers of the first Napoleon
did when the great Emperor's words were in their ears—"Soldiers, the Emperor has his eye on you." Du Bois–Reymond
adds that, consciously or unconsciously, every student felt
the winning influence of his great personality. With all this
he knew how to unbend, especially with favorite students,
and many a joke from him found its way around the laboratory even during working hours. He was not one to stand
on his dignity, and Virchow tells of him that even when
nearly fifty he was known to race with a student down the
corridor from one class-room door to another. He took up
skating at the age of forty-five, and though he had not many
friends and was too entirely devoted to his work to make

many acquaintances, it was always a source of pleasure to young men to be allowed to associate with him, and many eagerly sought the privilege.

How impressive a figure Müller made in his character of teacher can be gathered best, perhaps, from a note added to Virchow's panegyric during its progress through the press, in which the pupil tells his impressions of the master:

"I must confess that Müller, in his lectures and in his manner, reminded me of a Catholic priest, which might be accounted for by the impressions of his early childhood. When as the dean of the Faculty he mounted the *cathedra superior*, dressed in his official robes, and pronounced the Latin formulary of the proclamation of the doctors of medicine, with short, broken and contracted words; when he began his ordinary lectures in almost murmured syllables; or, when with religious earnestness he was discussing any of the abstruse questions of physiology, his tone and manner, his gestures and looks, all betrayed the traditional training of the Catholic priest."

Virchow adds, "Müller himself was what he styled one of his greatest predecessors—perpetually a priest of nature. The religion which he served attached his pupils to him as it were by a sacred bond; and the earnest, priest-like manner of his speech and gestures completed the feeling of veneration with which everyone regarded him."

In the recently issued life of von Helmholtz, the great German physicist, his biographer makes it very clear how much Helmholtz thought of Müller, one of the earliest teachers.[1] Helmholtz, Brücke, and Du Bois–Reymond were warm personal friends (college chums we would call them in America), and all fervent admirers of their greatest

[1] Herman von Helmholtz, von Leo Koenigsberger. Bd. 2, Braunschweig, Friedrich Viewig und Sohn, 1902–3

master, who showed them, as Helmholtz says, "how thoughts arise in the brains of independent thinkers." A half-century later, in his recollections of the time, he said: "He who has come in contact with one or more men of the first rank has his mental intellectual standard for all time broadened, and such contact is the most interesting thing that life can hold." Curiously enough, one of the most interesting things in Helmholtz's recollections is that, despite the fact that the poverty of his parents made it advisable for him to get through his medical studies as soon as possible, Müller persuaded him to take another year's medical work before going up for his graduation. This was mainly for the purpose of having his pupil complete an essay in physiology on which he was engaged. Müller offered him the use of his own laboratory and all his instruments for this purpose. His judgment was justified by Helmholtz's wonderful work on the conservation of energy made within a few years after his graduation.

Müller's death was sudden, though not entirely unexpected. He had been ailing for many months and had resolved to give up his lectureship. He had made most of his preparations for settling up his affairs, and had even sent for his son, who was practising medicine at Cologne, to come up to see him. He made a special engagement for a consultation with his physician for a certain morning, and having gone to bed in reasonably good spirits, in fact, feeling better than he had for a long while, was found dead in the morning. Some time before he had made his will forbidding an autopsy, and so the exact cause of death will never be known, though it is rather easy to surmise that it was due to apoplexy, as arteriosclerosis—that is, degeneration of arteries—had been noticeable in Müller for some years, and his temporal artery particularly had become hard and tortuous.

Müller was buried with all the rites of the Church, and as

in Germany the ecclesiastical authorities are very strict in this matter, there can be no doubt that the great physiologist had been a faithful Catholic. He was known for his edifying attendance at Mass on all the Sundays of the year. Many years afterward, in the midst of the Kulturkampf in the early seventies, a monument was erected to him in his native Coblentz, and the occasion of its unveiling was taken by the Catholic Rhineland for a celebration in honor of their great scientist.

For a time, in his younger years, Müller appears to have been not all unaffected by the materialistic tendencies so rife in the science of the time. His early anatomical investigations seem to have clouded somewhat his faith in things spiritual. One of the expressions attributed to him before his twenty-fifth year is that nothing exists in the human being which cannot be discovered by the scalpel. It was not long, however, before Müller repudiated this expression and came back to a realization of the importance of the immaterial. Another expression attributed to him, "Nemo psychologus, nisi physiologus," "No one can be a psychologist, unless he is a physiologist," has been often repeated as if Müller meant it in an entirely materialist sense. As a matter of fact, however, it is intended to convey only the idea that no one can really exhaust the science of psychology unless he knows the physiology of the brain, the organ which the mind uses in its functions in this life. The expression is really the foundation of the modern physiological psychology, which is by no means necessarily materialistic in its tendency, and has become a favorite subject of study even with those who appreciate thoroughly the importance of the immaterial side of psychology.

Müller seems never to have gotten so far away from the Church as that other great physiologist of the succeeding generation in France, Claude Bernard, who for many years allowed himself to be swamped by the wave of materialism so likely to seem irresistible to a scientist engaged in physiological researches.   But, even Claude Bernard came back to the Church before the end, and, under the guidance of the great Dominican, Père Didon, reached the realization that the only peace in the midst of the mysterious problem of life and the question of a hereafter is to be found in a submissive faith of the doctrines of Christianity.

Many years ago, when Virchow took it upon himself to say harsh words in public of Catholic scholarship, and to put forward the hampering influence of the Church on intellectual development as a reason for not allowing Catholics to have any weight in educational matters, the organ of the Catholics of Germany, *Germania,* reminded him that his own teacher, the great Johann Müller, the acknowledged father of modern German medicine, and the founder of the fecund scientific method to which so many discoveries in the biological and medical sciences are due, had been brought up and educated a Catholic, had lived all the years of his productive scholarship and fruitful investigation in her bosom, and had died as an acknowledged son of the great mother Church.

Müller is certainly one of the great names of nineteenth century science.   When many another that seems now as well, or perhaps even better known, shall have been lost, his will endure, for his original researches represent the primal step in the great movement that has made possible the advances in nineteenth century medicine.   He was honored by his contemporaries, venerated by the men of science who succeeded him; he has been enshrined in a niche for himself by posterity, and his name will remain as that of one of the great geniuses to whose inventive faculty the world owes some of those steps across the borderland into the hitherto unknown which seem so obvious once made, yet require a master mind to make and mean so much for human progress.

THEODORE SCHWANN, FATHER OF THE CELL DOCTRINE

My message is chiefly to you, Students of Medicine, since with the ideals entertained now your future is indissolubly bound. The choice lies open, the paths are plain before you. Always seek your own interests, make of a high and sacred calling a sordid business, regard your fellow-creatures as so many tools of trade, and, if your heart's desire is for riches, they may be yours; but you will have bartered away the birthright of a noble heritage, traduced the physician's well-deserved title of the Friend of Man, and falsified the best traditions of an ancient and honorable Guild. On the other hand, I have tried to indicate some of the ideals which you may reasonably cherish. No matter though they are paradoxical in comparison with the ordinary conditions in which you work, they will have, if encouraged, an ennobling influence, even if it be for you only to say with Rabbi Ben Ezra, " What I aspired to be and was not, comforts me." And though this course does not necessarily bring position or renown, consistently followed it will at any rate give to your youth an exhilarating zeal and a cheerfulness which will enable you to surmount all obstacles—to your maturity a serene judgment of men and things, and that broad charity without which all else is naught—to your old age that greatest of blessings, peace of mind, a realization, maybe, of the prayer of Socrates for the beauty in the inward soul and for unity of the outer and the inner man; perhaps, of the promise of St. Bernard, ' Pax sine crimine, pax sine turbine, pax sine rixa."—OSLER, *Teacher and Student, Aequanimitas.*

THEODORE SCHWANN, FATHER OF THE CELL DOCTRINE.

I⊤ is one of the curious features of history that genuine worth of human accomplishment is almost in inverse ratio to the popularity it obtains in the generation in which it is produced. Supremely great work is rarely appreciated at anything like its proper value, by contemporaries. This principle is true apparently in all fields of human endeavor. In literature and in art it is a commonplace. But also, surprising though it may be, in science and in social betterment the rule holds a prominent place. It is nearly always the sign of only passing merit when any work secures the plaudits of its own generation. Brilliant theories are often immediately hailed with universal acclaim, while groundbreaking observations that are really great discoveries are apt to be neglected. The really new discovery is so novel that men cannot appreciate it at once. It is so different from their ordinary modes of thinking that they cannot place it properly. Its complete significance fails them.

This has been true for our nineteenth century biology almost more strikingly than for any other department of knowledge. Our many avenues of publicity instead of heralding abroad the great observations as soon as they have been made, in order to enable others to continue the work that the master mind has begun, have been only too constantly crowded with new opinions, novel theories, taking hypotheses, all attracting attention that they did not deserve. Men like Theodore Schwann, the father of the cell doctrine, are not apt to be so well known as the suggestor of some striking bit of theory. Even the great biologists, such as Darwin himself, are known rather for their insubstantial theories than for their substantial additions to biological knowledge by patient observation and genial penetration into the secrets of nature. It is perhaps a warning to the modern physician who realizes this state of affairs, not to take the popular theories even in his own branch of biology as the current coin of truth. Theories pass, but observations endure. Auenbrugger's new method of tapping the chest in order to elicit its varying sounds looked even more childish than Galvani's acceptance of the position of dancing master to a frog, but their observations thus made continued the germs of undying truth.

While the name and the life of Theodore Schwann are but little known by the general public, his work is very thoroughly appreciated by those who have made special studies in biology, and few men in the progress of that science are considered to hold as high a place as that assigned to him. A study of the life of Schwann will serve to show not only that he eminently deserves this honor which has come to him, but will also bring into evidence the fact that his career deserves to be better known popularly, because it illustrates very well the typical mode of life in which great scientists are nurtured and the methods of investigation by which great discoveries are made.

Of the men who have made the biology of the nineteenth century there are three whose names stand out with special prominence. They are noted not for their controversial writing on mooted points, but for ground-breaking, original work of the highest scientific import. Their discoveries will preserve their memories for posterity long after the names of many of those to whom the glare of controversial publicity lent an ephemeral brightness for their own generation shall have been forgotten. They are: Theodore Schwann, the anatomist, to whom modern biology owes its foundation by the establishment of the cell theory; Claude Bernard, the physiologist, to whom we are indebted for the great biological ideas of nervous inhibition and internal glandular secretion; finally Louis Pasteur, the chemist-bacteriologist, to whom is due the refutation of the annihilatory abiologic doctrine of spontaneous generation, and the discoveries that have revolutionized modern medicine and promise to accomplish as great a revolution in modern manufactures and industries.

It has often been said that the Catholic Church is opposed to scientific advance. It has especially been insisted that in what concerns biological science the Church's attitude has been distinctly discouraging. Recently the definite assertion has been made that no original thinker in science could continue in his profession of faith. Now, it so happens that all three of these men were born in the bosom of the Catholic Church, and were educated from their earliest years to maturity under her watchful care. Schwann and Pasteur remained in the midst of their great scientific triumphs her faithful sons. For years Bernard withdrew from all his old religious associations and became indifferent to the spiritual side of life, but before the end he came back to the knees of the Mother whose fostering care meant so much to him in early life.

Theodore Schwann, the first to formulate the cell doctrine, to promulgate the teaching that all living tissues, whether plant or animal, are composed of a number of minute elements which under all circumstances are biologically equivalent—is the father of modern biology. Cells had been seen and recognized as such before, but their significance was first pointed out by him. His cell theory has now become the cell doctrine, the teaching of all the schools of biology. The generalization that forms the basis of the doctrine was the result of some of the most accurate and careful observation that has ever been made. The work was done when the mechanical helps to the analysis of tissues were in the most primitive condition. The microscope had just been introduced into general laboratory work. The microtome, the instrument by which tissues are cut into thin sections suitable for microscopic examination, and to which almost more than to the microscope itself we owe our detailed knowledge of the intimate constitution of tissues, was as yet unthought of. Despite these drawbacks Schwann's work was done with a completeness that leaves very little to be desired. He published, when not yet thirty, the story of his comparative investigation of the cellular constitution of plants and animals, and there is very little that can be added, even in our day, to make its scientific demonstration any clearer than it was. It was typical of the man that, heedless of disputatious controversy over details of his work, he should go calmly on to complete it, and then give it to the world in all its convincing fulness. The same trait crops out with regard to other subjects. His was one of the great scientific minds of the century, always immersed in a philosophic calm befitting the important problems he had in hand. His life is ideal in its utter devotion to science, and to the teaching of science, while no duty that could round it out and make it humanly complete for himself or others was despised or neglected.

Theodore Schwann was the fourth of a family of thirteen children, born in the little German town of Reuss, not far from Cologne. He received his college education in the Jesuit Gymnasium of Cologne, and passed thence to the University of Bonn. The lower Rhineland is largely Catholic, and to this day, though Bonn has become the fashionable exclusive German university to which the Kaiser and many of the scions of the great German families go for their higher education, the faculty of theology at the university remains Catholic. Schwann devoted some time here to the study of theology, but he came under the influence of Johann Müller, was allowed to assist in some of his experiments on the functions of the spinal nerves of frogs, and this seems to have determined him to a medical career.

After two years spent in medicine at Würzburg, another great Catholic university of Southern Germany, we find Schwann at the University of Berlin, once more working with Johann Müller, who had been invited from Bonn to fill the distinguished Rudolphi's place in the chair of anatomy at the rising Prussian university. Müller was one of those wonderful men—they turn up, unfortunately, all too rarely—who, though not great discoverers themselves, have the invaluable faculty of inspiring students with an enthusiasm for original observation which leads to the most brilliantly successful researches. A great teacher, in the proper sense of the word, he was not. In his public lectures and his ordinary lessons he was often arid and uninteresting, insisting too much on unrelieved details, "the dry bones of science." He seems to have failed almost completely in conveying the usual scientific information of his course with the air of novelty that attracts the average student. The true teaching faculties are not given to many. Müller had a precious quality all his own that has proved much more valuable for science than the most enlightened pedagogy.

To the chosen few among his students who were drawn into close intimacy with him and permitted to share his personal scientific labors, Müller proved a source of most precious incentive—a suggestive master, the inspiration of

17

whose investigating spirit was to be with them throughout
life. To no one, except perhaps to Socrates of yore, has it
been given to have sit at his feet as pupils so many men who
were to leave their marks upon the developing thought of a
great era in human progress. Beside Schwann, there studied
with Müller, during these years at Berlin, Henle the anatomist, Brücke the physiologist, Virchow the pathologist,
Helmholtz the physicist, Du Bois-Reymond the physiologist,
Claparède, Reichert, Lachmann, Troschel, Lieberkühn and
Remak. All these names are writ large in the scientific
history of the century. It is a remarkable group of men,
and of them Schwann, with the possible exception of Helmholtz, will be remembered the best by posterity; certainly
none of them would not have cheerfully resigned his hopes
of scientific renown for any work of his own to have made the
discovery which, as an enthusiastic biographer said, set the
crown of immortality on a young, unwrinkled forehead.

Schwann's thesis for his doctorate at Berlin showed the
calibre of the man, and demonstrated his thorough fitness
for success as an experimental scientist. The question
whether the growing embryo in the ordinary hen's egg con-
sumes oxygen or not had been in dispute for some time.
It was well known that an air-chamber existed in the egg
even at the earliest stages of embryonic life. It was understood that the mature chick just before its egress from the
egg must have air, and the porosity of the egg-shell was
sufficient to permit its entrance. Whether at the beginning
of embryonic life within the egg, however, oxygen was necessary, remained somewhat in doubt. It had been demonstrated that the gas existing in the air-chamber of an egg
became changed in composition during the progress of development. From being slightly richer in oxygen than ordinary
atmospheric air at the beginning of embryonic growth,

containing 24 to 25 parts of oxygen per 100, it became modified during comparatively early development so as to contain not more than 17 parts of oxygen per 100 and some 7 parts of carbon dioxide. This change of composition was, at least, very suggestive of the alteration that would take place during respiration. It was pointed out, however, that the argument founded on these observations was drawn only from analogy, and was by no means a scientific demonstration of the fact that the embryo not only consumed air during its growth, but actually needed oxygen for the continuance of its vital processes.

It was suggested that the change of composition in the air within the egg might be due not to any essential vital functions, but to chance alterations brought on by decomposition in the unstable organic material so abundantly present in the substance of the egg. Schwann settled the question definitely by a set of ingenious experiments. He exposed eggs for various periods to the action of other gases besides air, and also placed them in the vacuum chamber of an air-pump. When not in contact with the air the eggs developed for some hours if the temperature was favorable, and then development ceased. If after twenty-four hours' exposure to an atmosphere of hydrogen eggs were allowed free contact with the air, development began once more at the point at which it had ceased. After thirty hours of exposure to hydrogen, however, or to the vacuum, all life in the egg was destroyed, and it failed to develop no matter how favorable the conditions in which it was afterward placed. The completeness with which the points in dispute in this problem were demonstrated is typical of all Schwann's work. His conclusions always went farther than the solution of the problem he set out to solve, and were always supported by simple but effective experiments, often ingeniously planned, always carried out with a mechanical completeness that made them strikingly demonstrative.

One of Schwann's brothers had been a worker in metal, and Schwann himself had always shown a great interest in mechanical appliances. This hobby stood him in good stead in those days when laboratories did not contain all the intricate scientific apparatus and the facilities for experimentation so common now, with their workshop and skilled mechanics for the execution of designs. Many another worker in the biological sciences of that time owes his reputation to a similar mechanical skill. Experiments were impossible unless the investigator had the mechanical ingenuity to plan and the personal handiness to work out the details of appliances that might be necessary for experiments. It is told of Schwann that when Daguerre's discoveries in photography were announced, such was his interest in the new invention that he made a trip to Paris especially to learn the details of the method. Some daguerreotypes made by him according to the original directions of the inventor himself are still preserved by his family.

Schwann's investigation of the respiration of the embryo in hens' eggs led to further studies of the embryo itself, and to the discovery that it was made up of cells. Later came the resolution of other tissues into cells. When, after his graduation as doctor in medicine, the post of assistant in anatomy at Berlin fell vacant, it was offered by Johann Müller to Schwann. The position did not carry much emolument with it. The salary was ten German thalers—*i. e.*, about $7.50 per month—a pittance even in those days when the purchasing power of money was ever so much greater than now. His duties took up most of his time. The work was congenial, however, and Schwann remained here for five years. As Henle has said in his biographical sketch of

Schwann, in the *Archiv f. mikroskopische Anatomie,* just after his death in 1882: "Those were great days. The microscope had just been brought to such a state of perfection that it was available for accurate scientific observations. The mechanics of its manufacture had besides just been simplified to such a degree that its cost was not beyond the means of the enthusiastic student even of limited means. Any day a bit of animal tissue, shaved off with a scalpel or picked to pieces with a pair of needles or the finger-nails, might lead to important ground-breaking discoveries." For at that time almost everything as to the intimate composition of tissues was unknown. Discoveries were lying around loose, so to speak, waiting to be made. Schwann was not idle. The precious years at Berlin saw the discovery that many other tissues were composed of cells. The nuclei of the striped and unstriped muscles were found, and while the cellular character of these tissues was not demonstrated, their secret was more than suspected and hints provided for other workers that led very shortly to Kölliker's and Henle's discovery of muscle cells.

Besides his interest in histology, the branch of anatomy which treats of the intimate constitution of tissues, Schwann was working also at certain general biological questions, and at some knotty problems of physiology. Not long after his installation as an assistant at Berlin, from observations on fermenting and decomposing organic liquids, he came to a conclusion that was far in advance of the science of his day. He announced definitely *infusoria non oriuntur generatione aequivoca*—the infusoria do not originate by spontaneous generation. Under the term infusoria, at that time, were included all the minute organisms; so that Schwann's announcement was a definite rejection of the doctrine of spontaneous generation over thirty years before Pasteur's demonstrations finally settled the question. Schwann was never a controversialist. He took no part in the sometimes bitter discussions that took place on the subject, but having stated his views and the observations that had led up to them he did not ask for the immediate acceptance of his conclusions. He continued his work on other subjects, confident that truth would prevail in the end. When the congratulations poured in on Pasteur for having utterly subverted the doctrine of spontaneous generation, the great French scientist generously referred the pioneer work on this subject to Schwann, and sent felicitations to that effect when Schwann was celebrating the jubilee anniversary of his professoriate.

While studying ferments and fermentations Schwann became interested in certain functions of the human body that carry with them many reminders of the biological processes which are at work in producing the various alcohols and acids of fermentation. The changes that occur in the contents of the human stomach during the preparation of food for absorption had long been a subject of the greatest interest to physiologists. It had been studied too much, however, from the merely chemical side. The necessity for the presence of an acid in the stomach contents in order that digestion should go on led to the conclusion that the acid was the most important constituent of the gastric juice. By means of the scrapings of the stomachs of various animals Schwann succeeded in preparing an artificial gastric juice, and showed just how the action of the gastric secretions brought about the solution of the contents of the stomach. He isolated pepsin, and demonstrated that it resembled very closely in its action the substances known as ferments. He even hinted that digestion, instead of being a chemical was a biological process. Any such explanation as this was scouted by the chemists of the day, headed by Liebig. Most of the physiological functions within the human body were then triumphantly claimed as examples of the working of chemical laws.

Of the contradiction of his conclusions Schwann took practically no notice, but went faithfully on with his work. He could not be lured into controversy. For nearly five years he continued his work at the University of Berlin, receiving only the pittance that has been mentioned—less than ten dollars per month. Only the purest love of science for its own sake, and the satisfaction of his own enthusiastic spirit of investigation kept him at work. There was but little prospect of advancement at the University of Berlin itself. Schwann was one of the lowest in rank of the assistants; the professor was only just beyond the prime of life; and before Schwann on the list for promotion was at least one man, Henle, who had already done distinguished work. Germany had the good fortune to have all during the nineteenth century young men who, unmindful of present emolument, had been satisfied with the scantest wages for their support, provided the positions they occupied gave them opportunities for original work. Even at the present day young medical men are glad to accept what they consider the honor of the position of assistant to the professor and director of the clinic, and to remain in it for from five to ten years, sometimes even more, though the salary attached to it is only from $250 to $400 per year. They well know that if their original investigations into various medical questions are successful, advance in university rank is assured. Their promotion seldom comes from the institution where they have done their work, unless it should be one of the smaller universities; but the invitation to a chair at a university will come sooner or later for meritorious research.

Schwann's invitation came from Louvain. His work on cells had attracted a great deal of attention. In the midst of the rationalism and infidelity then so common among scientific men Schwann was known as a faithful, sincere Catholic. When the great Catholic University of Louvain, then, looked around for a professor of anatomy, he appeared to be the most suitable person. Henle, who had very little sympathy for Schwann's religious views, speaks most kindly of him as a man and a comrade. Schwann seems to have endeared himself to the "difficult" Prussians, as he did to those around him all his life. For the dominant note in the sketches of him by those who knew him personally is that of heartiest friendship, joined with enthusiastic admiration for his simple sincerity and unselfish devotion to his friends and to science.

A little incident that has been preserved for us by Henle shows how much his young contemporaries appreciated even at that early date, long before the full significance of the cell theory could be realized, the aspect of Schwann's work which was to make him immortal. At a little farewell dinner given him by his co-workers in various laboratories of the University of Berlin the feature of the occasion was a punning poem, by the toast-master, on the words Louvain and cells.

In German Louvain is Löwen, which also means lion; that is, it is the dative case of the name of the lion. Reference is made to the fact that as Samson found honeycomb (in German, bee-cells) in the lion, so now Louvain—i.e., in German, Löwen, the lion—finds a champion in the man of the cells. As Samson's riddle was suggested by finding the bee-cells, so will the new professor at Louvain solve the riddles of science by the demonstration of cells. The youthful jesting seer prophesied better than he knew. Schwann's first completed work at Louvain was the *Microscopical Researches into the Accordance in Structure and Growth of Plants and Ani-*

mals.[1] The theory it advanced was to prove the most potent element thus far introduced into biological science to help in the solution of the difficult problems that constantly occur in the study of the various forms of life.

At Louvain, Schwann remained for about ten years. The period is marked by a continuance of his fruitful investigation of cell-life, of the physiological biology of ferments and fermentation, and of the allied subject of digestion in animals. His researches in Berlin on this interesting and important subject, which was practically a complete mystery at that time, had been mainly concerned with the gastric juice. He now began the study of various secretions which aid intestinal digestion. He proved that bile, which used to be considered an excretion, was really an important digestive secretion. He was not able to demonstrate the function of bile as completely as he had done for the gastric juice. The problem of intestinal digestion is much more complicated than that of stomach digestion, and involves a number of factors for which allowance has to be made if the value of any one of them is to be accurately determined. Even in our own day all of the physiological problems in the functions of biliary secretion are not solved. The greatest step was the demonstration that bile is a thing whose presence in the intestines is to be encouraged, not because, as Horace said, mental trouble was imminent unless one were purged of black bile in the springtime, but because its presence insures the proper preparation of food, and neutralizes in the intestinal tract certain poisonous substances that if absorbed would prove sources of irritation to all higher tissues.

His work on bile practically closes Schwann's career as an investigator. The seven years between twenty and twenty-

[1] Mikroskopische Untersuchung über die Uebereinstimmung in der Structur und dem Wachsthum der Thiere und Pflanzen, 1839.

seven were so full of discovery that there seemed to be great promise for his mature years. Had Schwann died at thirty his biographies would have surely contained lengthy comments on the great discoveries that would undoubtedly have rewarded his efforts in the prime of his powers. Schwann's seeming inactivity has been a fruitful cause for conjecture. The fact of the matter is, however, that original work of a high order is accomplished mainly during the time when activity of the imagination is at its height. There are very few cases in which this acme of inventive effort has lasted more than ten years.

Besides this there were certain more material factors that hindered original work. Schwann was a German, yet had to give his lectures at Louvain in French. For several years most of his efforts were devoted to acquiring facility in the language of his adopted country. Then Schwann was not such a teacher as Müller, but the true pedagogue who took seriously to heart the duty of teaching all his students. To do this meant, in the rapidly advancing science of that day, unceasing toil on the part of a conscientious professor. For it was a time of great discoveries succeeding one another with almost incredible rapidity. For ten years Schwann faithfully devoted himself to his teaching duties in the anatomical course at Louvain. He then accepted the chair of comparative anatomy and physiology at Liège, where he continued to lecture for thirty years. As the result of his stay at Louvain there has always been special attention given to biological studies at that university. At the present time there is published there a very well and favorably known biological journal, *La Cellule*, through which many important contributions from the professors and students of the university find their way before the public.

During his stay at Liège Schwann was formally invited,

on three different occasions, to return to his German Fatherland to become professor at some of her great universities.
Professorial chairs in anatomy or physiology at Würzburg,
at Giessen, and at Breslau, were offered him between 1850
and 1860. He refused them, however, to continue his work
in Belgium. He found his adopted countrymen eminently
sympathetic. It seems clear that he felt more at home in the
midst of the profoundly Catholic sentiment that pervaded the
Belgian universities, and which was in such marked contrast
to the rationalistic spirit characteristic of the German
universities at that time. Schwann was penetrated with a
lively sense of the deepest religious feeling, which is noticeable
all through his life. His attitude in this matter greatly impressed his scientific contemporaries. His sense of duty in
matters spiritual was only equalled by his affectionate regard
for his relatives. His vacations were invariably spent with
his parents while they were alive, and later with his brothers
and sisters in the neighborhood of Cologne. It was while
making a Christmas visit to them that he suffered the fatal
stroke which carried him away.

Toward the end of his career Schwann was invited to be
a member of a commission to investigate the case of Louise
Lateau. It will be remembered that the report of recurring
bleedings from stigmata in this case attracted a great deal of
attention, not only among Catholics, but among all classes
throughout the world. After careful observation Schwann
refused to concur in the report that the bleedings were mani-
festly miraculous. At first it was announced that he had
declared them evidently beyond the domain of natural causes,
but this report he took occasion to correct immediately. The
circumstance led to the publication of some harsh words in
the religious press, but with his usual moderation Schwann
refused to enter into any discussion, and so the affair ended.

His thoroughly conservative attitude in the matter, and his application of the strictest scientific criteria to the case, prevented formal expression of approval on the part of those in authority. While such an opinion would have carried only personal weight with it, it might easily have been made a cause for unfortunate aspersions upon the Church.

The most marked feature of Schwann's career is the unfailing friendships that linked him to those with whom he was associated. At Louvain, and later at Liège, he was the personal friend of most of his students, while at Berlin he made friendships with some of the great men in German medicine which endured to the end of his life. When the celebration of his fortieth anniversary came around, the hearty tributes from all over Europe showed in what lofty reverence the kindly old man was held, who had sacrificed some of his chances for greater scientific fame in order to be a teacher of others, and a living exponent of the fact that the frame of mind which leads to great scientific discovery and that which bows humbly to religious truth, far from being hopelessly and essentially opposed to each other, may be peacefully united in the same person in their highest expression.

CLAUDE BERNARD, PHYSIOLOGIST

The experienced eye, the power of perceiving minute differences and fine analogies which discriminate or unite the objects of science, and the readiness of comparing new phenomena with others already treasured up in the mind— these are accomplishments which no rules can teach and no precepts put us in possession of. This is a portion of knowledge which every man must acquire for himself; nobody can leave as an inheritance to his successor. It seems, indeed, as if nature had, in this instance, admitted an exception to the will by which she has ordained the perpetual accumulation of knowledge among civilized men, and had destined a considerable portion of science continually to grow up and perish with individuals.—DR. JOHN BROWN, *Edward Forbes, Spare Hours.*

CLAUDE BERNARD, THE PHYSIOLOGIST.

With the recent development of post-graduate education the Collège de France has become a favorite shrine of pilgrimage for educators who visit Paris. It represents the oldest educational institution deliberately founded with the idea of combining teaching with investigation. The professors were not bound to teach definite doctrines, literary or scientific, but to give rather the results of recent investigations and personal meditation on great scientific and philosophic problems. The college was not meant, in a word, so much for students as for specialists. It was intended not to convey a definite body of knowledge on any subject, but rather to round out the knowledge acquired in the regular course at the University of Paris, and to dwell particularly on recent lines of advance in special subjects in a manner that would encourage original investigation.

In a word, the Collège de France was the first modern post-graduate school. We have learned in recent years how important are post-graduate departments for their influence on the regular work of a university. Unless original investigation of a high order is constantly done at a university, it is inevitable that the regular course will cease to be up to date. Modern educators are coming to realize very forcibly this quality of a successful teaching institution. Hence the interest that will surely continue to grow in the Collège de France, its foundation, its history, its teachers, and its methods.

To the great majority of those who come to pay their respects at this shrine of original investigation. it will prove a

distinct surprise to find the centre of the court of the Collège de
France occupied by a statue of Claude Bernard. Bernard is not
well known, and is still less appreciated out of scientific circles.
By many it is forgotten that the original free school, the
Collège de trois langues, in which Hebrew, Greek, and Latin
were the only chairs, has extended its scope, and that in our
day the natural sciences represent the most fertile field of its
achievements. The absolute freedom of opinion guaranteed
to professors originally, and which constituted the principal
reason for an educational institution apart from the University of Paris and its trammels, has proved a precious
heritage to later generations. Science has flourished vigor-
ously, and the memorial to its representative cultivator at the
college in this century has deservedly been given the place
of honor in its court.

To the initiate, however, for whom, in medicine and physiology and general biology, his work is still an inspiration,
many points of interest around the college will have all their
attraction from associations with Claude Bernard's career.
His neglect by the popular mind is more than compensated
for by the fervent admiration of all those who are occupied
with investigations along the lines he followed. For in him
they recognize a master mind such as is given to a branch of
science not more than once in a century; the veritable possessor of a magician's wand, who knows how to disclose the
hidden veins of precious ore, the exploitation of which will
prove a source of riches to so many faithful followers. For
these the dark little laboratory of the college in which Bernard
made so many of his ground-breaking discoveries will be in
the nature of a shrine to which one comes with grateful
memories of the *genius loci* that was. The apartment across
the street at No. 40 Rue des Ecoles, where Bernard lived for
years, will be the term of many a pilgrimage. Scientists

from all over the world will wander from here out to the
laboratory in the Jardin des Plantes, where Bernard's work
was done in his later years, and where the fundamental problems of life—plant and animal—usurped the attention that
had at first been devoted exclusively to human physiology
and its allied sciences.

Claude Bernard is another and a striking illustration of the
historical tradition that great men usually come from the
country, and not infrequently from poor parents. He was born
in 1813, at St. Julien, not far from Lyons, almost in the centre
of France. His father owned a small farm in the Beaujolais
wine district. The little estate came later into Bernard's
hands, and when he could afford the time he spent his
summers there. When the air is clear the white summits of
the Alps can be seen, and they make a pleasing contrast to the
plains along the Saone and the hill-sides of the immediate
neighborhood, all covered with vineyards. The physiologist,
who enjoyed nature very much, speaks enthusiastically of his
"little verdant summer nest."

He was educated at the Jesuit school of Villefranche. It
will be recalled that Theodore Schwann was also a student
of the Jesuits. In these days, when Jesuit educational
training is impugned, the facts are worth noting. It is
claimed especially that the old-fashioned training by means
of the classics is narrowing. The old method of a definitely
prescribed course of study for every student is said to hamper
development. Slavish devotion to old pedagogic methods,
it is urged, cannot but shackle and destroy initiative. The
subordinate place of the sciences in this scheme of education
is said to hinder progress in the sciences later in life, to
leave the powers of observation undeveloped until too
late, and to distract the mind of the student too much from
the practical side of life. Here are two men whose lives are

18

an open contradiction to all the allegations of the opponents of the old Jesuit system of training. Needless to say that they are but two of many.

Bernard pursued the course with the Jesuits at the Collège de Villefranche as far as it went. After this we find him at Lyons, at first pursuing studies in philosophy in preparation for his baccalaureate degree, evidently with the idea of eventually entering the university. Family reasons, mainly financial, compelled him to give up his studies, and for nearly two years he was an assistant in a pharmacy in Lyons. Here he developed a skepticism with regard to the effect of the drugs he compounded that led later in life to his important studies on the physiological action of remedies.

The science of therapeutics was at that time in a most inchoate stage. Very little was known of the exact action of drugs. Exaggerated claims were made for many, but mainly on uncertain clinical experience. The modern patent medicine was as yet unknown, but something not unlike it had become popular among the patrons of the Lyons pharmacy. One remedy was in constant demand by city patrons and by country people, who came from long distances especially to procure it. It was known as *la thériaque*—"the cure"—I suppose from some fancied connection with the root of the word therapeutics.

This remedy, according to the old women of the neighborhood and the countryside, was a panacea for every ill that flesh is heir to, and a few others besides (*pro morbis omnibus cognitis et quibusdam aliis*). The composition of this wonderworker was even more interesting than its universal curative efficacy. Whenever a drug spoiled from too long keeping, or an error in its manufacture made it unavailable for the purpose for which it was originally intended, or whenever an involuntary mistake in compounding occurred, the assistants in the pharmacy were directed not to throw the drugs away, but to reserve them for "la thériaque." "Mettez vous cela de côté pour la thériaque" (put that aside for "la thériaque") was a standing order in the shop. From a remedy of such varied ingredients the most wonderful effects could be expected and were secured. An unexpected action of the remedy, however, was that produced on Bernard's mind. This influence was later to lead to the healing of numberless ills in the system of therapeutics, and to bring about the establishment of the sciences of experimental pharmacology and physiology.

Bernard developed literary ambitions while at work in the pharmacy. He spent many of his free evenings at the theatre, and wrote a musical comedy, "The Rose of the Rhone," which was acted with some success. He worked at a prose drama, and, thinking the possibilities of life too narrow in Lyons, he resolved to go to Paris. With his play in his pocket, and a letter of introduction to the distinguished critic, St. Marc Girardin, he reached the capital. Bernard's drama, "Arthur de Bretagne," was published after his death, and shows that its author possessed literary talent of a high order. This must have been evident to Girardin, to whom it was given to read; but he very wisely advised its author to eschew literature, at least for a time, until he was able to make his living by some other means. Girardin advised Bernard to take up the study of medicine, for which his work in pharmacy had already prepared him somewhat.

Bernard, having once made up his mind to pursue medicine, threw himself, as was his wont, enthusiastically into the study of it. The utmost frugality was necessary in order to enable him to live on the scant income that could be allowed him from home. He lived with a fellow-student in a garret in the Quartier Latin. Their one room was study and sleeping room, and even, on occasion, kitchen. When a "box" came from home, utensils were borrowed from the laboratory for whatever cooking was necessary.

Bernard was especially interested in anatomy, and soon made himself known by the perfection of his dissections. Physiology attracted him not for what was known in the science, but for the many problems as yet unsolved. His was above all a mind not prone to accept scientific teaching on the *ipse dixit* of a professor. Except in the dissecting-room, his work attracted no attention. He was not looked upon as a brilliant student, and yet all the while he was unconsciously preparing himself thoroughly for his life-work. Later on his dissecting skill was to be a most helpful acquisition. Bernard's first promising opening came unexpectedly. The nicety with which he did certain dissecting work in preparation for one of Magendie's lessons attracted the attention of the professor, at that time the greatest living experimental physiologist. Magendie, in his bluff, characteristic way, without asking further about him, called out one day: "I say, you there, I take you as my *preparateur* at the Collège de France."

This position was gladly accepted by Bernard, for it provided him with an income sufficient to support himself. The work was congenial. His duty was to prepare the specimens and make ready the demonstrations for Magendie's lectures. His career as a physiologist dates from this appointment. He had to give some private lessons, and do what is called "coaching," or "tutoring," to eke out his slender income, but in the main his time after this was entirely devoted to investigation and experiment.

His first investigation concerned stomach digestion. It was important mainly because it directed his mind to digestive questions. In these he was to make his great discoveries.

His first independent investigation concerned the differences to be found in the digestive apparatuses and functions of the carnivora and herbivora—that is, of the meat and plant-eating animals. The differences in the natural habits of these two classes of animals had long been noted. While the meat-eaters invariably bolt their food, the plant-eaters chew theirs very carefully. Many of these latter, like the cow, are ruminants—that is, they bring up their food to chew it over again at their lesiure. The instinct that makes them do this is most precious. Their food is mainly composed of starch, in the digestion of which the saliva takes a large part. The thorough mixture of the food with saliva, then, is an extremely important matter. Human beings, who are both herbivorous and carnivorous, must learn to masticate thoroughly at least the starch-containing portions of the food. Bernard's first researches concerned the nerves that supplied the salivary glands, and which consequently influence the flow of saliva. Curiously enough, the conclusions of his first experiments were erroneous. The topic led him, however, into the general subject of the influence of nerves upon glandular secretion, a problem that he was destined to illustrate in many ways.

After the salivary glands the most important structure for the digestion of starches in the animal economy is the pancreas. It was early evident, however, that the pancreatic secretion effected more than the conversion merely of starch into sugar. Its most important rôle, that of influencing the digestion and absorption of fats, was only recognized as the result of a classical observation of Bernard's upon the rabbit. He noticed that fat introduced into the digestive tract of a rabbit undergoes no change until it has advanced a considerable distance beyond the stomach. When fat is introduced into the dog's digestive apparatus a marked change

begins in it almost as soon as it leaves the stomach. At first
this seemed very mysterious. Observations were made over
and over again, always with the same result. There was evidently some important distinction between the intestines of the
two animals. Careful investigation showed that the difference
between the behavior of the fat in the rabbit and the dog was
due to the presence or absence of the pancreatic fluid from
the intestinal contents. In the dog the pancreatic duct which
carries the secretion of the gland to the intestine empties into
the intestine just beyond the stomach. In the rabbit the duct
and its secretion empty into the intestine only some eight
to ten inches below the intestinal orifice of the stomach. It
is just beyond where the pancreatic duct reaches the intestine
in both animals that the digestion of fat begins. This observation solved the seeming mystery of fat digestion, and at
the same time made clear the importance of the pancreatic
secretion in the general work of digestion.

Bernard's attention was directed by this first observation
to the other properties of the pancreatic fluid. He soon
demonstrated by experiment, not only that it split up fats
into fatty acids and glycerin, and so made their absorption
possible, but that it had a powerful action upon proteids—
that is, upon the albuminous portions of the food, and also
upon the starches and sugars. Up to this time the principal
rôle in digestion had been assigned to the stomach and the
gastric juice. After Bernard's observations it was evident
that the action of the stomach was mainly preliminary to
intestinal digestion, and that the chief work in the preparation
of food for absorption into the system was really accomplished
by the secretion of the pancreas. It took some years to make
all this clear. Much of the advance in our knowledge of the
effect of pancreatic juice upon proteids—that is, upon meat
and other albuminous materials—is due to Kühne, a pupil

of Bernard; but not only did the inspiration for the pupil's work come from the master, but the important fundamental principle of pancreatic proteolysis—*i.e.*, the solution of proteids by pancreatic secretion—was clearly laid down in Bernard's original publications on the subject. Only in our own day has come the greatest confirmation of the notion then first introduced into physiology, of the surpassing importance of intestinal digestion. The removal of the whole stomach for malignant disease is now undertaken without any fears as to the ultimate result on the patient's general nutrition. The operation has been done many times, and the surgeon's confidence that the intestines would compensate, as far as digestion of food was concerned, for the absent stomach has been amply justified. Patients who survived the operation have all gained in weight, and some of them have enjoyed better health than for years before the removal of their stomachs.

From his studies of the pancreas, Bernard, whose mind was always of a very practical bent, was very naturally led to the study of that puzzling disease, diabetes. The question of how sugar was absorbed into the system was an interesting one even at that time. It was not realized, as it is now, that saccharine material was a most valuable food-stuff. Its use in the world's great armies of recent years has brought sugar very prominently before the medical profession of to-day. The bone and sinew for hard fighting and exhausting marches would not seem to be derivable from the favorite dainty of the child, which has besides fallen into such disrepute as a health disturber; yet tons upon tons of sweets are now shipped to fighting armies, and are distributed in their rations when especially hard work is required of them. Bernard did not quite realize that he was attacking, in the question of the digestion and consumption of sugar in the system, one of the most important problems of nutrition, especially as far as regards the production of heat.

Sugar is a substance that dissolves easily and in considerable quantity in water. When in solution it easily passes through an animal membrane by osmosis, and so the question of its absorption seemed simple enough. The disease diabetes showed, however, that sugar might exist very plentifully in the blood and yet the nutrition of an individual suffer very much for the lack of it. Something else beside its mere presence in the system was necessary to secure its consumption by the tissues. Bernard thought that the liver was active in the consumption of sugar, and that disease of this organ caused diabetes. He therefore secured some of the blood going to the liver of a living animal and some of the blood that was just leaving it. To his surprise the blood leaving the liver contained more sugar than that entering it. After assuring himself that his observations were correct, he tried his experiments in different ways. He found that even in the blood leaving the liver of an animal that had been fed only on substances containing no sugar, sugar could be demonstrated. Even in a fasting animal the liver itself and the blood leaving it showed the presence of a form of sugar. The only possible conclusion from this was that the liver was capable of manufacturing this form of sugar out of non-sugar-containing material, or even from the blood of a fasting animal.

This was the first time in physiology that the idea of an internal secretion was advanced. Glands within the body that gave off a secretion always possessed a duct by which this secretion was conducted to where it was to produce its effect. The idea that glands exist which pour their secretion directly into the blood-stream had not occurred.

This branch of physiology has developed wonderfully since

Bernard's discovery. The chapter of the functions of the ductless glands is one of the most interesting and most practical in modern medicine. The spleen, the thyroid, the suprarenal glands have taken on a new significance. Mysteries of disease have been solved, and, most wonderful of all, we have learned that many of the substances derived from these glands, when not present in the human body, may be effectually supplied by corresponding substances from animals, with results upon suffering human beings that are little short of marvellous. To mention but one example: the stunted, idiotic child that, because of congenital absence of the thyroid gland, formerly grew up to be a repellent, weak-minded man or woman, can now in a few short months be made the peer of most of its kind. All the modern tissue-therapy, with its hopeful outlook, is due to Bernard's far-reaching conclusions from his experiments upon sugar digestion and absorption.

His studies on sugar logically led Bernard to the investigation of heat production and heat regulation in the human body. Glycogen, the sugary substance produced by the liver, occurs abundantly in all the muscles of the body, and it was evident that muscular movement leads to its consumption and the consequent production of heat. Sugar is a carbon-containing substance, and its combustion always produces energy. The question of heat regulation was a much more complicated problem. Heat is always being produced in the human body and always being given off. Very different amounts of heat are required to keep up the temperature of the human body in the winter and summer seasons. Near the pole or at the equator man's temperature in health is always the same. To secure this identity of temperature some very delicately balanced mechanism is required. Without the most nicely adjusted equilibrium of heat production and dissemination human tissues would soon freeze up at a temperature of 70° below zero, or the albumin of the body fluids and muscular tissue coagulate at a temperature above 110° F.

While engaged in the investigation of this interesting problem Claude Bernard found that the cutting of the sympathetic nerves in the neck of a rabbit was followed by increased heat on the side of the head supplied by the nerve, and that this increased heat coincided with heightened sensibility and greater blood-supply in the parts affected. Here was an important factor in heat regulation laid bare. It was evident that the sympathetic nerve trunk supplied filaments to the small arteries, and that when these nerves no longer acted, as after the cutting of the nerve trunk, these arteries were no longer controlled by the nervous system and became dilated. The presence of more blood than usual in the tissues and its slower flow gave occasion to more chemical changes in the part than before, and consequently to the production of more heat.

These vasomotor nerves, as they have been called, because they preside over the dilatation and contraction of the walls of the bloodvessels (vasa) of the body, are now known to play an important rôle in every function. When food enters the stomach, it is dilatation of the gastric arteries, brought on by the reflex irritation of the presence of food, that causes the secretion of the gastric juices necessary for digestion. It is the disturbance of this delicate nervous mechanism that gives rise to the many forms of nervous dyspepsia so common in our day. It is its disturbance also that makes digestion so imperfect at moments of intense emotion, or that makes severe mental or bodily exertion after the taking of food extremely inadvisable. The vasomotor nerves, however, control much more than heat processes and digestion. The familiar blushing is an example of it, and blushes may occur in any organ. Excitement paralyzes the efforts of some individuals, but renders others especially acute. It is probable that the regulation of the blood-supply to the brain has much to do with this. While one student always does well in an oral examination, another, as well gifted, may always do poorly. Just as there are those who cannot control the vasomotor nerves of the face, and blush furiously with almost no provocation, so there are brain-blushers in whom the rush of blood interferes with proper intellection. On the other hand, there are those, and they are not always unaware of it, in whom the slight disturbance of the facial vasomotor mechanism only gives rise to a pleasing heightened color, and in the same way the increased blood-supply to the brain only gives them more intellectual acumen.

These two discoveries by Bernard—the formation of sugar by the liver and the nervous vasomotor mechanism—are, in their far-reaching application and their precious suggestiveness for other investigators, the most significant advances in physiology of the nineteenth century. They are directly due to a great imaginative faculty informing a most fertile inquiring spirit. Bernard was very different from his master, Magendie, in his applications of the experimental method. Magendie's researches were made more or less at random in the great undiscovered regions of physiology. He made his experiments as so many questions of nature. He cared not what the answer might be. He seldom had an inkling beforehand where his experiments might carry him. As he said himself, he was a rag-picker by the dustheap of science, hoping to glean where others had missed treasures, and not knowing what his stick might turn up next. Bernard's experiments were always made with a definite idea as to what he sought. Not infrequently his preconceived theory proved to be a mistake. It is of the very genius of the man that he was able to recognize such errors, and that he did not attempt to divert the results of experiments so as to bolster up what looked like eminently rational theories. The imaginative faculty that had come so near perverting him to literature was a precious source of inspiration and initiative in his scientific work. It was not followed as an infallible guide, however, but only as a suggestive director of the course investigation should take.

Besides the important discoveries made by Bernard there are two minor investigations, successfully accomplished, that deserve a passing word. To Claude Bernard we owe the use of curare in physiological experimentation. Curare is an Indian arrow poison which absolutely prevents all muscular movement. If artificial respiration is kept up, however, the animal lives on indefinitely, and no motion will disturb the progress of the most delicate experiment. In Bernard's time it was thought that the drug did not affect the sensory nervous system at all, and that as a consequence, though absolutely immobile, the animal might be suffering the most excruciating pain. We now know that the sensory system is also affected, and that the animal in these experiments suffers little if at all.

Bernard's investigation of the effect of carbonic oxide gas will probably be of more practical benefit to this generation and the next than it was to his. Like most of Bernard's discoveries, this one threw great light on important questions in physiology quite apart from the subject under investigation. Carbonic oxide is the gas produced by incomplete combustion of coal. The blue flames on the surface of a coal fire when coal is freshly added are mainly composed of this gas in combustion. From burning charcoal it is given off in considerable quantities. The gas is extremely poisonous. Unlike carbon dioxide, which does harm by shutting off the supply of oxygen, carbonic oxide is actively poisonous. After death the blood of its victims, instead of being of a dark reddish-blue, is of a bright pinkish-red. Bernard's study of the change that had taken place in the blood showed that the hemoglobin of the red blood-cells had united with the carbonic oxide present in the lungs to form a stable compound. The usual interchange of oxygen and carbon dioxide in the tissues could not take place. The combinations formed between oxygen and carbon dioxide and the hemoglobin of the blood readily submit to exchanges of their gaseous elements, and so respiratory processes are kept up.

Before Bernard's discovery it was thought that the respiratory oxygen was mostly carried dissolved in the blood-plasma —that is, in the watery part of the blood—or at least that its combination was a physical rather than a chemical process. This idea was overthrown by the discovery that the carbonic oxide combination with hemoglobin was very permanent. The rôle of the red blood-cell in internal respiration took on a new importance because of the discovery, and the comprehension of anæmic states of the system became much easier.

About the middle of his career Bernard suffered from a succession of attacks of a mysterious malady that we now recognize to have been appendicitis. Once at least his life was dispaired of, and recurring attacks made life miserable. After a year of enforced rest on the old farm of his boyhood, now become his own, he seems to have recovered more or less completely. His health, however, was never so robust as before. Toward the end of his life he lived alone. His wife and daughters were separated from him, and one of the daughters devoted her time and means to suffering animals in order to make up, as she proclaimed, for all her father's cruelty.

Bernard lived almost directly opposite to the Collège de France, in a small apartment in the rue des Ecoles. An old family servant took care of him, and his life was one of uttermost simplicity, devoted only to science. Once at court, in 1869, Napoleon III insisted on knowing, after an hour's conversation with him, what he could do for him. Bernard asked only for new facilities for his experimental work, and new apparatus and space for his laboratory.

Honors came to him, but left him modest as before. He was elected a member of the French Academy—one of the forty immortals. Only five times in the history of the Academy has the honor of membership been conferred upon a medical man. Before Bernard, Flourens, the father of brain physiology, had occupied a *fauteuil*, while Cabanis and Vicq d'Azyr are two other names of medical immortals.

Bernard was elected to the 24th *fauteuil*, which had been occupied by Flourens, and according to custom had to pronounce his predecessor's panegyric. The conclusion of his address was the expression: "There is no longer a line of demarcation between physiology and psychology." Physiology had become the all-ruler for Bernard in human function, and he drifted into what would have been simple materialism only for the saving grace of his own utter sanity, his active imagination, and the unconscious influence of early training. During his most successful years of scientific investigation, wrapped up in his experiments and their suggestions, Bernard was drawn far away from the spiritual side of things. This partial view of man and nature could not endure, however. In an article on Bernard in the *Revue des Questions scientifiques* for April, 1880, Father G. Hahn, S. J., says of him: "A man of such uprightness of character could not be allowed to persist to the end in this restless skepticism. His mental condition was really a kind of vertigo caused by the depths of nature that he saw all around him. At the threshold of eternity he came back to his true self and his good sense triumphed. The great physiologist died a true Christian."

Bernard was one of the great thinkers of an age whose progress in science will stamp it as one of the most successful periods of advance in human thought. He accomplished much, but much more he seemed to have divined. He seldom gave out the slightest hint of the tendencies of his mind, or of his expectations of discovery in matters of science, until fully satisfied that his theoretic considerations were justified and confirmed by observation and experiment. In one thing, however, he allowed favored friends to share some of his anticipations, and the notes published after his death show that he was on the very point of another great discovery in biology which has since been made. He was a firm friend of Pasteur's, and had ably seconded the great chemist-biologist's efforts to disprove spontaneous generation. Bernard's demonstration that air passed through a tube heated red hot might be suffered with impunity to come in contact with any sort of organic material, yet would never cause the development of germ life, was an important link in the proof that if life were carefully destroyed, no life, however microscopic in character, would develop unless the seeds of previously existent life were somehow brought in contact with the organic matter.

With regard to fermentation, too, Bernard was for many years in close accord with Pasteur, who taught that fermentation was the result of the chemical activity of living cells, the ferments. Toward the end of his life Bernard came to the view, however, that the action of ferments was really due to the presence in them of chemically active substances called diastases. These substances are of varied chemical composition, but each one has a constant formula. Their presence in a fermentescible solution is sufficient of itself, even in the absence of living cells, to bring about fermentation. It has since been shown that after this substance is removed from ferment-cells by pressure, and the liquid carefully filtered so that absolutely no cells remain, fermentation will yet take place.

This does not disprove the necessity for life to produce the diastases originally, though it advances science a step beyond the theory that it is the actual vital interchange of nutritious substances within the ferment-cell that causes fermentation. With each step of advance in biological science the mystery of life and its processes deepens.

No one has done more to bring out the depths there are in vital function than Bernard. His early training was of the type that is, according to many prominent educators of our day, least calculated to develop originality of view, or capacity for initiating new lines of thought. Our pedagogic Solons would claim that the narrow orthodoxy that wrapped itself around his developmental years must surely stifle the precious genius for investigation that was in him. It is due, on the contrary, very probably to the thorough conservatism of his early training and the rounded fulness of the mental development acquired under the old system of classical education, that we have to chronicle of Bernard none of the errors by exaggeration of personal bias that are so common among even great scientific men. Few successful men have ever owed less to luck or to favoring circumstances in life. He was in the best sense a self-made man, and he owed his success to a large liberality of mind that enabled him to grasp things in their true proportions. With an imaginative faculty that constantly outstripped his experimental observations he was singularly free from prejudgment and was able to control his theories by what he found, never allowing them to warp his powers of observation. Bernard is without doubt the greatest example of the century that a fully rounded youthful training is much more favorable to successful investigation than the early specialization which is falsely supposed to foster it.

PASTEUR, FATHER OF PREVENTIVE MEDICINE

More than two hundred and fifty years ago, Descartes, the most original mind of the modern age, who, more than any other thinker, has determined the course both of speculative and of scientific inquiry, declared that if any great improvement in the condition of mankind was to be brought about, medicine would provide the means, and what he foresaw we see.—BISHOP SPALDING.

PASTEUR, FATHER OF PREVENTIVE MEDICINE.

Louis Pasteur is the most striking figure in nineteenth century science. In biology, in chemistry, in physics, in medicine and surgery, and in the important practical subjects of fermentation, spontaneous generation and sanitation, he has left landmarks that represent great advances in science and starting-points for new explorations into the as yet un-mapped domain of scientific knowledge. His was a typically scientific mind. His intuitions were marvellous in their pro-phetic accuracy, yet were surpassed by his wonderful faculty for evolving methods of experimental demonstrations of his theories. His work has changed the whole aspect of biology and medicine, and especially the precious branches of it that refer to the cure and treatment of disease.

To such a man our generation owes a fitting monument. It has been given him. He was modest in life with the sincere modesty of the true man of science, who knows in the midst of great discoveries that he is only on the edge of truth, who realizes that "abyss calls to abyss" in the world of knowledge that lies beyond his grasp. Pasteur's monument, very ap-propriately for a man of his practical bent, is no idle orna-mental memorial. It is a great institution for the perpetual prosecution of his favorite studies and for the care of patients suffering from the diseases to whose investigation the best part of his life was devoted.

In this Institut Pasteur repose his ashes. They find a suitable resting-place in a beautiful chapel. Situate just below the main entrance a little lower than the ground floor,

(293)

of the institute proper, this chapel seems to form the main
part of the foundation of the building. It is symbolic of the
life of the man in whose honor it was erected. He who said,
"The more I know the more nearly does my faith approach
that of the Breton peasant. Could I but know it all my faith
would doubtless equal even that of the Breton peasant
woman." On a firm foundation of imperturbable faith this
greatest scientific genius of the century raised up an edifice
of acquisitions to science such as it had never before been
given to man to make.

Above the entrance of this chapel-tomb, and immediately
beneath the words "Here lies Pasteur," is very fittingly placed
his famous confession of faith:

"Happy the man who bears within him a divinity, an ideal
of beauty and obeys it; an ideal of art, an ideal of science,
an ideal of country, an ideal of the virtues of the Gospel."[1]

When we turn to the panegyric of Littré in which the
words occur we find two further sentences worth noting here:
"These are the living springs of great thoughts and great
actions. Everything grows clear in the reflections from the
infinite."[2]

These words are all the more striking from the circumstances in which they were uttered. When a vacant chair
(*fauteuil*) in the French academy is filled by the election of
a new member of the Forty Immortals, the incoming academ-
ician must give the panegyric of his predecessor in the same
chair. Pasteur was elected to the fauteuil that had been
occupied by Littré. Littré, who by forty years of unceasing
toil made a greater dictionary of the French language than

[1] Heureux celui qui porte en soi un dieu, un idéal de beauté et
qui lui obéit; idéal de l'art, idéal de la science, idéal de la patrie,
idéal des vertus de l'Evangile.

[2] Ce sont les sources vives des grandes pensées et des grandes
actions. Toutes s'éclairent des reflets de l'infini.

the Academy has made in the nearly two hundred years devoted
to the task, was the greatest living positivist of his day. He
and Pasteur had been on terms of the greatest intimacy.
Pasteur's appreciation of his dead friend is at once sincere and
hearty, but also just and impartial. Littré had been a model
of the human virtues. Suffering had touched him deeply
and found him ever ready with compassionate response.
His fellow-man had been the subject of his deepest thoughts,
though his relationship to other men appealed to him only
because of the bonds of human brotherhood. Pasteur called
him a "laic" saint. For many of us it is a source of genuine
consolation and seems a compensation for the human virtues
exercised during a long life that the great positivist died the
happy death of a Christian confident in the future life and
its rewards.

But Pasteur himself rises above the merely positive. The
spiritual side of things appeals to him and other-worldliness
steps in to strengthen the merely human motives that meant
so much for Littré. Higher motives dominate the life and
actions of Pasteur himself. In the midst of his panegyric of
the great positivist the greatest scientist of his age makes his
confession of faith in the things that are above and beyond the
domain of the senses—his ideals and his God.

There is said to exist a constant, unappeasable warfare
between science and religion. Perhaps it does exist, but
surely only in the narrow minds of the lesser lights. In no
century has science developed as in the one that has just
closed. Faraday the great scientific mind of the beginning
of the century, said, at one of his lectures before the Royal
Academy of Sciences of England, when the century was
scarcely a decade old: "I do not name God here because I
am lecturing on experimental science. But the notion of
respect for God comes to my mind by ways as sure as those

which lead us to physical truth." At the end of the century
the monument of a great man of science is a chapel with an
altar on which the sacrifice of Him that died for men is com-
memorated on Pasteur anniversaries.

The walls of the chapel are inscribed with the scientific
triumphs of the master whose ashes repose here. It is a
striking catalogue. Each heading represents a great step
forward in science:

1848, Molecular Dissymmetry.

1857, Fermentations.

1862, So-called Spontaneous Generation.

1863, Studies in Wine.

1865, Diseases of Silk Worms.

1871, Studies in Beer.

1877, Virulent Microbic Diseases.

1880, Vaccinating Viruses.

1885, Prophylaxis of Rabies.

Apparently these various sub $\vdots$ s are widely separated
from one another. It might seen that Pasteur was an erratic
genius. As a matter of fact, each successive subject follows
its predecessor by a rigid logic. Pasteur's life-work can be
best studied by a consideration of these various topics and
an appreciation of the advance made in each one.

Pasteur was first of all and always a chemist. He was
interested in chemistry from his early years. In the decade
from 1840 to 1850 organic chemistry—or as we prefer to call
it now, the chemistry of the carbon compounds—was just
opening up. Great discoveries were possible as they were
not before or since. Pasteur, with a devotion to experimental
work that amounted to a passion, was a pupil at the Ecole Nor-
male, in Paris. Bruited about he heard all the suggestive
questions that were insoluble problems even to the great men
around him. He was especially interested in the burning

question of the day, the internal constitution of molecules and the arrangement of atoms in substances which, though they are composed of exactly the same constituents, exhibit very different physical and chemical qualities. The subject is, almost needless to say, a basic problem in chemistry and remains to our own day the most attractive of scientific mysteries.

Mitscherlich, one of the greatest chemists of the time, had just announced that certain salts—the tartrates and paratartrates of soda and ammonia—"had the same chemical composition, the same crystalline form, the same angles in the crystalline condition, the same specific weight, the same double refraction and, consequently, the same inclination of the optic axes. Notwithstanding all these points of similarity, if the tartrate is dissolved in water it causes the plane of polarized light to rotate while the paratartrate exerts no such action." Pasteur could not believe that all the chemical and physical qualities of two substances could be identical and their action to polarized light be so different. Mitscherlich was known, however, as an extremely careful observer. For several years Pasteur revolved all the possibilities in Mitscherlich's observations and, finally, came to the conclusion that there perhaps existed in the paratartrates, as prepared by Mitscherlich, two different groups of crystals, the members of one of which turned the plane of polarization to the right, the other to the left. These two effects neutralized each other and apparently the paratartrates have no influence on the polarized beam of light.

Pasteur found that the paratartrates were composed of crystals that were dissymmetrical—that is, whose image reflected in a mirror cannot be superposed on the crystal itself. This idea Pasteur makes clear by reference to the mirrored image of a hand. The image of the right hand as

seen in a mirror is a left hand. It cannot be superposed
on the hand of which it is the reflection any more than the
left hand can be superposed on the right and have corresponding parts occupy corresponding places. Pasteur found
that the paratartrates were not only dissymmetrical, but
that they possessed two forms of dissymmetry. The mirrored
image of some of the crystals could be superposed on certain
of the other crystals just as the mirror image of the right
hand can be superposed on the actual left hand. He con-
cluded that if he separated these two groups from each other
he would have two very different substances, and so the
mystery propounded by Mitscherlich would be solved.

With Pasteur to conceive an idea was to think out its
experimental demonstration. He manufactured the paratartrates according to the directions given by Mitscherlich, and
then proceeded to sort the two varieties of crystals by hand.
It was slow, patient work, and for hours Pasteur strove
feverishly on alone in the laboratory. At length, the crystals
were ready for solution and examination as to their effect
upon polarized light. If Pasteur's idea as to the dissymmetry
of crystals were confirmed, a great scientific advance was
assured. Tremblingly the young enthusiast adjusted his
polariscope. He tells the story himself of his first hesitant
glance. But hesitation was changed to triumph. His
prevision was correct. There were two forms of crystals with
different effects on polarized light in Mitscherlich's supposed simple substance. Pasteur could not stay to put his
instrument away. The air of the laboratory had become
oppressive to him. Drunk with the wine of discovery, as a
French biographer remarks, he rushed into the open air
and almost staggered into the arms of a friend who · as
passing. "Ah," he said, "I have just made a great discovery.
Come to the Luxembourg garden and I will tell you all about

it." It was characteristic of the man all through life to have no doubt of the true significance of his work. He was sure of each step in the demonstration and his conclusions were beyond doubt.

Pasteur's discovery made a profound sensation. The French Academy of Sciences at once proceeded to its investigation. Among the members who were intensely interested, some bore names that now belong to universal science —Arago, Biot, Dumas, De Senarmont. Pasteur told long years afterward of Biot's emotion when the facts were visibly demonstrated to him. Greatly moved, the distinguished old man took the young man's arm and, trembling, said: "My dear child, I have loved science so well that this makes my heart beat." How deeply these men were bound up in their work! How richly they were rewarded for their devotion to science! There were giants in those days.

Pasteur's discovery was much more than a new fact in chemistry and physics. It was the foundation-stone that was to support the new science of stereochemistry—the study of the physiochemical arrangement of atoms within the molecule—that took its rise a few years later. Much more, it was a great landmark in biology. Pasteur pointed out that all mineral substances—that is, all the natural products not due to living energy—have a superposable image and are, therefore, not dissymmetrical. All the products of vegetable and animal life are dissymmetrical. All these latter substances turn the plane of polarization. This is the great fundamental distinction between organic and inorganic substances—the only one that has endured thus far in the advance of science. Dissymmetry probably represents some essential manifestation of vital force. Often there seem to be exceptions to this law; but careful analysis of the conditions of the problem shows that they are not real.

An apparent contradiction, for instance, to this law of demarcation between artificial products and the results of animal and vegetable life is presented by the existence in living creatures of substances like oxalic acid, formic acid, urea, uric acid, creatine, creatinin, and the like. None of these substances, however, has any effect on polarized light or shows any dissymmetry in the form of its crystals. These substances, it must be remembered, are the result of secondary action. Their formation is evidently governed by the laws which determine the composition of the artificial products of our laboratory, or of the mineral kingdom properly so called. In living beings they are the results of excretion rather than substances essential to life. The essential fundamental components of vegetables and animals are always found to possess the power of acting on polarized light. Such substances as cellulose, fecula, albumin, fibrin, and the like, never fail to have this power. This is sufficient to establish their internal dissymmetry, even when, through the absence of characteristic crystallization, they fail to manifest this dissymmetry outwardly.

It would scarcely be possible to indicate a more profound distinction between the respective products of living and of mineral nature than the existence of the dissymmetry among living beings and its absence in all merely dead matter. It is strange that not one of the thousands of artificial products of the laboratory, the number of which is each day growing greater and greater, should manifest either the power of turning the plane of polarization or non-superposable dissymmetry. Natural dissymmetrical substances—gum, sugar, tartaric and malic acids, quinine, strychnine, essence of turpentine, and the like—may be and are employed in forming new compounds which remain dissymmetrical though they are artificially prepared. It is evident, however, that all these new products only inherit the original dissymmetry of the substances from which they are derived. When chemical action becomes more profound—that is, becomes absolutely analytic or loosening of the original bonds imposed by nature—all dissymmetry disappears. It never afterward reappears in any of these successive ulterior products.

"What can be the causes of so great a difference?" We quote from Pasteur's life by his son-in-law: "Pasteur often expressed to me the conviction," says M. Radot, "that it must be attributed to the circumstance that the molecular forces which operate in the mineral kingdom and which are brought into play every day in our laboratory are forces of the symmetrical order; while the forces which are present and active at the moment when the grain sprouts, when the egg develops, and when under the influence of the sun the green matter of the leaves decomposes the carbonic acid of the air and utilizes in diverse ways the carbon of this acid, the hydrogen of the water and the oxygen of these two products are of the dissymmetrical order, probably depending on some of the grand dissymmetrical cosmic phenomena of our universe."

For the first few years after this discovery Pasteur endeavored by every possible means to secure experimental modifications of some of these phenomena of dissymmetry. He hoped thus to learn more fully their true nature. Magnetic influences especially would, he hoped, enable him to pierce, at least to some degree, this fundamental mystery of nature. While acting as professor at Strasburg, he procured powerful magnets with the view of comparing the actions of their poles and, if possible, of introducing by their aid among the forms of crystals a manifestation of dissymmetry. At Lille, where he was for several years dean of the scientific faculty, he contrived a piece of clockwork intended to keep a plant in continual rotary motion, first in one direction and then in the other. "All this was crude," he says himself, "but further than this I had proposed with the view of influencing the vegetation of certain plants to invert, by means of a heliostat and a reflecting mirror, the motion of the solar rays which should strike them from the birth of their earliest shoots. In this direction there was more to be hoped for."

He did not have time, however, to follow out these ingenious experiments. He became involved, as we shall see, in labors more than sufficient to take up all his time and all his energy. These labors were of great practical importance for France. Pasteur always insisted, however, that great discoveries will yet be made in following out this order of ideas, and that there is in this subject magnificent opportunity for young men possessed of the genius of discovery and the power of persistent work.

When, only a few years ago, Professor Duclaux, Pasteur's successor as the head of the Pasteur Institute, and himself one of the greatest living authorities on biological chemistry, wrote the story of the mind of the master,[1] he said, of this subject of dissymmetry: "A living cell appears to us, then, as a laboratory of dissymmetrical forces, a bit of dissymmetrical protoplasm acting under the influence of the sun—that is to say, under the influence of exterior dissymmetrical forces. It presides over actions of very different kinds. It can manufacture, in its turn, new dissymmetrical substances which add to or take away from its energy. It can, for instance, utilize one of the elements of a paratartrate without touching another. It can manufacture crystalline sugar at one moment and consume it at another, laying by stores for itself to-day using them up to-morrow. In a word, the living cell

_____
[1] L'Histoire d'un esprit, par M. Duclaux, Paris, 1896.

presents a marvellous plasticity, which exerts itself without the slightest disturbance by minimal deviations of forces due to dissymmetrical influence. Ah, if spontaneous generation were only possible! If we could only create living matter, raise up in the midst of inactive mineral material a living cell, then it would be easy for us to understand something more of vital manifestations and to comprehend better the mystery of dissymmetry."

But spontaneous generation is as far off as ever. Pasteur's discoveries in dissymmetry have brought us closer than ever before to the mystery of life. Scientists still hope, but it is with ever-waning confidence, that they may pluck out the heart of the mystery. Pasteur's own thoughts with regard to dissymmetry rose above even the lofty heights of mere earthly biology. He saw in it the great force that links the universe together. On one occasion, at the Academy of Sciences, he expressed himself as follows:

"The universe is a dissymmetrical whole. I am inclined to think that life, as manifested to us, must be a function of the dissymmetry of the universe or of the consequences that follow in its train. The universe is dissymmetrical; for, placing before a mirror the group of bodies which compose the solar system with their proper movement, we obtain in the mirror an image not superposable on the reality. Even the motion of solar light is dissymmetrical. A luminous ray never strikes in a straight line. Terrestrial magnetism, the opposition which exists between the north and the south poles of a magnet, the opposition presented to us by positive and negative electricity, are all the resultants of dissymmetrical actions and motions."

This raising of his thoughts far above the sordid realities he is concerned with into the realms of suggestive theory is typical of Pasteur. His was a true creative mind—poetic in its highest sense. The imagination properly controlled is of as great value to the scientist as to the poet. Pasteur's theories were ever pregnant with truth to be. All his life he kept this question of dissymmetry before his mind and hoped to get back to work at it. But opportunity failed. Other and more practical work was destined to occupy the busy half-century of investigation that followed.

Most of Pasteur's work, after this first thrilling discovery and its possible significance, is very well known. His meditations on the distinction between material derived from living and non-living sources led him to investigate certain processes called fermentations—before his time considered merely chemical. It is well known that if a dilute solution of sugar be exposed to the air anywhere in the world it will ferment—that is, certain changes will take place in the liquid, some gas will escape from its surface and alcohol will be formed. There are changes that take place in other organic substances—milk, meat solutions, butter, etc.—that resemble quite closely alcoholic fermentations, though the end-product of the process is not alcohol. Pasteur showed that all these supposed chemical changes are really due to the presence of minute living cells, called ferments. During the growth of these cells they split up the substances contained in the material in which they occur, using parts of them for their nutrition. He proved this very clearly for the lactic acid and butyric acid fermentations. Milk was supposed to become sour and butter rancid because they are unstable organic compounds, liable to change in the presence of the oxygen of the air. These changes were now shown to be due to minute living things that grow in the milk and the butter.

When Pasteur offered the same explanation of the origin of vinegar he found a strenuous opponent in Liebig, the great chemist. Liebig admitted the existence of specific substances,

called ferments, but said that they were nitrogenous compounds in unstable equilibrium as regards their composition, and with a marked tendency to undergo alteration when
exposed to the air or free oxygen. These alterations, once
begun, affect also the liquids in which the ferments are
contained—milk, blood, sugar solutions and the like.
Theodore Schwann had shown the existence of certain yeast-
like bodies in fermenting liquids, but these were considered
to be effects, not causes, of the fermentation, and even
Schwann, himself, believed that they originated in the liquids
in which they were found. It remained for Pasteur to
demonstrate, as he did by a brilliant series of ingenious and
conclusive experiments, that ferments are living cells, that
they never originate except from previous cells of the same
species, and that no fermentation takes place unless they are
present.

The changes that take place in organic liquids when exposed to the air and the frequent development in such liquids
of moving bodies evidently possessed of life constituted,
before Pasteur's time, the principal reason for believing that
life might originate from some special combination of chemical
forces, and without the necessity for preceding life of the same
species as its efficient cause. The new explanation of fermentation greatly weakened the position of those who believed in spontaneous generation—that is, the origin of life
from dead matter under certain specially favorable circumstances. Pasteur proceeded to show, by rigid demonstration,
that if all life were destroyed in organic substances, living
beings never originated in them unless living seeds from the
air gained access to them. After a meat solution has been
thoroughly boiled nothing living develops in it, even though
the air is allowed free access, if the air admitted has been
previously filtered through cotton. He showed that even the

20

bending of the neck of the tube into the shape of an "S," so as to prevent the entrance of dust particles, suffices to protect the most changeable organic material from the growth of 'micro-organisms in it. His teaching was not accepted at once. Details of his experiments were impugned. Apparently complete counter-demonstrations were made, but Pasteur knew how, by his marvellous intuition, to detect the fallacy of supposed demonstration, and to invent new crucial tests of the proof of biological succession.

These studies in minute life and in fermentation led him almost naturally to the study of disease. Two centuries before, Robert Boyle, of whom his notorious descendant the great bullster, Sir Boyle Roche, had said that he was the father of chemistry and the brother of the Earl of Cork, made use of an expression wonderfully prophetic in its accurate penetration of the future. "He that thoroughly understands the nature of ferments and fermentations," said Boyle, "shall probably be much better able than he that ignores them to give a fair account of divers phenomena of certain diseases (as well fevers as others) which will perhaps be never properly understood without an insight into the doctrine of fermentations." The marvel is that the very first man who understood the nature of fermentation proved to be the one destined to unlock the mystery of contagious disease and its origin.

Pasteur's first investigations in the field of disease concerned a mysterious malady that affected the silkworm and was ruining the silk industry of France. This disease was first noted seriously about 1850. When a colony of silkworms had been attacked it was useless to try to do anything with them. The only resource for the silk farmers was to get the eggs of an unaffected race of worms from some distant country. These became infected after several generations, and untainted eggs had to be brought from a distance once more. Soon the silkworm plague invaded most of the silk-growing countries of Europe. In 1864, only the races of silkworms in China and Japan were surely not infected. Great suffering had been entailed on many departments of France by the failure of the silk industry. The most careful investigation failed to reveal any method of combating the disease. Acute observers had been at work and some very suggestive observations on the affected worms had been made, but the solution of the problem of the prevention of the disease seemed as far off as ever. In 1863 the French minister of agriculture formally agreed to pay 500,000 francs (about $100,000) to an Italian investigator who claimed to have found a remedy for the disease, if his remedy proved efficient. The offer was to no purpose. In 1865 the weight of cocoons of silk had fallen to 4,000,000 kilos. It had formerly been nearly 30,000,000 kilos. This involved a yearly loss of 100,000,000 francs (about $20,000,000).

Pasteur showed that the failure of the silkworm was not due to one disease, but to two diseases—pebrine and flacherie. These diseases are communicated to the eggs of the worms, so that the young begin life handicapped by the maladies. The crawling of the worms over leaves and stems makes these liable to communicate the diseases. The prevention of the diseases is accomplished by procuring absolutely healthy eggs and then never letting them come in contact with anything that may have been touched by diseased worms. If, at the egg-laying period, worms show any signs of disease their eggs are to be rejected. These simple suggestions were the result of rigid experimental demonstration of the spread of the diseases from worm to worm, including the demonstration of the microbic causes of the two diseases. These precautions proved effective, but their introduction met with opposition. The strain of the work and the worry of controversy brought Pasteur to the brink of the grave by a paralytic stroke. From this he never entirely recovered and was always afterward somewhat lame. After the severest symptoms had passed off he was given the opportunity to make a crucial test of preventing the silkworm diseases at the villa of the French Prince Imperial. The products obtained from the silkworms on the estate had, for years, not sufficed to pay for the fresh supplies of eggs obtained from a distance. Pasteur was given full charge of the silk industry on the estate. The sale of the cocoons at the end of the year gave a net profit of 26,000,000 francs (over $5,000,000). This decisive demonstration effectually ended all opposition.

His attention was next naturally directed to the diseases of animals and human beings. His studies in fermentations and in silkworm diseases had taught him the use of the microscope for such investigations. Splenic fever—known also as anthrax—a disease that attacks most species of domestic animals and may also prove fatal to man, was the first to yield the secret of its origin. The cause proved to be a bacterium—that is, a small, rod-shaped plant. This was but the first of a series of similar discoveries, until now the science of bacteriology has become one of the most important branches of knowledge. Pasteur's investigations included much more, however, than the mere discovery of the germ of the disease. He showed that a series of diseases which passed under different names in different animals were all due to the same cause. Further, he discovered one of the methods of distributing the disease. When the carcasses of animals that have died from the disease are not buried deeply below the surface of the ground, animals grazing above may become infected with the disease.

The germs of the disease can be shown to occur in the grass above the graves. It is carried to the surface in the bodies of earth-worms. This important observation was the first hint of the methods of disease distribution by some living intermediary. Modern medicine has come to understand that these biological distributing agents are far more important than the fabled transmission through the air.

Pasteur overturned the notion of spontaneous generation of life. Then his work eradicated the idea of the spontaneous generation of disease. It opened up a new era by showing that the origin of many diseases is not due to changes in the atmosphere nor to some morbid productivity of soil or water under favoring circumstances, but to minute living organisms whose multiplication is encouraged by the conditions that were supposed to produce disease. Finally, came the precious suggestion that living things always convey and distribute disease; man to man, for epidemics travel not with the velocity of the wind but only as fast as the means of communication between distant points; animal to man, as is well known, for many diseases now; and, lastly, insects, worms and the like were also shown to be real carriers of disease.

In investigating chicken cholera Pasteur discovered another great basic principle in the knowledge of disease, especially of its treatment. After considerable difficulty he succeeded in finding the germ of this disease which was causing great losses in the poultry industry of France and other European countries. This germ was cultivated for a number of generations on artificial media and never failed to produce the disease when fowls had been inoculated. During the course of his studies in the malady Pasteur was called away to a distant part of France in connection with his investigation of anthrax. He was away from his laboratory for several months. When he returned he inoculated some fowls with the cultures of chicken cholera which he had left behind. To his surprise and annoyance the inoculations failed to produce the typical symptoms of the disease. The fowls suffered from some slight symptoms and then recovered. When he left his laboratory inoculations had been invariably fatal. It took considerable time and trouble to procure fresh cultures of the chicken-cholera microbe. Meantime, the fowls which had been only slightly affected by the old cultures were carefully preserved. When these birds were inoculated with the fresh virulent cultures they failed to take the disease. Other fowls promptly died, exhibiting all the characteristic symptoms of chicken cholera. Those that had suffered from the mild form of the disease produced by the old cultures were protected from further attacks of the disease.

One of the great mysteries of medicine, the varying virulence of disease, had been thus solved by what seemed an accident. There are no accidents in the lives of great investigators. There are surprises, but genius knows how to reconcile their occurrence with the principles they are working out. Pasteur understood at once the wonderful utility there might be in this discovery for the protection of men and animals from disease. He proceeded to practical applications of the new theory by providing old cultures for the inoculation of fowls in districts where chicken cholera produced serious ravages. Then, working on the same lines as for chicken cholera, he proceeded to elaborate vaccine material for anthrax.

Vaccine was the name deliberately selected for the inoculating substance in order to honor the genius of the English physician Jenner, who had discovered the power of vaccination to protect from smallpox. The weakening of the germs of anthrax, so as to produce only a mild form of the disease, was a much more intricate problem than for chicken cholera, because the anthrax bacillus does not weaken with age, but enters a resting or spore stage, resembling the seed stage in large plants. After a patient series of investigations Pasteur accomplished his object by some ingenious methods that served to show, perhaps better than any other details of his career, how thoroughly practical was his inventive genius.

Unfortunately the absorption in his work proved too much for his health. He was seized by a series of apoplectic attacks which for a time threatened to put an end to his invaluable career. When he did begin to recover his health one of the most serious problems in his regard was to keep him from hindering his convalescence by a return to his old-time absorption in the important problems of the cure and the prevention of disease, at which he had been so happily engaged. The keynote of Pasteur's life was to prevent human suffering as far as possible, and any time not given to this important duty seemed to him to be utterly wasted. With regard to this unfortunate break in Pasteur's work Dr. Christian Herter, in his address on the "Influence of Pasteur in Medical Science," delivered before the Medical Society of Johns Hopkins University,[1] has an interesting passage, in which he discusses the significance of the master's work up to this time, and the interest that his illness awakened among all the distinguished medical scientists of Europe at the time:

"It is likely that excessive work and mental stress in some degree contributed to the onset of the series of paralytic seizures which in October, 1868, threatened the life of Louis Pasteur. During the critical period of his illness, many of the most distinguished scientific men of France vied with each other to share with Mme. Pasteur the privilege of nursing the man they loved so well and of rescuing the life

[1] New York: Dodd, Mead & Co., 1904.

that had already placed science and a nation under enduring obligation through discoveries which were either of the greatest practical utility or appeared susceptible of almost unlimited development. Had Pasteur died in 1868, he would have left a name immortal in the annals of science. Others would in some degree have developed his ideas. Already inspired by the researches on fermentation, Lister would have continued to develop those life-saving surgical methods which will forever be associated with his name. But we may well question whether investigations in biology and medicine would not have been for a time at least conducted along less fruitful paths. Who shall say how soon the great principle of experimental immunity to pathogenic bacteria, the central jewel in the diadem of Pasteur's achievements, would have been brought to light?"

When Pasteur recovered sufficiently to resume work, it was soon clear to apprehensive friends that he had no intention of leaving his ideas to be worked out by other men. The miseries of the Franco-Prussian War deeply affected him, and could not fail to inhibit his productiveness, but after a time the unquenchable love for experimental research was once more ascendant and there began a new epoch, the epoch of great discoveries relating to the origin and cure or prevention of the infectious diseases of man and the domestic animals. As in the case of Ignatius Loyola, it seems as if the lamp of the genius shone with a larger and more luminous flame after the onset of bodily infirmity in defiance of the physical mechanism which is too often permitted to master the will.

After his illness Pasteur devoted himself even more than before to the study of the various biological problems connected with human diseases. There was one exception to this, in his series of studies on beer, undertaken shortly after the Franco-Prussian War. Pasteur was an ardent patriot, so much so, indeed, that after the war he sent back to the German government certain decorations and diplomas that had been conferred upon him. He thought that his country had been overreached by a scheming, political statesman, bent on the aggrandizement of the kingdom of Prussia. To the end of his life this feeling of hostility never entirely vanished. It was his hope, then, that by improving the character of French beer it might not only be made more wholesome in the best sense of the word, but also that the French brewing industry might be made a serious rival of its German competitors. Pasteur's discoveries are the most important for the brewing industry that have ever been made. The Germans proved, however, even more capable of taking advantage of them than his French compatriots.

After this Pasteur devoted himself without further interruption to the study of the microbic diseases of man. His greatest practical triumph was undoubtedly with regard to hydrophobia, or, as it is more properly called, rabies. The mystery of the disease was most illusive. Pasteur could not succeed in finding the germ of the disease. Even down to our own day it has not been satisfactorily demonstrated. In spite of this lack of an important element of knowledge, which might be supposed absolutely essential for the successful therapeutics of rabies from a biological standpoint, Pasteur succeeded in producing material that would protect those bitten by rabid dogs from developing the affection

Long and bitter was the opposition to the introduction of his method of treatment. The greatest living German bacteriologist said that it was idle to provide "remedies of which we know nothing for diseases of which we know less." The reference was to the failure to find the germ of the disease and the claim, nevertheless, of having discovered a cure. Wherever the Pasteur treatment for rabies was introduced, however, the number of deaths following the bites of mad animals fell off. In Russia, where the mad wolves of the Steppes so often inflict fatal bites, the power of the new treatment was soon recognized. In Hungary its value was appreciated without delay. Then the British government, after a most careful investigation, introduced it into the Indian army. Then Austria took it up officially. At the International Medical Congress at Moscow, in 1897, Americans, who expressed doubts as to the efficiency of the Pasteur treatment for rabies, were laughed at by the medical representatives of nations who have the most opportunities for studying the disease. Shortly after the Moscow congress the German government officially announced its intention of treating all persons bitten by rabid animals by the Pasteur method. A Pasteur institute for the treatment was opened in connection with the University of Berlin. With this the last serious opposition disappeared. The Germans are now enthusiastic advocates of the value of the Pasteur treatment. The statistics of the Berlin Pasteur Institute are pointed to as demonstrating beyond doubt the possession of power to cope with one of the most fatal diseases man is liable to. Alas, that this should not have come during the master's lifetime! It would have been the happiest moment of Pasteur's life to have had his ideas triumphant in Germany. Unlike the generality of great men, however, Pasteur enjoyed the meed of almost unstinted appreciation during life.

Geniuses are often said to be neglected by their contemporaries. The expression is exemplified much less frequently in our own time than formerly. The rapid diffusion of ideas, and the consequent control and confirmation of scientific claims by many minds, enable the present generation to recognize merit before its possessor has starved.

Pasteur's career was certainly an exemplification of the fact that true genius, though it may meet with opposition, will be well rewarded. The son of the poor tanner of Dole, by the mere force of his intellectual energy, lifted himself to the level of earth's great ones. His funeral obsequies were a pageant in which French officialdom felt itself honored to take part. The President of the French Republic, the members of both houses of the legislative department, the officials of the city of Paris, the members of the faculty of the university, of the French Academy, and of the various scientific societies of the French capital, gathered to honor their mighty dead. Never has it been given to anyone without family prestige or political or ecclesiastical influence to have a great world-capital and a great nation accord such glorious obsequies, while all the world extended its sympathy and added pæans of praise.

Nor was it only at the moment of death that the expression of sincere respect and merited honor was paid. When there was question of erecting a Pasteur institute, in which the master's great work could be carried on more effectually, contributions poured in from every part of France and from all over the civilized world. Two of the world's greatest hereditary rulers made it a point to visit the humble laboratory of the great scientist whenever they came to Paris. Alexander II, the Czar of the Russians, was the intimate friend of the tanner's son, who became the world's benefactor. Dom Pedro II, the late Emperor of Brazil. was another royal visitor to Pasteur. In the library of the *Institut Pasteur* at Paris, the busts of these two and of two other great friends of his, scarcely less in worldly importance and greater in their beneficence, keep watch above the ashes of the dead scientist. They are Baroness Hirsch, the world benefactress, and Baron Albert Rothschild, the head of the French branch of the great banking family.

All united in honoring the marvellous genius whose work has proved of such practical utility for mankind, and whose discoveries are as yet only beginning their career of pregnant suggestiveness to scientific men. His genius has brought the great ones of earth to his level or raised him to theirs. His own thought on the equality of man is a confession of the faith that was in him. It was expressed in his discourse of reception into the French Academy in the midst of the panegyric on Littré, from which we quoted at the beginning of this sketch: "Where are the true sources of human dignity, of liberty and of modern democracy, if not in the infinite, before which all men are equal? The notion of the infinite finds everywhere its inevitable expression. By it the supernatural is at the bottom of every heart."

Pasteur, the man, is, however, if possible, even more interesting than Pasteur, the greatest of living scientists. In the midst of all his work and his wonderful success, amid the plaudits of the world, Pasteur remained one of the simplest of men and the kindest of friends to those who knew him. Dr. Roux's expression is well known: "The work of Pasteur is admirable; it shows his genius; but one must have lived on terms of intimacy with him in order to know all the goodness of his heart." He was kindness personified, and those who think of him as a cruel vivisector and encourager of experiments upon animals that cause suffering, belie him and his humanity very much. He would never permit animals to be used in experiments without an anesthetic, and even then only when he deemed that use absolutely necessary for the furtherance of projects that promised great benefit to humanity. Nothing was harder for him to do than to walk the hospitals and see human suffering when he was studying the causes of disease in human beings. Even the slight pain inflicted during the injections for hydrophobia was a source of great discomfort to him, and his anxiety with regard to these patients was one of the main causes of the breakdown in health that shortened his life.

One of the most beautiful things about Pasteur's personal life is the relation to his family, and especially to his children, and their union in religious simplicity. On the occasion of the death of his father, whom Pasteur loved very deeply and for whom he had instilled the deepest affection into the hearts of his children, he wrote to his daughter, whose first communion was to occur on that day. His letter is that of a man deeply affectionate, sincerely religious, and eminently trustful of the future that faith alone points out. His letter runs:

"He died, my dear Cecelia, the day of your first communion. Those are two memories which will, I hope, never leave your heart, my dear child. I had a presentiment of his death when I asked you to pray particularly on that morning for your grandfather at Arbois. Your prayers will surely be very agreeable to God at such a time, and who knows if grandpa himself did not know of them and did not rejoice with our little Jeanne [a daughter who had died the year before] over the pious sentiments of Cecelia?"

It is not surprising, then, to find many other expressions of Pasteur's extreme interest in spiritual things, though they might have been little expected fom a man so deeply immersed in scientific investigations as he was. After all, it must not be forgotten that his discoveries, by solving the mystery that surrounds the origin of disease, cleared some of the ways of Providence of that inscrutable character which is supposed in shallow minds to constitute the greatest part of their impressiveness. With epidemics explained, not as dispensations of Divine Providence, but as representing the sanction of nature for the violation of natural laws, one of the

reasons for which mankind worshipped the Deity seemed
to be gone. The man who had done most to make clear
these mysterious processes of nature was, however, himself
far from thinking that materialism offers any adequate explanation of the mysteries of life, or of the relations of man to
man, and of man to his Creator. Impatient at the pretensions
of such pseudoscientists, Pasteur once said: "Posterity will
one day laugh at the sublime foolishness of the modern
materialistic philosophy. The more I study nature, the
more I stand amazed at the work of the Creator. I pray
while I am engaged at my work in the laboratory."

For Pasteur, death had no mysteries. He had written
to his father, once, on the death of his little daughter Jeanne:
"I can only think at this moment of my poor little one so
good, so full of life, so happy in living, and whom this fatal
year, now drawing to a close, has snatched from us. After a
very short time she would have been for her mother and for
me, for all of us, a friend, a companion, a helpmate. But
I ask your pardon, dear father, for recalling to you such sad
memories. She is happy. Let us think of those who remain,
and let us try to prevent for them, as far as lies in our
power, the bitternesses of life." So, when it came to the
hour of his own death, Pasteur faced it with the simple confidence of a sincere Christian, and the undoubting faith of a
lifelong son of the Church. For many hours he remained
motionless, one of his hands resting in that of Madame
Pasteur, while the other held a crucifix. His last conscious
glance was for his lifelong companion, his last conscious
act a pressure of the image of his Redeemer. Thus, surrounded by his family and disciples in a room of almost
monastic simplicity, on Saturday, September 28, 1895, about
five in the afternoon, passed peacefully away the greatest
of the nineteenth century scientists

Almost needless to say, the life of a man like Pasteur contains the most wonderful lessons for the young scientists of the twentieth century. Few men have lived their lives so unselfishly, and with so much preoccupation for the good that they might accomplish, as he did. To have remained in the midst of it all simple, earnest and faithful to duty, without self-seeking, is a triumph worthy of recording, and makes a career well deserving of emulation. When Pasteur made his discoveries with regard to fermentation the Empress of the French asked to be shown just what his investigations had demonstrated. Pasteur went to Court for the purpose, and after the Emperor and Empress had been shown the ferment cells, and expressed their interest, Eugenie said: "Now, you will develop this discovery industrially, will you not?" Pasteur replied. "Ah, no, that will be left for others. It does not seem to me that it would be worthy of a French scientist to allow himself to be diverted to the industrial applications of his discoveries, even though it might prove eminently lucrative for him." As a matter of fact, had Pasteur allowed himself to be allured into the foundation of an immense manufactory constructed and directed on the great principles which he had discovered, there seems no doubt that this would have been a wonderful money-making scheme. Certain it is that the capital for such an adventure would have been readily available. Had Pasteur yielded to the solicitations made him he might have died worth many millions, instead of the very modest competency which came to him in the ordinary course of his scientific labors. The money might have seemed a temptation for the sake of his children, but the world would have lost all the great discoveries with regard to human diseases. It is not unlikely that these would have been made even without Pasteur. There is no doubt, however, that their discovery would have been very much delayed and that as a consequence almost untold human suffering that has been prevented would have occurred. It must never be forgotten that such men as Lister and Koch derived their most fertile suggestions from the discoveries made by Pasteur.

Pasteur's life may very well be held up, then, as a model to the present and future generations of what the highest ideals of a scientific career can be. Dr. Christian Herter, in the discourse already quoted from, has stated this so well and at the same time has joined with it so felicitously a quotation from Pasteur's advice to young men, that we can find no better way in which to close this consideration of Pasteur's career than by quoting him once more:

"To have fought the long battle of life with unwavering constancy to the loftiest ideals of conduct, toiling incessantly without a thought of selfish gain; to have remained unspoiled by success and unembittered by opposition and adversity; to have won from nature some of her most precious and covert secrets, turning them to use for the mitigation of human suffering;—these are proofs of rare qualities of heart and mind. Such full success in life did Louis Pasteur attain, and from the consciousness of good achieved his noble nature found full reward for all his labors.

"Of the children whom nature has endowed with splendid gifts there are few whose lives have affected so profoundly and so beneficently the fate of their fellows, few who have earned in equal degree the gratitude and reverence of all civilized men. Although not many can hope to enrich science with new principles, all of us may gain from Pasteur's life the inspiration to cultivate the best that is in us. Let us keep living in our memories the inspiring words which the master spoke on the seventieth anniversary of his birthday:

" 'Young men, young men, devote yourselves to those sure

and powerful methods, of which we as yet know only the first secrets. And I say to all of you, whatever may be your career, never permit yourselves to be overcome by degrading and unfruitful skepticism. Neither permit the hours of sadness which come upon a nation to discourage you. Live in the serene peace of your laboratories and your libraries. First, ask yourselves, What have I done for my education? Then, as you advance in life, What have I done for my country? So that some day that supreme happiness may come to you, the consciousness of having contributed in some manner to the progress and welfare of humanity. But, whether our efforts in life meet with success or failure, let us be able to say, when we near the great goal, 'I have done what I could.' "

JOSEPH O'DWYER, THE INVENTOR OF INTUBATION

I have hope and wish that the nobler sort of physicians will advance their thoughts, and not employ their time wholly in the sordidness of cures; neither be honored for necessity only; but that they will become coadjutors and instruments in prolonging and renewing the life of man.— BACON

JOSEPH O'DWYER, THE INVENTOR OF INTUBATION.

At the beginning of the nineteenth century a young medical practitioner, working faithfully in the wards of his hospital in Paris, pitying especially the patients who suffered from pulmonary disease, and realizing how hopeless was their treatment, since medical science knew so little of the real nature of the ailment from which they suffered, invented the stethoscope and established the principles on which modern physical diagnosis is based in a method so complete that after the lapse of three-quarters of a century very little has been added to what was then discovered. This genius was the famed Laennec, of whom we have written in a preceding chapter, who was wont to spend his days walking the wards of the Necker Hospital in Paris, caring more for his poor patients than for the nobility and members of the wealthy classes, who willingly would have taken advantage of his clinical knowledge so conscientiously gained. Laennec made possible progress in medicine that places him among the five or six greatest medical men of all times.

At the end of the nineteenth century a man of about Laennec's age was touched with pity for the sufferings of the poor children whom he saw dying from suffocation because of the ravages of laryngeal diphtheria. Nothing could be done for them except, perhaps, to benumb their senses by means of narcotics, while nurse and medical man stood idly by suffering excruciatingly themselves while their little patients bore all the lingering, awful pains of death by asphyxiation.

For years Joseph O'Dwyer labored at the problem of relieving these little patients, and finally achieved similar success to Laennec with his stethoscope. The modern doctor, moreover, was quite as patient in his work of research as Laennec, and though his discovery had not so wide an application as the latter's it was accomplished through the same tireless, persevering labor, and through the same instinct of genius that finally led to the culminating invention which no one has been able to improve, and which has made its inventor's name a familiar word to medical men over the world. American medicine has no more shining light than the name of Joseph O'Dwyer, and the record of his simple, sincere, straightforward life, faithful during his successful career to the simple religious principles imbibed in the bosom of an old-fashioned Catholic family, who, during a long career, thought little of self and mainly of the possibilites for good presented by his profession, cannot but prove one of the standard biographies in this country's medical history.

Dr. Joseph O'Dwyer, the inventor of intubation, was born in 1841, in Cleveland, Ohio. Shortly after his birth his parents, who were only moderately well to do, moved to Canada, so that O'Dwyer's boyhood was passed not far from London, Ontario. There he received his early education, and there also, as was the custom in those days, he began his medical studies by becoming a student in the office of a Dr. Anderson. After two years of apprenticeship, he came to New York and attended lectures in the New York College of Physicians and Surgeons, where he was graduated in 1866, at the age of twenty-five. Immediately after graduation he obtained the first place in the competitive examination for resident physician and sanitary superintendent of the Charity or City Hospital of New York City, on Blackwell's Island. Shortly after his appointment an epidemic of cholera broke out in the workhouse (under his charge), and Dr. O'Dwyer nobly devoted himself to the care of the patients. While engaged in this work he contracted the disease himself, but fortunately recovered completely without suffering from any of its usual after-effects.

When, not long subsequently, another epidemic of cholera occurred in New York, and a number of cases of the disease were transferred to Hart's Island and there quarantined, volunteers for their medical attendance were asked from among the members of the medical staff of the Charity Hospital. Dr. O'Dwyer was one of the first to come forward and offer his services. Again he contracted the disease, but recovered from it as completely as from typhus. Years afterward he described to a friend his feelings as he lay in one of the hospital tents, the only accommodation that could be provided for him owing to the crowded condition of the wards. His attack was rather severe and yet left him his consciousness, while as he lay expecting death at almost any moment, the thought (as he was wont to relate) sometimes came to him that it was perhaps foolish of him to have volunteered in so dangerous a service. This thought was always put away, however, and he assured his friend that at no time had he ever regretted his exposure to the disease in the cause of suffering humanity. The risks that usually come with professional obligations (it appeared to him) are not to be avoided at the cost of the consciousness of a duty refused.

During his service at the Charity Hospital, Dr. O'Dwyer endeared himself to all those with whom he came in contact. In examination for the position of resident on the Island he had passed first, and during his service there it was generally conceded that he towered above his companions in his efficiency and attention to duty. Some of those who were residents with him afterward made names that are distinguished in the history of the practice of medicine in New York City, yet all of them were ever ready to acknowledge that O'Dwyer had been a leader among them in the service. With a very practical turn of mind, he united the capacity for patient work that enabled him to master difficulties, while his devotion to his profession gave him a deep interest in every department of medicine. The foundation of his future success as a practitioner of medicine was laid in these fruitful years of hard work among the poor charity patients of New York City, for whose welfare, as is evident from what we have said, he was ready to make any sacrifice.

After about two years of service on Blackwell's Island, Dr. O'Dwyer, who had attracted no little attention by his faithful fulfilment of duty, was appointed examiner of patients—applicants for admission to the hospitals under the control of the City Board of Charities and Correction. He therefore resigned his position on the Island, and in partnership with Dr. Warren Schoonover opened an office on Second Avenue, between Fifty-seventh and Fifty-eighth Streets. With his colleague, he devoted himself especially to obstetrical practice, in which he had great success, delivering in one year, it is said, over three thousand patients.

In 1872 Dr. O'Dwyer was appointed to the staff of the New York Foundling Asylum, in connection with which his real life-work was to be accomplished. While there Doctors Reynolds and J. Lewis Smith were his colleagues, and all three of them have added no little distinction to American medicine by the careful observations made at that asylum.

At this time one of the most fearful scourges that could afflict a foundling asylum or children's hospital was an epidemic of diphtheria. Those who pretend not to believe in the efficacy of the antitoxin treatment of diphtheria should listen to the account given by some of the Sisters, who for long years were in service in the New York Foundling Asylum, of the fear that came over them when it was announced that diphtheria had entered the wards in their charge. It was always certain beyond doubt that this disease would spread very extensively, and, in spite of all precautions and the enforcement of whatever quarantine was possible, the mortality rate would be very high. Usually forty or fifty per cent. of those who were attacked by diphtheria would perish from the disease, nor was it easy to foresee the end of any epidemic.

In not a few cases death took place from that most excruciating of all fatal terminations—asphyxia. The false membrane, characteristic of diphtheria, would form, in a certain proportion of cases, in the larynx and upper part of the trachea of the little patient, the inflammatory swelling that accompanied it further decreasing the naturally small lumen of the child's undeveloped air passages. Gradually dyspnœa would set in, the dreaded croup begin to be heard, and difficulty of breathing developed at times to such a degree that the little one would use every effort to secure breath, the aeration of the blood growing less and less, and cyanosis— that is, an intense blueness of the face and hands—becoming evident, till finally the child died slowly in all the agonies of asphyxiation, while doctor and nurse stood sadly by, absolutely powerless to do anything to relieve the heart-rending symptoms.

About the middle of the nineteenth century tracheotomy— that is, the surgical opening of the trachea, or wind-pipe, below the larynx, for the purpose of admitting air to the lungs through such artificial opening—had been introduced by Trousseau, of Paris. In many cases this afforded relief;

at least the little patients did not die the awful death by asphyxiation, though not many recovered from the diphtheria or the results of the operation. O'Dwyer himself, when asked what had led him to think of intubating the larynx, said that he had been aroused to experimentation in this direction by the complete failure of tracheotomy during the years from 1873 to 1880 at the New York Foundling Asylum.

In 1880, Dr. O'Dwyer began to devise some method of providing a channel for the passage of air and secretions through the larynx. He knew that tracheotomy, as a serious, bloody operation, always is put off until the condition of the patient is quite alarming, if not hopeless, and that some device for holding the larynx open, if not too difficult of application, would surely prove life-saving in a great many cases. His first thought was that the introduction of a wire spring within the larynx might serve to hold the inflamed sides apart. He realized, however, that the edema and false membrane would force their way around the wires, and so gradually occlude the throat passage in spite of the presence of the spring.

His next thought was a small bivalve speculum, that is to say, two portions of tubes cut longitudinally and fastened together in such a way that the ends could be forced apart. Such instruments are used very commonly for the examination of various cavities in the human body. The laryngeal spring, or speculum, was more successful than the wire, but it had one of the faults of the wire spring. Into the slit between the two portions of the speculum the inflamed mucous membrane was apt to force itself, so that before long difficulty of breathing would recur. Besides, if the spring which kept the blades of the speculum apart were weak, the instrument would fail of its purpose in keeping the mucous membrane apart, while, if it were strong, the pressure of the blades would cause ulceration.

Notwithstanding its faults, however, the bivalve laryngeal speculum accomplished somewhat of the purpose intended. In one case it kept a child alive until the dangerous period of the disease was passed, and thus was the means of saving the first little patient suffering from membranous croup in the thirteen years that the Foundling Asylum had been in existence. Dr. O'Dwyer continued to experiment with the speculum for some time, but finally gave it up and began to study the detailed anatomy of the human larynx. These studies included not only the normal larynx, but also its conditions under the influence of various pathological lesions. Finally (as one of Dr. O'Dwyer's assistants at that time says), he appeared one day in the autopsy-room with a tube. This tube was a little longer than the speculum that before had been in use. It was somewhat flattened laterally, and had a collar at its upper end. This tube was very soon to prove of practical value.

In the first case in which it was employed it was a failure, inasmuch as the patient died from the progress of the diphtheria, though the notes of the case show that after the introduction of the tube the dyspnœa was relieved and the child breathed with comparative ease for the sixteen hours that elapsed before death took place. To any one who knows the harrowing agony of death from asphyxiation, and who appreciates the fact that this form of death was now to be definitely done away with, the triumph of this first introduction of the tube will be at once clear. Dr. O'Dwyer himself was very much encouraged. The relief afforded the patient was for him a great personal satisfaction, since one of the severest trials to his sensitive nature in the midst of his professional work had always been to have to stand helplessly by while these little patients suffered.

The fact that this tube had been retained for sixteen hours demonstrated definitely that the larynx would tolerate a foreign body of this kind without any of the severe spasmodic reflexes that might ordinarily be expected under such circumstances, while the fact that the tube had not been coughed up showed definitely that the inventor was working along the proper lines for the solution of his life-problem. The second case in which the tube was employed resulted in recovery, and Dr. O'Dwyer's more than a dozen years of labor and thought were rewarded by not only relief of symptoms, but the complete recovery of the patient without any serious complications and without any annoying sequelæ.

As the first case (alluded to above) is now a landmark in the history of medicine, the details relating to it seem worth giving. The little patient was a girl of about four years of age, who on the fifth or sixth day of a severe laryngeal diphtheria developed symptoms of laryngeal stenosis, with great dyspnœa. Hitherto the only hope would have been tracheotomy, but Dr. O'Dwyer introduced one of his tubes. The little patient was very much frightened and, as might be expected, in an intensely irritable condition because of the difficulty of breathing. She absolutely refused to permit any manipulations, and it was only with great difficulty that he finally succeeded in introducing the tube. After its introduction the little one shut her teeth tightly upon the metallic shield which the doctor wore on his finger for his protection, and he was absolutely unable to withdraw it from her mouth. It was only after chloroform had been given to her to the extent of partial anesthesia, with consequent relaxation of muscles, that he succeeded in freeing himself.

This proved to Dr. O'Dwyer the need of another instrument (to be employed in the introduction of tubes)—an apparatus by which the mouth could be kept widely open so as to allow of manipulation without undue interference by the patient. For this purpose he contrived the mouth-gag —a very useful little instrument that has been found of service in many other surgical procedures about the mouth besides intubation.

His first tubes, however, were not without serious defects. For instance, in order to permit of the extraction of the tube afterward, there was a small slit in the side of the tube, into which the extractor hooked. Into this slit the swollen and edematous mucous membrane was apt to force its way, and (as can readily be understood) in the removal of the tube considerable laceration in the tissues usually was inflicted. Accordingly the tubes subsequently made were without this slit. Moreover, the first tubes that were employed were not quite long enough, a defect which led to their being rather frequently coughed up. This inconvenience was not wholly obviated even by the lengthening of them.

O'Dwyer continued his studies, and finally hit upon the idea of putting a second shoulder on the tubes. This, it was hoped, would fit below the vocal cords, and with the cords in between the two shoulders the tubes would surely be retained. This improved tube was actually retained, but the drawback to its adoption (as shown in practice) proved to be that it was retained too tightly. When the time for its removal came it was almost impossible to get it out. It was evident then that some other model of tube would have to be constructed in order to make the process of intubation entirely practical, and thus do away with certain dangers.

One of O'Dwyer's assistants at this time at the Foundling Asylum tells of the amount of time the doctor gave to the study of the problem involved in these difficulties and of his ultimate success therein. Putty was moulded in various ways on tubes, which were inserted in specimen larynxes, and plaster casts were taken, with the idea of determining just the form of tube which would so exactly fit the average normal larynx as to be retained without undue pressure, yet at the same time keep the false membrane from occluding the respiratory passages and furnish as much breathing space as possible. Finally Dr. O'Dwyer decided that the best form of tube for all purposes would be one with a collar, or sort of flaring lip at the top, which was to rest on the vocal cord, with, moreover, a spindle-shaped enlargement of the middle portion of the tube, which lay below the vocal cords, fitting more or less closely to the shape of the trachea. To avoid the pressure and ulceration at the base of the epiglottis—a very sensitive and tender portion of the laryngeal tissues—a backward curve was given to the upper portion of the tube. On the other hand, the lower end, which rests within the cricoid ring and which was likely to be forced against the mucous membrane of the trachea occasionally, was somewhat thickened to avoid the friction and leverage that might be exerted if there were any free-play allowed. At the same time the lower end of the tube was thoroughly rounded off.

Thus Dr. O'Dwyer, realizing all the difficulties of this new method of treatment, solved them, as experience proved that the tubes could be made of still smaller calibre than had been hitherto supposed and yet be efficient in relieving respiratory dyspnœa. Experience also proved that the metal tubes at first used had a number of serious disadvantages. They were heavier than those which could be made of hard rubber in the same size and shape, while the metal tubes besides had a tendency to encourage the deposition and incrustation on their surfaces of calcium salts. These incrustations, roughening the surface of the tube, increased its tendency to produce pressure ulceration, as well as added to the difficulty of its removal, and consequently to the liability of producing laceration of tissues after convalescence had been established. Accordingly tubes were made of hard rubber, which could be allowed to remain in the larynx almost for an indefinite period without any inconvenience. While at first intubation was looked upon as a merely temporary expedient, clinical experience showed that sometimes in neurotic patients it was necessary to let the tube remain in the throat for several weeks or even months.

Dr. O'Dwyer's originality in the invention of intubation has sometimes been doubted. The idea of some such instrumental procedure as he finally perfected seems to have occurred to practitioners of medicine a number of times in medical history. No one reduced the idea to practice in any successful degree. O'Dwyer's invention was not some chance hit of good fortune in lighting on a brilliant idea, but the result of years of patient investigation and shaping of means to ends. Often failure seemed inevitable, but he continued to experiment until he forced the hand of the goddess of invention to be favorable to him. The history of intubation is interesting mainly because it brings out clearly O'Dwyer's success where others had failed.

The evolution of intubation forms, moreover, a very interesting chapter in the story of medicine. It is curious to learn that the Greeks of the classical period, and very probably for a long time before, knew something of the possibility of putting a tube into the larynx in cases of stenoses or contractions which threatened to prevent breathing. It is clear that they thus secured patency of the air-passages after these had become occluded. Hippocrates mentions canalization of the air-passages, and suggests that in inflammatory croup with difficulty of respiration, canulas should be carried into the throat along the jaws so that air could be drawn into the lungs. This is probably diphtheria, the first mention of the disease in medical literature, though it is usually said to have been first described in Spain at the beginning of the nineteenth century. There is evidence, too, in Greek medical history that these directions were followed by many practising physicians of those early times. Considering that intubation of the larynx is usually thought to be a very modern treatment, this tradition in Greek medical history serves to show how transitory may be the effect of real progress in applied science. After a time the Asclepiades, and some centuries later Paulinus of Æginetus, rejected the teaching of Hippocrates in this matter, while the latter suggested even the employment of bronchotomy.

After this episodic existence among the Greeks, there is no mention of anything like intubation of the larynx until about the beginning of the nineteenth century. In 1801, Desault, a French surgeon, while attempting to feed a patient suffering with a stricture of the œsophagus through a tube passed down the throat, inadvertently allowed the tube to pass into the larynx. This brought on a severe fit of coughing, but after a time the tube was tolerated and an attempt was made to feed the patient through it, with the production (as can be readily imagined) of a very severe spasmodic laryngeal attack. Desault realized the probable position of the tube then, and, taking a practical hint from this accident, suggested that possibly tubes could be passed down into the lungs even through a spasmodically contracted or infiltrated larynx, with the consequent assurance of free ingress of air. As these cases were otherwise extremely

hopeless, it was not long before he found the opportunity
to put his hypothesis to the test, and in some half a dozen
cases he succeeded in lengthening patient's lives and making
them more comfortable for some hours at least.

Desault's suggestion was followed by similarly directed
experiments on the part of Chaussier, Ducasse and Patissier.
All these came during the first quarter of the century in
France, while, in 1813, Finaz of Seyssel, a student of the
University of Paris, in writing his graduation thesis for the
faculty of medicine, suggested the use of a gum-elastic tube
that should be passed down into the larynx in order to allow
the passage of air in spasmodic and other obstructive conditions.   In 1820, Patissier suggested that some such remedy
as this should be employed for edema of the glottis.   This
affection, which is apt to be rapidly fatal, is a closing of the
chink of the glottis, or *rima glottidis*, as it is called, which
occurs very rapidly as the result of inflammatory conditions,
especially in patients who are suffering from some kidney
affection.

There was no doubt in the mind of practitioners generally
of the necessity in many cases for some such expedient as
the intubation of the larynx, but there was a very generally
accepted notion that the mucous membrane of the larynx
was entirely too sensitive to permit of a tube remaining for
any considerable length of time in contact with the vocal
cords and the very sensitive mucous membrane of the
epiglottis. Meantime many precious lives were lost. Our
own Washington was a sufferer, perhaps, from inflammatory edema of the larynx, complicated by a kidney trouble,
though this was thirty years before Bright's work, and (as a
matter of course) we have no definite data in the matter;
or, as seems not unlikely, he suffered from a severe attack
of laryngeal diphtheria, and, after hours of intense dyspnœa,

22

suffocated while his physicians stood hopelessly by, unable to do anything for him.

There are many other names in the history of attempts at intubation during the first half of the century, two of the most important of which are Liston and John Watson, who, as the result of chance observations in cases in which feeding-tubes were inadvertently passed into the larynx, came to the thought that the larynx might tolerate a tube much better than had been previously imagined. About the middle of the nineteenth century there was no little discussion with regard to the possibility of applying remedies within the larynx after the insertion of a tube, and a large number of medical articles appeared thereon. Diefenbach, the great German surgeon, interested himself in this matter particularly, and protected his left index-finger by a shield that acted also as mouth-gag in inserting the tubes. This technique was afterward to be made use of by O'Dwyer.

The first great step in intubation, as we know it at the present time, however, came from Bouchut, who suggested the use of a tube about the size of a thimble meant to be inserted into the larynx. At the upper part of this tube there were a pair of rings, between which the vocal cords were supposed to rest and hold it in place. Bouchut operated in seven cases with his tube, but five of his patients died, while two of them recovered only after tracheotomy had been performed. Bouchut succeeded, however, in showing that the larynx would tolerate a tube, though he made exaggerated claims for his method, while the very imperfect instruments he employed foredoomed his inventions to failure. It happened, moreover, that the time was unpropitious. Trousseau had not long before re-invented tracheotomy, and had employed it with considerable success in cases of croup. Under Trousseau's influence, a committee of the Academy of

Medicine of Paris declared Bouchut's method unphysio-
logical and impracticable. Moeller, of Koenigsberg, tried
to reintegrate Bouchut's method with certain ameliorations,
but failed. The field of intubation—and a very discouraging
one it seems, strewn as it was with failures made by many
excellent workers—was left for O'Dwyer to exploit. How
thoroughly he worked out his methods can best be appreciated
from the fact that no improvement of importance has come
since he presented to the medical profession the intubation
system as he had eloborated it some fifteen years ago.

How thoroughly Dr. O'Dwyer realized all the difficulties
attached to the practice of intubation may be gathered from
some of his articles on details of the treatment of patients
necessary in order to make intubation a success. One of
the great difficulties in the matter was the liability, when a
tube was in place, for food and drink to find their way,
during the process of swallowing, into contact with sensitive
tissues of the larynx. To overcome this difficulty, Dr.
O'Dwyer made many modifications of the upper part of
the tube. Accordingly he made many wax models of the
larynx, and studied the function of the epiglottis and its
method of covering the larynx in order to facilitate the complete protection of the laryngeal tissues during the process
of swallowing. Finally, he succeeded in making a tube that
enables most patients to learn how to swallow without much
difficulty.

In the mean time O'Dwyer was full of practical suggestions with regard to the management of these cases. His
clinical experience showed him that it was better to teach
the patients to swallow rapidly and then cough up any
material that might find its way into the larynx rather than
to take small sips with a spasm of coughing after each sip.
He showed that, notwithstanding the apparently great danger

of portions of food being carried past the larynx into the trachea, and so to the lungs, there was not nearly so much risk in this matter as had been anticipated. The almost inevitable occurrence of pneumonia was supposed to be one of the serious objections to the use of the intubation methods. Careful pathological investigations, however, soon showed that pneumonia developed much less frequently than had been expected, and, as a rule, when it did develop, it was due to an extension of the diphtheritic processes from the throat rather than to any infection by material that, because of the presence of the tube, had been inadvertently allowed to find its way into the respiratory tract.

However, O'Dwyer's work was not done without considerable opposition. Bouchut's original invention of tubes for the larynx had failed to attract attention because of its condemnation by the Academy of Medicine of Paris, under the influence of Trousseau. When O'Dwyer's tubes were first suggested, then, there were not lacking critics, who said at once that his method was not new, that it had been fairly tried already and found wanting, and that it was hopeless to expect that any intubation method would succeed, since the larynx would not tolerate such a foreign body. There are always those who are sure, on *a priori* grounds, that a new invention cannot succeed because it infringes on certain well-known physical laws that make it impossible. Similarly there were a number of experienced clinicians who were sure that O'Dwyer's reported results could not be as represented.

It was not only from members of the medical profession that O'Dwyer met with discouragement. His work at the Foundling Asylum was carried on in spite of many difficulties and disappointments. His first contrivances for keeping the larynx open in spite of the inflammatory swelling were all failures, and, as owing to unfamiliarity considerable difficulty was experienced in the insertion of the various mechanical appliances, he seemed to be adding to the torture of his little patients. Many of the attendants at the hospital became discouraged and almost dreaded to see any attempt made to save the children. From one of the sisters attached to that institution O'Dwyer received the greatest possible encouragement. Sister Rosalie had often been known to weep at the death of her little charges, orphans though they were, and, though death frequently seemed a welcome relief from suffering, she hoped against hope that something would be accomplished to make deaths by asphyxiation rarer; so that even in the face of repeated failure she was ever ready to encourage O'Dwyer in further attempts in the accomplishment of his humane purpose. Not a little of his ultimate success is due to her sympathy and the enthusiastic faith inspired by her motherly love for the little homeless waifs who had come to occupy places in her heart.

At the beginning, some of the specialists in children's diseases gave the new method a trial, yet without obtaining satisfactory results. Professor Jacobi, our most distinguished specialist in that field in America, to whom the German government offered the chair of pediatrics at the University of Berlin, contended, in writing his article on diphtheria for Pepper's *System of Medicine*, that intubation could not be expected to accomplish all that was claimed for it. It was not long, however, before Jacobi realized his mistake in this matter and handsomely made up for it. While he was president of the Academy of Medicine, in opening a discussion on intubation before the academy, in 1886, he said that O'Dwyer's work deserved all possible praise, and that his untiring devotion to the subject, in silent patience until he had brought it to perfection, was a model that might well be held up for the emulation of American physicians, commonly only too prone to announce discoveries even before they were made.

Besides the application of O'Dwyer's tubes in acute diseases affecting the larynx and causing difficulty of breathing, the method of intubation has proved of special service in the treatment of stenotic diseases of the larynx. There are certain diseases in which deep ulcerations of the vocal cords, and of the laryngeal structures in their neighborhood, are followed by persistent contraction. This contraction may extend so as to cause serious narrowing of the chink of the glottis, producing difficulty of breathing, and an intense breath-hunger that usually causes excruciating agony. Such patients formerly were objects of very special pity, but unfortunately very little could be done for them. Since the introduction of O'Dwyer's tubes, the lot of these patients has been made not only more tolerable, but, in course of time, even actual cures have been obtained, the tendency to contraction in the scar-tissue in the larynx being eventually overcome, with consequent relief of all the symptoms.

Dr. O'Dwyer himself tells the story of the first patient thus treated. It was a woman, about forty years of age, the innocent victim of a dissolute husband, who came suffering with labored, stridulous breathing. The morning of the previous day she had visited a prominent laryngologist of New York City, who advised her to have tracheotomy done before the sun went down. A colleague suggested that she should go to Dr. O'Dwyer to see if he could not give her relief by means of his process of intubation. The stricture in the larynx had resulted after the healing of frequently repeated ulcerations. The tissue all around the site of the old ulcers was densely cicatricial, with a very marked tendency to contract. The aperture through which the breathing had to be done was just sufficient to admit air enough to allow the patient to continue on her feet, but it was becoming ever narrower, while her discomfort was very marked. The stenosis had been coming on for two years, and was slowly progressive in spite of every form of treatment then known to the medical profession.

At this time there was no such thing as intubation tubes suited for adults. Dr. O'Dwyer, therefore, had a set made, using as models casts taken from a series of various-sized bodies, and furnishing directions to the instrument-maker from careful measurements of adult larynxes. The tubes were made in various sizes for different-sized people, but none of them was small enough to be of service in this case, and even the largest of the tubes that had been made for children could be inserted only after the use of considerable force. This tube was inserted and allowed to remain for several days and then the next larger size was introduced. As considerable irritation had been set up by the previous tube, however, an interval of several days' rest was allowed. At the end of about eighteen days, breathing had become quite comfortable and the patient was allowed to return to her home in a suburban town. In two months and a half, however, all her symptoms had returned.

Another course of dilatation was then undertaken, and the patient was instructed to return thereafter every week for some time, until the tendency to contraction had been over-come. After a time, the intervals between dilatations were increased to a month, and then to six weeks, without any return of the dyspnœa. It is characteristic of O'Dwyer's very conservative view of things to find his prognosis of this case as given to the "Laryngological Section" of the Ninth International Medical Congress. He said:

"It is now one year and nine months since I began the

dilatation of this patient's larynx, and there is scarcely any doubt that it will be necessary to continue it during the rest of her life."

Later, however, we find the report:

"The cicatricial tissue in the larynx (as reported by the doctor) lost its tendency to contract, and the patient has remained now for over five years free from any return of the stenosis."

This last sentence is from Dr. O'Dwyer's note of the case, when by special invitation he discussed the subject at the annual meeting of the British Medical Association, held at Bristol, England, in July, 1894.

Interesting as is the career of Dr. O'Dwyer as an investigator and discoverer in medicine, his character as a man is still more worthy of attention.   For nearly thirty-five years he was a member of the staff of the New York Foundling Asylum; during which time he endeared himself to sisters and nurses, to his brother-physicians on the staff and to his little patients. He was eminently conscientious in the fulfilment of his duty, and had a tender sympathy that made him feel every slightest pain of his child-patients almost as personal.

One very stormy evening, in the closing years of his life, after his more than twenty years' service as a member of the asylum staff, a little child fell ill and he was sent for. Though not well himself, the doctor came out into the night and the storm to attend the little patient. As he was leaving the hospital, long after midnight, one of the sisters, who had been longest in the hospital and who knew him very well, said to him:

"But Doctor, why did you come out on such an awful night? The house physician might have gotten on very well without you until morning, even though the little one was much worse than usual."

"Ah, sister," he said, "it was a child suffering, and I couldn't stay home and think that perhaps there was something I might suggest that would relieve that suffering even a little during the night."

It was this beautifully tender sympathy that urged him on against many discouragements to continue his investigations with regard to the possibility of intubation, and finally led him to his brilliant and perfected discovery. Yet it is even more interesting to find that after all these years of labor, just as soon as antitoxin was introduced, and it became clear that a new and great advance in therapeutics had probably been made, O'Dwyer immediately took up the new remedy in order to test fully its possibilities. If antitoxin were to prove the success that was claimed for it abroad, if cases of diphtheria were to recover under its influence as they apparently had done in France and Germany, then the rôle of intubation would soon be a very small one and O'Dwyer's years of patient investigation would go for very little. Such considerations, however, had no weight with him, and it may be said that during his superintendency at the New York Foundling Asylum antitoxin had for the first time a full, unrestricted opportunity given it to demonstrate its power for good.

Notwithstanding discouragements of many kinds, the test of the efficacy of diphtheria serum was persevered in when others with more apparent reason for interest in it became disheartened and were ready to give it up, if not even actually deprecating its use. The medical profession understands very well now how unfavorable were the conditions under which diphtheria antitoxin was used at first. The original experiments had been made in the laboratory with small animals, and the amount of antitoxin necessary to produce good effects in human beings was not well understood. As a distinguished authority in children's diseases, who is himself a great advocate of the efficacy of antitoxin, once said: "It can practically be admitted that when first antitoxin was introduced its use was scarcely more than expectant treatment." That is to say, so little of antitoxic power was contained in the serum injected at first that the children were practically only kept from other and more exhausting forms of treatment, while the physicians awaited the results with nature as the only really active therapeutic agent.

After all, it must not be forgotten that the first doses of antitoxin contained at most 50 to 100 antitoxin units, as we now measure serum efficacy for the treatment of diphtheria. At the present time no one would think of using less than five hundred units as a beginning dose, and those who obtain the best results begin with 1000 to 1500, or in severe cases with 2000 to 3000 units of antitoxic strength. It is almost providential that, notwithstanding this failure to understand the serum properly, the verdict of the profession did not go so generally against antitoxin as to condemn its use hopelessly. It is owing to O'Dwyer and a few other sympathetic souls, who "hoped almost against hope," that finally experience succeeded in demonstrating the true value of diphtheria antitoxin.

There was another difficulty, however, in the way of the adoption of antitoxin that had to be overcome, one that proved no little source of discouragement to many of those who were testing the remedy. The original diphtheria serum employed was not concentrated; so when a sufficient amount of antitoxic units to neutralize the toxins of the disease under treatment was employed, a large quantity of serum had to be injected. Experience shows that the injection of any foreign blood serum into an animal is followed by a certain amount of hæmolysis, or blood destruction, and by

certain cutaneous manifestations, such as urticaria, erythe-
mata, the familiar hives-like eruption and red itchy spots,
which prove a great source of annoyance. In very susceptible
cases the injection of even a small amount of foreign serum
is followed by some fever, by restlessness, and red and swollen
joints. In the early days of the employment of diphtheria
antitoxin, all of these complications were noted in many
cases. They were sufficient to make many who were interested in the demonstration of the value of antitoxin so
disappointed and discouraged that they gave up the task.
Not so, however, with O'Dwyer, who continued its use,
and encouraged others by his example so that in spite of these
objections antitoxin obtained a firm foothold.

Dr. O'Dwyer's conduct, with regard to the continued use
of antitoxin under the discouraging conditions we have
sketched, stamps him as a great member of his humanitarian
profession, whose only purpose was the relief of suffering
and the cure of disease, without any thought, moreover, of
self-glorification. The use of antitoxin has made the necessity for intubation occur much less frequently than before,
and thus has undone some of the good contemplated by Dr.
O'Dwyer, but has accomplished it in a way which he eminently approved and helped on as far as lay in his power,
even at the time when others were doubtful, not without good
reasons, as to the results that were being obtained from the
use of antitoxin.

Perhaps the best index of the sincere simplicity and frank
goodness of O'Dwyer's character is to be found in his relations to the religious community of which he had been so
long a medical attendant. In the words of one of their
superiors, he was looked upon by the sisters at the Foundling
Asylum as the father of the house, who had, as might be
expected, the confidence and trust of every member of the

community.   His relations to Sister Irene, the famed superior
of the asylum, became those almost of brother to sister.
Sister Irene (as is well known), though a woman who accomplished some of the best philanthropic work that, at least,
our generation has known, was always in delicate health.
For several years before his death, Dr. O'Dwyer scarcely
ever let an evening go by without coming to see her personally.   He, better than anyone else, realized how much she
had done for the Foundling Asylum, and how much her
wonderful influence was still accomplishing in making the
extension of that work possible.

There is, of course, another side to this story of Dr.
O'Dwyer's solicitude for Sister Irene that deserves to be
noticed.   Few women have ever accomplished work of the
extent and character that Sister Irene succeeded in doing
with so little friction.   In the parlor of the Foundling Asylum
there is an engrossed scroll—a tribute to her memory from
the medical board of the Asylum—which shows how well she
was appreciated.   As a bit of hospital history it deserves a
place here, especially as there seems no doubt that O'Dwyer's
mutual relations to the sisters and to the medical staff were
of a kind that helped wonderfully in securing the frictionless
co-operation that meant so much for the institution.   The
memorial scroll reads as follows:

"Tribute to the memory of Sister Irene—to the Sister
Superior who secured friends and funds for the building of
the first and largest foundling hospital in America.

"To the sweet-souled woman—the friend of the foundling
and fallen; to the best friend any medical board ever had,
this tribute is presented with their sympathies to the Reverend
Mother and the Sisterhood of the Sisters of Charity by the
Medical Board of the New York Foundling Hospital."

While an extremely modest man himself, and one of very

few words, Dr. O'Dwyer delighted in teaching others anything he felt that he knew well himself. His conduct with
regard to the teaching of intubation was especially admirable. He was ready to show any serious-minded physician
just how the operation was accomplished, and many a young
doctor obtained precious training in the exercise of the rather
difficult manipulation involved in placing a tube in a child's
larynx from the hands of O'Dwyer himself. He never lost
patience with the awkward ones and never seemed to consider that too many calls were made on his time. He might
easily have made money on the operation or the instruments, but deemed such considerations unworthy of his
professional dignity. Personally he was a very reticent man,
but, as a number of friends have said of him, "he made
every word count;" and those who knew him best justly
appreciated the expression of an opinion from him, since it
was always sure to be the fruit of mature consideration and
the result of personal clinical experience, usually extending
over long periods.

The opinion held of Dr. O'Dwyer by his colleagues in
the profession—and, be it well understood, there is no more
searching appreciation of practical methods and theoretical
opinions than that obtained by brother-physicians—is the
best possible tribute to his greatness as an investigator, his
honorableness as a practitioner, and his distinction as a
man. We quote the summing up of his character given by
Dr. Northrup, who had been his colleague for a score of
years at the New York Foundling Asylum, and whose paper
on the subject was read before the New York Academy of
Medicine shortly after O'Dwyer's death:

"What the world knows of O'Dwyer," said Dr. Northrup,
"is his genius as an inventor, his achievement in adding a
great operation to the equipment of the profession, and thus

making the most conspicuous real contribution to medical
progress within the last fifty years. This the world knows
and has acknowledged. To us there is another and a pleasant duty to testify, that with this genius there was all that
goes to make a man. His home life, his religious life, his
civic life, his professional relations with both colleague and
patient, his hospital relations, were such as befit a high-prin-
cipled man. As highly as we esteem him as an inventor and
genius and practitioner of wide knowledge, as much as we
valued his superior medical judgment, we would write upon
the monument of his achievements, 'O'Dwyer the Man.' "

In a previous passage of his address before the Academy,
Dr. Northrup had said:

"If I were asked what most contributed to Dr. O'Dwyer's
medical excellence I would say his habit of thinking and his
good logic. He had a good medical mind, an excellent
medical judgment. Above all, that quality of intellect which
allows a man to grow after the age of forty. To the New
York Foundling Asylum, with which Dr. O'Dwyer was
connected for twenty-five years, he was everything; to the
maternity service he was the expert obstetrician; in intubation he was the inventor and teacher; in the general medical
service he was the constant consulting mind, whose opinion
in times of difficulties and in the midst of puzzling clinical
problems every one voluntarily sought. To the Sisters of
Charity he was physician and friend, consulted with regard
to every important concern of the house, whether medical
or not. All adored him."

Dr. O'Dwyer's domestic life was most happy. He had
married, very suitably, a woman of bright disposition, who
was a foil to his own soberer and more melancholy ways,
and the relations between husband and wife growing tenderer
with the progress of years, their home-life became the model

of an ideal Christian family. When he lost her through death, more than half of his life seemed to have gone, and he never quite recovered from the blow. The circumstances of her death added to his sense of loss, as it must have increased his appreciation of her worth. She died a martyr to what she considered her duty as a Christian mother. During the course of a pregnancy she was taken with what is known as pernicious vomiting, an affection that is likely to prove fatal unless the irritated uterus should be relieved of its burden—a means that neither she nor her husband would consent to adopt. Her death thus was the result.

During the years after the death of the doctor's wife, intimate friends found out what an effort of Christian fortitude it was for him to keep up his spirits and his work. Though he was one of the busiest of professional men, in very active practice, not a week passed but he found time to go to her grave and put flowers thereon. Just after her death he was as a man stricken by some dazing mental affection. Yet his sense of duty was so great that on his return from her funeral, being informed that a little child suffering from diphtheria needed his services for the performance of intubation, he at once made haste to comply with the untimely demand on him, and had given the little patient relief within the quarter of an hour after he had alighted from the funeral carriage.

Personally, Dr. O'Dwyer was of cold exterior, nor had he many close friends. Those who knew him well understood that beneath the layer of ice there was a warm, considerate, tender heart for those whom he admitted to the penetralia of his intimacy. On the other hand, few men have ever had friends more devoted than were O'Dwyer's. He was, however, of an extremely sensitive disposition. His conclusions in medicine had always been worked out with the greatest care, and were the results of personal observations. To have them criticised then by those who had much less experience, or who had never thought along the same lines, was always intolerable to him, and generally kept him out of medical discussions. Those who knew him best realized that his opinions were of the greatest value, nor ever failed to contain a germ of original thought, the result of his personal experience. After his long years of work at intubation, many of his medical brethren refused at first to accept his new method of treatment, claiming that it did not reduce the mortality, even though it did for a moment relieve the sufferings of the patient. This position was a source of the keenest disappointment and depression to O'Dwyer.

After the method of treatment by intubation had been for some time before the medical profession of the country, a thorough discussion of it was held at one of the meetings of the Academy of Medicine of New York. Authorities in children's diseases from several of the large Eastern cities were invited to be present to give their opinions of intubation. Most of them were agreed that O'Dwyer's invention was of very little service. It was not a novelty in the history of medicine to have a really great and helpful discovery thus at first rejected by those who were later to be its ardent advocates. To O'Dwyer, however, who was present and took part in the discussion, the criticism of his method of treatment was a source of veritable torment. He did not show at the meeting how deeply wounded was his spirit, but for three days afterward he practically shut himself up in his room and refused to see anyone.

Naturally he was of a rather melancholic tendency, prone to dwell on the sadder side of things, and was constantly interested in sad stories and songs. He liked sad music, and usually refused to listen to the livelier airs that others, especially of his race, were apt to find so refreshing. Something of this sterner side of his character entered into all his relations with others, and even with his own family. Though deeply affectionate, he very seldom permitted them to see and appreciate that fact. He was rather apt to be stern than otherwise, fearful lest his affection should in any way spoil them. To the very young children, in whose regard he did not consider this objection to hold, he was almost demonstratively affectionate, and those who knew his love for little children appreciated the sacrifice he made in denying himself demonstrations of affection to his own.

With all his sadness there was, as might be expected from his racial descent, a vein of dry humor, not infrequently manifest, though only to very near friends. He appreciated a good story, though the slightest tendency to vulgarity was extremely displeasing to him. He is said to be the originator of the humorous expression that has since been used often enough. While one day calling at a friend's house, in the absence of the friend, the servant asked him to leave his name, but was met with the reply (from the doctor) that "he preferred not to, as he thought he might have use for it before he got home."

The religious side of O'Dwyer's character is intensely interesting, because it represents a successful professional man—the maker of an important discovery in medicine; a logical, scientific thinker, whose opinion was valued by all his professional brethren—as one of the simplest of believers, tenderly pious and faithful. The sexton of the church near which he lived tells (since his death) of frequently seeing him steal in during the day to say his prayers at the foot of the altar. He was one of the most faithful attendants at the communions and retreats of the Xavier Alumni Sodality

23

of New York City, of which he was an enthusiastic member. His deep piety can, perhaps, be best appreciated from a characteristic incident, which illustrates his faith in prayer—his confidence in Providence. He had asked for something with regard to one of his children over and over again, and finally thought that his prayer had been heard. Later on he had reason to regret the fact that his wish had been granted, and to a friend, to whom he told the circumstances, he said:

"All that we can do is to say with resignation, 'Thy will be done,' and then we shall be sure that whatever happens will be for the best."

The story of O'Dwyer's death serves to illustrate some of the weaker points of modern medicine. During the nearly ten years after his wife's death he had never been quite the same man, but had succeeded in doing a large amount of work and had continued to care for a very large practice. In December, 1897, he began to develop some anomalous symptoms, pointing to a serious pathological condition within the skull. He seemed to have had what are known as "Ménière's symptoms," that is, a tendency to vertigo, some ringing in the ears and other unpleasant feelings. Toward the end of that month some hemiplegia, or at least some weakness of one side of his body, developed. He was rather neglectful of his personal health, as most physicians are, and until this time had paid very little attention to his symptoms. Most of the prominent New York consultants and nervous specialists were called in, but there was a marked disaccord as to the cause of the symptoms.

After some days in bed, comatose symptoms began to manifest themselves, and on January the seventh following, after having been lethargic for some days, Dr. O'Dwyer died. The *antemortem* diagnosis of his case was dubious, lying amid the possibilities of tubercular meningitis, secondary infection after otitis media, and secondary infection from some external cause. During the previous December, O'Dwyer had been treating a patient with carbuncle, and developed himself a small carbuncle on his chin. By some it is thought that infectious material from this lesion had been carried by emissary veins or their accompanying lymphatics to the inside of the skull, affecting the meninges, and perhaps portions of the brain-substance itself.

The *postmortem* examination did not entirely clear up the doubts of diagnosis. The lateral sinus was found thrombosed, while there were some suspicious signs in the middle ear, but no distinct inflammatory condition. Just how the infection took place, then, is not clear, but O'Dwyer's condition of lowered resistive vitality was evidently at fault, to an important degree, in permitting infection to take place and in not throwing it off afterward.

At the time of his death he was about fifty-seven years of age. He had reached the maturity of his powers, and with the consciousness of having accomplished one good work was ready for further original investigations in practical medicine. A thought that had occupied him very much toward the end of his life was the possibility of a mechanical method of treating pneumonia. He had made a series of experiments on the lungs, and many clinical observations with regard to the possibility of producing over-inflation by mechanical measures. He confided to one of his physician friends, who had been closest to him during life, that he hoped thus to secure a method of treating pneumonia successfully. This, after all, is the most serious problem in present-day medicine. Our death-rate from pneumonia is at least as high now as it was a century ago. O'Dwyer started from the observation that those suffering from emphysema seldom develop true pneumonia. And he hoped to prevent the progress of the disease, or to abort it in its inception, by producing artificial emphysema for the time being. Had he lived, it seems not unlikely that we would have had further original work of a high order from him.

Though of Irish descent, Dr. O'Dwyer illustrated very well the expression that was used of the English nobility who went to Ireland in Elizabeth's time, and who are said to have become "more Irish than the Irish themselves." O'Dwyer became an American of the Americans. He believed in meeting Americans on their own ground, cultivating their acquaintance, and making them realize the worth of new citizens of the republic by showing them how sincere was the patriotism of their recently admitted compatriots.

Dr. O'Dwyer was in everything the model of a Christian gentleman, and an exemplary member of the great humanitarian profession whose charitable opportunities he knew how to find and take advantage of at every turn in life. The American medical profession has never had a more worthy model of all that can be expected from physicians in their philanthropic duties toward suffering humanity, nor a better exemplar of what Christian manhood means in the widest sense of that expressive term. With an inventive genius of a high order, that gave him a prominent place in a great generation and that has stamped his name on the roll of medical fame for all time, there were united the simple faith, the earnest purpose, the clear-sighted judgment and the feeling kindness—those supreme qualities of head and heart that will always secure for him a prominent place in the small group of great medical men.

INDEX.